Llanelli
Story of a Town

LLANELLI STAR

Llanelli
Story of a Town

John Edwards

breedon **books**
PUBLISHING

First published in Great Britain in 2001 by
The Breedon Books Publishing Company Limited
Breedon House, 3 The Parker Centre, Derby, DE21 4SZ.
Updated 2007.

ISBN 978-1-85983-551-7

Printed and bound by
Cromwell Press, Trowbridge, Wiltshire.

Contents

Preface

AT LAST we have a definitive history of Llanelli. It has been a long wait, but at least John Edwards has made it worthwhile. It is the English version of *Llanelli – Hanes Tref*, published last year. His book has been three years in preparation, and the verdict must be that his time could not have been better spent. The problem, which in itself is a tribute, is to frame a preface of conventional length that fairly reflects the contents of a wide-ranging work of research extending from the Ice Age to the new Millennium.

Moreover, there is much more in it than a bare recital of facts larded with dates and figures. Indeed, in some chapters, particularly those devoted to the 19th century, there is a rich seam of information suitable to be translated into a quality of drama superior to much nowadays featured on our television screens. The murder and mayhem in local forays of the Rebecca rioters provide a case in point.

On a personal note, I welcomed the opportunities offered by the author to get to know more about characters first encountered in John Innes's *Old Llanelly* (1902), notably the Revd Ebenezer Morris, Vicar of Llanelly Parish, 1820-67, a man noted for his large size, muscular physique and volcanic temper. He was arrested, handcuffed, taken to court, fined £20 and, a bizarre fate for a cleric, "bound over to keep the peace". Yet, what redeems him is that his ministry was so effective, his preaching in Welsh and English so powerful, and the congregations at the Parish Church so large there was once a service when an overcrowded gallery "cracked under the strain".

In sad contrast to present times, it was a period when the various Nonconformist causes were also flourishing to such an extent that, at Capel Als, the Revd David Rees, incidentally the Vicar's inveterate foe, felt obliged to send 116 members to help found Siloa, 40 to Bryn Chapel, and finally 80 to establish Park Church.

But as we expect from the progenitor and editor of *Tinopolis* (pub.1995), the author's principal concern in the later chapters has been to detail over the past two centuries the establishment, development and subsequent contraction of Llanelli's basic industries together with the economic and social consequences; in this respect he has left little if anything of import to be added by those who might in future be similarly inclined. This is a book which richly deserves a place in every Llanelli home.

Harry Davies

Introduction

WRITING this book was a labour of love over a period of three years and it was a privilege to be able to do such detailed research into the history of Llanelli, the town in which I was born and bred and lived my entire life.

Let me make it clear that it is a history of Llanelli town, not of Llanelli and district, and the town, more or less, within its present-day boundaries. The late lamented Borough Council, in its time, was very supportive of local history and published books on specific subjects as well as works on several surrounding villages. I felt that it was high time that a new history of Llanelli was written.

My object was to write a general history of the town in preparation of the Eisteddfod 2000. This meant that no subject could be treated in any great detail. To compensate for this essential requirement I have drawn attention to appropriate books and articles in the notes for those who require further information. Other subjects one may find omitted altogether because trying to include everything would have resulted in a catalogue rather than a history. The omissions will provide a challenge for others to tackle.

There is no such thing as objective history and my personal views and interests will become apparent here and there. I hope I shall be forgiven for this because it is *my* story. Other people's perceptions might be different. Although important names will be found throughout the book, it should be remembered that the history of any community is forged by its ordinary citizens and this is certainly true of Llanelli. Their names might not be mentioned, but it is the workers and their families who created the story of this town from the beginning.

It is good to be given the opportunity of providing an English version of the book launched at the Eisteddfod in August 2000. Having a second bite at the cherry, as it were, also meant that minor corrections could be made to the original. Many English speakers have looked forward to this book, and I am grateful to the *Llanelli Star* for making its publication possible.

Llanelli is an unique town. It has a remarkable character of its own. It generates great pride and loyalty. I trust that I have done justice to it. It gave me tremendous pleasure writing the book and I sincerely hope that it gives you pleasure in reading it.

Acknowledgements

Firstly, I owe a great debt of gratitude to the staff of Llanelli Public Library who gave me such prompt and courteous attention while I delved into local books, magazines and newspapers. It was at Llanelli Library, in fact, where most of the research was done. It is a place I have known since childhood and is very near to my heart. I also wish to thank the Record Office in Carmarthen, the National Library at Aberystwyth and the National Museum at Cardiff. The Llanelli Town and Rural Councils were also a source of willing help as were the Millennium Park Authority and the Carmarthenshire County Council's Economic Development Department.

Elwyn Jones was a delightful companion on many research expeditions and readily assumed responsibility for preparing the maps. I am also grateful to Sid Norton for his interest and help at all stages of the work. I have to thank Elizabeth Cox and Carol Lloyd for helping to put the work on disk and Robert Lloyd, editor of the *Llanelli Star*, for undertaking the publication.

I am also indebted to a number of individuals acknowledged in the book and to many more nameless friends who unwittingly jogged my memory in countless convivial surroundings.

Introduction to new edition

IT WAS gratifying to learn that Breedon Books wanted to reprint my book, *Llanelli – Story of a Town*. The original text is fundamentally the same except for additions made in the light of more recent research. Breedon also asked me to add an extra chapter to bring the history up to the present day and this I have done within a restricted word limit. Most of the research was done at Llanelli Public Library where the Regional Manager allowed me to use a room not currently used. The room was just off the Reference Library where I was very well looked after by the staff. I was particularly indebted to Mrs Yvonne Jones who so kindly brought me a cup of tea each morning; this was above and beyond the call of duty but typical of the attitude of the staff as a whole.

I was dragged kicking and screaming into the 20th century when I was persuaded to buy a computer. All my previous work had been done by pen and paper and finished on a portable typewriter and the computer has proved to be a difficult proposition. My progress has been facilitated by entry to a Beginners' Course at Coleg Sir Gar, conducted by Mrs Susan Owen and by regular distress calls to my friend, David Lloyd, who was always ready to help me out of any technical difficulties, and they were very many.

It was difficult to get hold of modern photographs of Llanelli. There were hundreds available of bygone ages but very few contemporary photographs so that I was compelled to tramp around the town snapping various buildings which I needed to include in the new chapter. Photographs of a better quality, however, were provided by Derek Newton-Goverd and by Carmarthenshire County Council through the help of Philip Fitzsimmons, and for these I am very grateful.

The addition of a chapter covering only seven years was, frankly, not an easy task. There were no vast themes to explore as in the previous chapters. There were, instead a series of smaller events, the recital of which could have ended up as a boring catalogue. After ploughing through local papers and other documents I felt as if I was in possession of hundreds of jig-saw pieces which needed to be put together to complete a picture. It was largely a matter of trial and error combined with stringent editing to comply with the required number of words. I just hope it pleases.

Chapter I
From the Age of Ice to the Age of Saints

LLANELLI stands on the shore of the Loughor estuary sheltered by the long arm of the Gower peninsula. From the slopes of Mynydd Sylen, the river Lliedi runs through it on its way to the sea though its course through the town is more or less invisible today. Before approximately 15,000 years ago, the Llanelli area was covered by ice 200ft thick, higher even than the top of Bigyn Hill. From this period onward, the ice gradually retreated.[1] For thousands of years afterwards, the sea covered most of the present site of the town and lapped around the foot of Bigyn Hill and Bryncaerau (Parc Howard) before gradually finding its present position.[2]

Before 10,000 BC we can imagine the earliest inhabitants of the area living in caves similar to the one discovered in Paviland on Gower. They would be living among strange animals like the mammoth which have long become extinct. The climate would have improved by about 8,000 BC with the natives living along the shore line far enough away from the dense forests. They would fish and collect shellfish such as cockles and mussels and also collect seaweed and make a kind of laverbread from it. These are foods still enjoyed by local people today. By hunting animals together, they would ensure a plentiful supply of meat as well as eating the fruits and roots of plants. From about 2,500 BC onwards, they became much more skilled at making tools and weapons of stone and they could plough the soil. They lived in huts of wood and stone, grew crops and herded tamed animals. Instead of wearing animal skins they wore woven clothes. They also used clay vessels for cooking. From this period onward, we can imagine life in the area becoming much more civilised.

The Iberians came to Britain around 2,000 BC by way of Spain and France. This marks the beginning of the Bronze Age, bringing obvious improvements to standards of living by using metal. A number of bronze objects have been found not far from Llanelli, in Llannon, Gorslas and Kidwelly and there are almost 100 burial chambers from this period in Carmarthenshire alone. Travelling by sea was much easier than by land and there was much trading along the coast in wooden boats and coracles. This was the period when Stonehenge was built with the bluestones being transported by river and sea all the way from Preseli. Perhaps some of them were seen by Llanelli fishermen on their way past Gower![3]

The Celts came to Britain from the middle of Europe about 500 BC and, by 100 BC, they had made themselves masters over the whole of the British Isles. By this time they had divided into two groups – the Goidels in Ireland, Isle of Man and Scotland (except for the south) and the Britons (or Brythons) in the rest of the country. With the Celts came the Iron Age. Their heavy iron axes were ideal for clearing new ground for ploughing. With their iron weapons, especially their powerful swords, they proved to be fearsome warriors. They were experts at handling horses and used them skilfully in everyday work as well as in war.[4]

One of the features of this age was the hill fort. A system of ditches and walls was used to defend these forts and the remains of many of them can be seen up and down the country. Here, in Carmarthenshire, can be seen the most impressive of them all, Garn Goch near Llangadog. The site here covered 20 acres and the thick protective walls stood 20ft high. There are traces of Celtic hill forts along the high ground between Pwll and Kidwelly and, without doubt, Bryncaerau (Parc Howard) was one of them and, probably, Bigyn Hill another. Hill forts were well-sited to spy out the surrounding land and, in times of war, they were safe shelters for both people and animals.

By this time, the people of the Llanelli area would be living in settled communities. They would be growing crops and working iron. Their primary occupation was farming, keeping cattle and sheep and using dogs and horses to help in their work. They would also fish and trade a little by sea and land. They would weave and wear clothes of colourful cloth and wear beautiful jewelry on special occasions. We don't know what language the Iberians spoke but Brythonic was the language spoken by the Celts. This was the earliest form of the

Welsh language. The Celts lived in tribes ruled by a chief who could well be a woman. They were followers of a nature religion and Druids played an important part in society, not only as priests but also as teachers and judges. The Celts of our area were a part of the Demetae tribe. Demetae is a Roman word approximating to Dyfed with a border very similar to the late county

Coin of the reign of Diocletian (Carmarthen Museum) discovered in Llanelli Parish Churchyard in 1855.

A stone spearhead (5.7 inches long) discovered in St Paul's vicarage garden. Sir Cyril Fox suggested it might be a copy of a bronze weapon. (Carmarthenshire Antiquary, 1924)

of Dyfed and comprising the counties of Carmarthen, Ceredigion and Pembroke.

The standards of the Roman army were first seen in Britain in the year 55 BC.[5] Leading the army was Julius Caesar who later became the best-known Roman in history. He came again in the following year, 54 BC, before returning to France to complete the conquest of the Gauls. Almost a century passed before the emperor Claudius, in 43 AD, sent four legions to invade Britain under the command of general Aulus Plautius. Caradog (Caratacus) led the neighbouring Silures in South Wales before fleeing to Yorkshire where he was betrayed by the tribe of the Brigantes and taken to Rome as a prisoner. One of the Romans' main forts in Britain was Caerleon. It was a legionary fortress and, from it, roads ran westward along the south coast. Llanelli stood between Loughor (Leucarum) and Carmarthen (Moridunum). It appears that a branch of the road connecting these two forts ran through the present site of Llanelli entering, from Loughor, by way of the old Swansea Road and leaving, via Old Road, in the direction of Trimsaran.

In the work of some earlier local historians there are references to a Roman camp on the site between John Street and Murray Street flanking Station Road. John Innes speaks of a 'square green camp'. The chapel nearby is called Greenfield. One of the adjoining fields is called Castle Field on old maps and the most prominent building now on the site is called Castle Buildings. The site is still obvious today as a raised mound.[6] Another tumulus-shaped site is seen on old maps near the site of the Old Castle tinplate works. Other historians say this was the site of the Roman camp. To obscure the point further, Old Castle Road virtually links both places. The likelihood is that it lay on the first site.

The Romans were here for over 350 years, a period of time which, today, would take us back to Cromwell's time and it is certain that they must have influenced the lives of the natives, however far removed they were from the centres of Roman life. This can be clearly seen by Latin words adopted by the Welsh language especially in the fields of building, mineral extraction, farming, cooking and writing. Here is just one example from each category; ffenestr-fenestra-window, aur-aurum-gold, ffrwyn-frenum-bridle, padell-patella-pan, llyfr-liber-book. At this time in history, Llanelli lay at the westernmost limits of the mighty Roman empire which stretched from the Middle East to Wales.

Celtic religion was a nature cult and its followers worshipped sun and moon, sea and rivers, wind and rain, trees and plants. Early on during the Roman occupation, news came of a new religion – Christianity. It is likely that it was introduced by soldiers and merchants. Israel and Britain, after all, belonged to the Empire. By the end of the fourth century, Christianity was recognised as the official religion of the Roman Empire.

By 410 AD, the city of Rome had fallen to the Goths and the last contingent of Roman troops had left Britain. The Saxons were invading the eastern shores, the Picts had broken through from the north and the Goidelic tribes of Ireland were attacking the western approaches. The Brythonic tribes fought bravely, but in vain, against their enemies. Large tracts of present-day Pembrokeshire and Carmarthenshire were occupied by the Irish. The Barbarians were at the gates and the countries of the old Empire were sinking into the Dark Ages.

During the same period, however, a little light was shed on the darkness by Christian missionary activity across the Celtic lands. Monks started moving about the Celtic countries, preaching the gospel, from Scotland in the north to Brittany in the south. Many Britons had fled to Brittany to escape the Barbarian invaders. Samson, for example, journeyed from Northern Ireland by way of the Isle of Man, Wales, Cornwall and the Channel Islands before settling in Brittany and becoming its most revered saint. Early in the fifth century, Patrick was seized by Irish raiders and taken from Britain as a slave before becoming Patron Saint of Ireland.[7]

Very many of these monks became active in Wales. Probably the first were Dyfrig and Illtud. Illtud became head of a famous school for monastic students at Llanilltud Fawr, or Llantwit Major. Monasteries were subsequently established by David at Saint David's and by Teilo at Llandeilo, albeit in rudimentary wooden buildings in keeping with their simple, saintly way of life. Even so, these monastic communities were organised to provide pastoral care to the surrounding areas and to be the centres of missionary activity. The name for this kind of community was 'clas' (classis monastica) and 'clas' churches were known as mother-churches. This period of history is known as the Age of the Saints and it extends into the sixth century.

'Llan' was the word used for the place where a monk settled. It meant a piece of enclosed land as used to this day in modern Welsh as in 'perllan' for orchard and 'gwinllan' for vineyard. It is likely that there was such a site where our Parish Church stands today which was consecrated, some centuries later, to Saint Elli. But who was this Elli who gave his name to our town? Reference to Elli is found in the *Book of Llandaff* which was written in the 11th century. There he is described as the most beloved disciple of Cadog who was the head of the monastery of Llancarfan in the Vale of Glamorgan. Indeed, after Cadog's retirement in old age, Elli himself became head of the monastery. In the *Book of Llandaff*, there are tales of Elli performing miracles, as one might expect in a manuscript written centuries after the events. The same is true of Rhigyfarch who was writing about Saint David several centuries after his death. Cadog is described as sailing to the island of Grimbul where he met a queen who was very distressed because her husband was angry with her for being unable to bear him an heir. She implored the saint to help her through prayer and promised that, if she bore a child, she would hand it over to his care to be brought up in the service of God. No one knows where the island of Grimbul is and it seems very strange that a queen, desperate for an heir, would then be prepared to abandon the child to Cadog.[8] In fact, it is possible that Elli was Cadog's own son or a son to one of his family. It is possible, also, that the whole story is a complete fabrication. The feast of Saint Elli is held on 23 January with Saint Cadog's Day on 24 January.

There are some who believe that Elli was a woman and a grandchild of Brychan Brycheiniog, ruler of the kingdom of Brecknock. It is said that she was a virgin whose father wished her to marry a prince in spite of her desire to become a nun. In order to escape marriage, she took her own life, an act which conferred on her the status of martyrdom. The likelihood is that it is Elli, the man, who is our saint and that Elli, the woman, belongs to Llanelly in Gwent.

Notes to Chapter I

1 The authoritative book on the geology of Llanelli is D.Q. Bowen: *The Llanelli Landscape* (Llanelli Borough Council, 1980).

2 There is a lingering belief in Llanelli that the doorstep of the Thomas Arms marks sea-level in the town. It is obviously untrue today but it was true during this period.

3 For a general book on this period see R.E.M. Wheeler; *Prehistoric and Roman Wales* (Oxford, 1925).

4 The classical work by Sir John Rhys, *Celtic Britain* (1904) has recently been reprinted by Random Press (1996).

5 Among numerous books on the Romans, see I.A. Richmond: *The Romans in Britain*, (Penguin, 1958.) For a unique survey, it is worth reading M.P. Charlesworth: *The Lost Province* (University of Wales Press, 1948).

6 Five Roman coins, at least, have been found in Llanelli. These are the recorded finds.
   a) one from the reign of Claudius near St Paul's Church in 1950.
   b) one from the reign of Domitian at Maesarddafen in 1963.
   c) one from the reign of Antoninus Pius in Tŷ'rfran in 1946.
   d) one from the reign of Diocletian in the Parish churchyard in 1855.
   e) one undetailed found while work was in progress on the Trostre Works site in 1951.

7 See E.G. Bowen: *The Settlements of the Celtic Saints in Wales* (University of Wales Press, 1954).

8 This story in full, can be read in J.G. Evans and John Rhys (eds.): *Liber Landavensis* (Oxford, 1893).

Chapter II
Wales and the Invaders

BY THE middle of the 6th century, the English had occupied most of the territory known as England today and, in 577, they defeated the Britons at the battle of Deorham, near Bath, thereby cutting off the connection with the Britons of south-west England. Early in the 7th century, the Britons were again defeated at the battle of Chester in 613, this time severing the link with the Britons of north-west England and southern Scotland. These losses were crucial to the future history of our country. From now on, we can envisage Wales ready to develop within its own geographical boundaries as a country on its own with its people changing gradually from being British to being Welsh.[1]

In the North, two kingdoms were slowly evolving – Gwynedd and Powys. In the South, there was Dyfed,[2] for a long time under Irish influence before becoming part

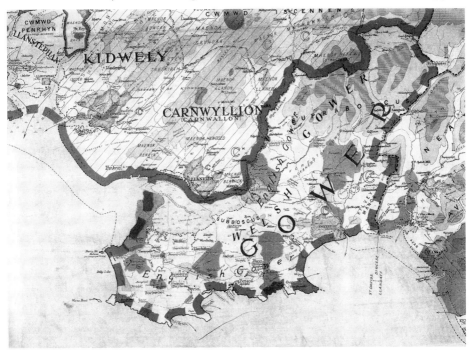

Map showing the three commotes – Kidwelly, Carnwallon and Gower. From William Rees, *South Wales and the Borders in the 14th century* (Ordnance Survey, Southampton, 1933)

The Gower Peninsula from Llanelli. (Carmarthenshire County Council)

of Deheubarth (the Southlands) which came into being through the fusion of Ystrad Tywi (Carmarthenshire) and Ceredigion. Other kingdoms in the South were Brycheiniog (Breconshire), Morgannwg (Glamorgan) and Gwent (Monmouthshire). The hundred of Eginog[3] comprised three commotes – Kidwelly, Carnwallon[4] and Gower. Carnwallon, more of less, consisted of the present parishes of Llanelli, Llannon, Llangennech and Llanedi. Notice that the river Loughor was no barrier to the close link between our commote and Gower. Even today as we look across from Llanelli and cast our eyes on that pearl of a peninsula, we experience the feeling that we are still closely related in spite of belonging to different counties.

The name, Machynys, was chronicled a very long time before there was any mention of Llanelli. In a charter of the *Book of Llandaff*, we see the following: 'An estate named Machinis with six modii of land (about 250 acres) given to Berthwyn, Bishop of Teilo (that is Llandaff).' Professor Wendy Davies has dated this charter as 735. Machynys is shown as an island on Camden's map and also on the Stepney Estate map as late as 1761[5] and there is persistent reference to a monastery being established there by Saint Pŷr (or Piro) the founder of the monastery at Caldy Island, off Tenby. In the middle of the eighth century, Wales acquired an eastern border when Offa, king of Mercia, constructed a dyke running from near Prestatyn in the north to Chepstow in the south, to mark the border between Mercia and Wales.

When Rhodri the Great became prince of Gwynedd in 844, he succeeded in adding Powys and Deheubarth to his lands, thus conjuring up the vision of a Wales united by one ruler. The dream was never realised, mainly because of the tradition of dividing land among the sons at the death of the father.[6] This is what happened after Rhodri's death but he was also frustrated during his lifetime by spending much of his time fighting a new enemy from Scandinavia. From about 850 onwards, the Vikings began ravaging the coasts of Wales. They already had settlements in Ireland, especially in Dublin, and from there they plundered possessions and took slaves captive. Gradually they started trading and even settled in some places, though they have left very little trace. Place-names, however recall their presence, such as Burry Holms nearby and Worms Head at the end of Gower and the town of Swansea itself -Sweyn's Ey- the settlement of the Viking chieftain Sweyn.[7]

When Rhodri's son, Cadell, died in 910, his son Hywel came to rule. He added Dyfed to his territory through marriage. He later extended his dominion to include Gwynedd and Powys and so ruled the whole of Wales with the exception of Brycheiniog, Morgannwg and Gwent. Hywel's centre of power was the stronghold of Dinefwr, near Llandeilo. Peace was Hywel's priority and so he set up friendly relations with the kings of Wessex, especially with Athelstan. He called an assembly of wise men to meet at Whitland to rationalise the country's laws. Up until now, there were different laws in different parts of Wales. He set up a committee of 12, comprising clergy and laymen, to sift through the laws, keeping the best, making alterations to some, deleting others and making new laws in their place. For the first time, there would be one law covering almost the whole of Wales. This achievement, more than any other, began to inspire a sense of Welsh nationality among the population. There was peace in the land throughout his long reign of 40 years until his death

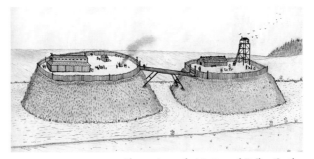

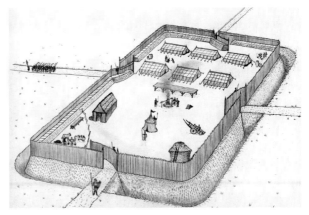

Above: An early Motte and Bailey Castle.
Below: A Roman Marching Camp.
(Drawings by Neville Tonge)

in 950. On this account, he was known as Hywel Dda – the Good – the only king in Welsh history to be so named. And he did, indeed, consider himself a king and had silver coins minted with the inscription 'Howael Rex'. He was one of our nation's finest leaders.

William of Normandy became king of England after the Battle of Hastings in 1066 and soon conquered the whole of that country. He, himself, did not attack Wales but he gave his barons permission to do so and to keep what land they could seize. The easiest lands to subdue were along the border between Wales and England, along the valleys of Severn, Wye, Usk and Dee into mid-Wales and along the coastal plains of north and south Wales. They advanced more or less along even routes, suitable for Norman military tactics, using armour-clad soldiers and heavy horses. The Welsh method of fighting favoured lightly-armed infantry making lightning raids on the enemy before retreating into the hills.

The Normans raised wooden castles as they advanced and it is possible that a castle of this type was built here. There are two sites under consideration. One is at Old Castle where a round island rises from the pond, which was the tinworks' reservoir.[8] Until comparatively recently, and before changing the course of the river to run into the Carmarthenshire Dock, the Lliedi flowed into the sea at Sandy, roughly where the bridge is today.[9] It is a low-lying site very much like the site of Ogmore castle in the Vale of Glamorgan. Apart from the Old Castle Tinplate Works, there was an Old Castle Colliery and farms called Hen Gastell Fawr and Hen Gastell Fach near the site. One of the Stradey

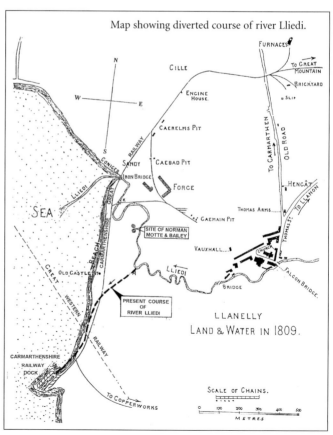

Map showing diverted course of river Lliedi.

LLANELLY
LAND & WATER IN 1809.

SCALE OF CHAINS.

Estate maps shows a mound near a field called Beili (Bailey); and motte (mound) and bailey castles were exactly what the Normans built. The Ordnance Survey of 1880 describes the site as a 'Camp' with a motte measuring 28 metres in diameter. Later, the motte was measured by a Royal Commission and found to be six metres high with traces of a ditch surrounding it. The second site to be considered is Pencastell where Station Road meets John Street and Murray Street. The Stepney Estate map of 1761 shows a rectangular site there and the place has been marked on successive maps up to the Ordnance Survey of 1880.[10] Pencastell was the name of a field, a part of Llanelly Park which lay behind Llanelly House in the centre of town. Later on, a doctor's surgery there was called Pencastell and Castle Buildings are still situated on the site. It is more likely that this site was a small Roman camp since its outline on maps forms the classical playing-card shape of Roman forts.

By the beginning of the 12th century, the Normans occupied large tracts of low-lying land in Deheubarth with the Welsh still occupying the higher ground, generally speaking, land above about 100 metres. By this time, the Welsh princes were expected to pay homage to the English kings, but they were by no means subdued. They would rise in revolt from time to time when they sensed that any advantage could be gained from political difficulties in England. This was especially true of the reign of the weak king Stephen who reigned from 1135 to 1154. Thus, in 1136, Hywel ap Maredudd of Brycheiniog went on the offensive and won an important battle at nearby Penllergaer. Hywel's victory encouraged

Gruffydd ap Rhys to travel to Gwynedd in a attempt to prevail on his brothers-in-law, the sons of Gruffydd ap Cynan, to help him regain lands he had lost to the Normans in Deheurbarth. It was while Gruffydd was away in the North that his wife Gwenllian raised an army to attack Kidwelly castle. The brave Gwenllian lost the battle and both she and her son were killed. The event, however, was never forgotten and, to this day, the field of battle is known as Maes Gwenllian and can be seen from the northern walls of Kidwelly castle.

Aerial photograph (1936) showing possible remains of Motte and Bailey Castle on Old Castle Tinworks' pond. (Ministry of Defence)

By 1155, Rhys, the son of Gruffydd and Gwenllian, had become the ruler of Deuheubarth after his two brothers, Cadell and Maredudd, had died while still quite young. Maredudd and Rhys had already put Loughor castle to the torch and raided Gower where the Normans had established Flemish settlers, as in Pembroke. We read, in *Annales Cambriae* (1190) the following words: 'Gouhir predatus est, castellum Carnawillian destruxit', that is 'Gower ravaged and the castle of Carnwallon destroyed.' Again, in the *Red Book of Hergest* (1215) we read: 'The young Rhys gathered together a large force, over-ran Kidwelly and Carnwallon and burned the castle'. It is true that there is a slight ambiguity here and that it might be understood that it was the castle at Kidwelly which was burnt. In that case, why was the order not 'Carnwallon and Kidwelly'? The castle of Carnwallon, almost certainly, is the castle of Llanelli, just as any reference to the church of Carnwallon means the church at Llanelli during this period.

After the death of Stephen in 1154, Henry II became king of England. He was one of the most powerful of all the English kings but a bitter quarrel arose between him and the Church, a quarrel which, later on, led to the murder of Archbishop Becket. Rhys took advantage of the situation to extend his dominions. He thus became the most powerful prince in the whole of Wales and Deheubarth was the strongest power in Wales until almost the end of the century. By 1160, the year of Becket's murder, Henry had decided that it would be better for him if he could come to some agreement with Rhys. At Pembroke, therefore, in 1171, Henry was forced to confirm Rhys's authority over Deheubarth and other lands he had added to it.

In 1172, after meeting Henry at Laugharne, Rhys was appointed Royal Justiciar of South Wales. Rhys was now on equal terms with the great barons of England and would, henceforward, be known as the Lord Rhys. He was now the King's deputy in south Wales and it was a great advantage for him to have Henry's trust so that peace could prevail in his lands. There was no question of betraying his Welshness, however, and over the Christmas season, in 1176, he called on poets and musicians from all the countries of Britain to compete at the very first Eisteddfod held at Cardigan. The chief prizes were both won by Welshmen, the best poet came from north Wales and the best musician from the south. In 1188, Rhys welcomed Giraldus Cambrensis (Gerald the Welshman) and Archbishop Baldwin when they came to preach the Third Crusade in Wales. Gerald mentions that the Archbishop, and the august entourage accompanying him, crossed the rivers Loughor and Gwendraeth before staying the night at Kidwelly castle. It is almost certain, therefore, that they passed through Llanelli.

Rhys was very supportive of the Church and, especially of the monasteries of Deheubarth and they, in turn, helped to keep alive the spirit of independence and of nationhood. Deheubarth was raised to a status of great importance during Rhys's reign but, after his death in 1197, the fate of Wales would lie in the hands of Gwynedd into the next century. The glory that was Dinefwr had come to an end.

Notes to Chapter II

1   John Davies: *History of Wales* (Penguin, 1992) is the latest of several books on Welsh history. It is suitable as a general reference throughout.
2   Dyfed, at this time, is the present Pembrokeshire, more or less.
3   Eginog is a delightful name which disappeared after the Norman Conquest. It deserves to be reclaimed.
4   There are several forms of the name but Carnwallon is my personal preference. Also to be found are Carnwyllion and Carnawllon. There is an interesting article by D.G. Jones in *Carmarthenshire Historian*, 1980: 'Commote of Uncertain Name'. There are two farms near Pontyberem called Carnawllon Fach and Carnawllon Fawr. The first reference in 1100, is Carnoguatlaun in *Vitae Sancti Cadoci*, the Life of St Cadog in Latin and the next is Carnwathlan in *Cartae et Munimenti de Glamorgan* in 1148.
5   It was an island when the tide was in.
6   This was the difficulty in attempting to create a unified kingdom. The English law was primogeniture when everything was left to the eldest son. Notice, on a lesser scale, that Welsh fields are smaller than those of England.
7   We also have Skokholm and Skomer in Pembrokeshire. Worm was a Viking chieftain. In April 1999, on a beach near Swansea, a ringed pin, a foot long, was found. It was Scandinavian in origin.
8   All that remains today is a tree-covered island in the middle of a pond at the bottom of People's Park.
9   The course of the river was changed in 1834.
10   The place is marked on maps by the classical playing-card shape of Roman forts.

Chapter III
Church and Castle

HERWALD was Bishop of Llandaff for a long period of almost 50 years from 1056 to 1104. A passage in the *Book of Llandaff* states that he consecrated five priests to the church of Carnwallon, that is, to the church at Llanelli. The priests were named Umel, Uchtryd, Jonas, Gwasdiui and Aeddan.[1] In 1130, Maurice de Londres became Lord of Kidwelly in succession to Roger, Bishop of Salisbury, the first lord. The de Londres family were Lords of Ogmore who had raised and supported a Benedictine Priory in nearby Ewenny. The Normans showed favour towards the Benedictines while the Welsh princes supported the Cistercians, an order which emphasised solitude, frugality and physical toil. Towards 1140, the churches of Llanelli and Pembrey were given to Ewenny by Maurice de Londres and, a little later, charges payable to Ewenny were sanctioned by Anselm le Gras, Bishop of St David's. Every year, Llanelli church was to pay 20 shillings and the church at Pembrey (in the commote of Kidwelly) was to pay 10 shillings. Ewenny Priory was, in turn, connected with the church of St Peter at Gloucester, and St Peter's maintained the right to nominate priests to the church at Llanelli. By this time, it is clear that Llanelli lay firmly within the diocese of St David's. In all likelihood, Llanelli had been the mother-church of the commote of Carnwallon under the old Welsh ecclesiastical system. Now it found itself within the deanery of Kidwelly and the archdeaconry of Carmarthen, under the rule of Norman bishops and subject to the authority of Canterbury. Gerald the Welshman tried in vain to get the Pope to acknowledge St David's as a metropolitan see but Wales was destined to wait until 1920 before obtaining ecclesiastical independence.[2]

From a political standpoint, it is quite clear that the old hundred (cantref) of Eginog had vanished from the face of the earth. By this time, the commote of Gower

Site of Old Castle. Now an island in the pond of the same name. (J.E.)

was in the hands of the de Breos family and Kidwelly and Carnwallon were, for the most part, under Norman rule apart from sporadic incursions from independent Welsh princes. In 1216, for example, Llywelyn I attacked south Wales and placed Rhys Grug in power for some years over Kidwelly and Carnwallon, among other territories. Again, in 1257, Llywelyn II swept down to the south and undermined the authority of William de Breos in Gower and Patrick de Chaworth in Carnwallon. By this time, de Chaworth was lord of Kidwelly by marriage with Hawys de Londres.[3]

The influence of the de Londres family throws some light on the situation in Llanelli during this period. At first glance, it would appear that the site of Llanelli's Norman castle is not a very suitable one.[4] People think of castles as standing firmly

The low-lying site of Ogmore Castle. (J.E.)

on a hill high above the surrounding land. But this is not true of all castles. The Normans sometimes built castles on river sites, often near the last fording-point before reaching the sea. In Llanelli, the site is on the bank of a river, on flat ground and less than a mile from the sea. Ogmore castle was rebuilt in stone and its ruins can still be seen on the river bank, on flat land, within a mile of the sea. Ogmore strengthens the argument for the existence of Llanelli's castle because the de Londres family were also lords of Ogmore. We can also compare the little cluster of houses which grew up around the church in Llanelli with the village of Ewenny around the Priory there – both settlements within a mile of a castle. Not all Norman settlements sheltered under the shadow of their castle walls.

It is therefore tempting to consider our town's position, in this period, as a tiny Norman island in the sea of Welshness that was the commote of Carnwallon. The situation is similar, though on a smaller scale, to the relationship, which existed between the town of Kidwelly and the commote of the same name. The difference is that Kidwelly castle was rebuilt in stone whereas Llanelli's castle was abandoned. It is probable that our massive church tower was raised as a defensive position in its place. It was built in the 13th century, the period when most stone constructions

The Church Tower from the top of Gelli Onn. (J.E.)

took place; the tower is 71ft high and 26½ft square and as Wirt Sykes observed: 'Along the entire coast of Wales, certain striking characteristics are observed in the churches. Look at their towers-each more ponderous than the rest… there is no question that they were defences as well as bell-towers.' [5]

After the fall of Llywelyn II in 1282 which tolled the death-knell of Welsh independence, the commote of Carnwallon came directly under the control of the lords of Kidwelly, though it is only fair to point out that the commote had been accounted an extension of Kidwelly at times in the past. Patrick de Chaworth died in 1283 and his daughter Matilda succeeded him. In 1298, Matilda married Henry, Duke of Lancaster and grandson of Henry III. Matilda's granddaughter married John, Duke of Lancaster, known as John of Gaunt, and their son became Henry IV. Thus, the lordship of Kidwelly came into the Kings's own hands and Llanelli was now under royal patronage. It is doubtful that this made any difference to the lives of the town's inhabitants. The same is true of Owain Glyndwr's rebellion at the beginning of the 15th century. Even though Owain recaptured great tracts of Wales, the revolt had little effect on Llanelli. It is true that he captured Carmarthen castle and that

Kidwelly Castle. (Llanelli Library)

his forces threatened Kidwelly castle, but he never came near Llanelli. Perhaps the reason for this was that he had received a warning from Hopcyn ap Tomas ab Einon of Ynystawe that he might be captured between the rivers Tywi and Llwchwr. Although the prophecy was never realised, it is just possible that Owain kept away from the area-just in case!

In order to raise money for a Crusade in 1291, Pope Nicholas IV levied a tax on every Christian church with Llanelli's share assessed at £10. In 1364, the right to nominate priests to the church was transferred from Gloucester to the church of St Mary at Leicester – a situation which continued until the Protestant reformation of the 16th century. Apart from the Parish Church itself, there were several chapels-of-ease attached to it. These were generally used to hold services for people who lived some distance away from the main church or when travelling conditions made it difficult for them to attend. Services were conducted by unbeneficed clergy and there are tales of monks from Neath Abbey returning home and spending the night at a hospice on the banks of the Llwchwr at the present site of Spitty (Hospitum) in Bynea. Four of these chapels are easily identifiable; Capel Dewi in Llwynhendy, Capel Ifan in Pontyberem, Capel Dyddgen on the slopes of Sylen and Capel Gwynllyw where Capel Isaf farm stands today. There are claims for a chapel at Llangennech and there may have been a Lady chapel in the Parish Church. It is interesting to note that John Innes's *Old Llanelly* written in 1902, observed that old people referred to the Parish church as St Mary's.[6] Not many of the hallowed stones of these chapels remain today although Capel Ifan (St John's) was rebuilt in the 19th century. Even though facts are scarce, we can safely assume that the religious life of the area continued in the Catholic tradition up until the Reformation.

Notes to Chapter III

1 *Liber Landavensis* op. cit. The spellings of the names vary.
2 See H.E. Butler (ed.): *The Autobiography of Gerald* (London, 1937).
3 J.E. Lloyd: *History of Carmarthenshire*. Two volumes, 1935 and 1939, remains a standard work. A more recent account is A.G. Rhys Jones; *The Story of Carmarthenshire* (Llandybie, 1959).
4 John Innes; *Old Llanelly* (1902) says that the site is singularly unsuitable for a castle. Other publications on the history of Llanelli are:
   D. Bowen: *Hanes Llanelli*. 1857.
   J.L. Bowen: *History of Llanelly*. 1886.
   A.Mee: *History of Llanelly Parish Church*. 1885.
   J.H. Morgan: *History of Llanelly*. 1930. In manuscript form.
   All these are available for reference at Llanelli Public Library.
5 Sikes was a US consul. He wrote 'The Wild Welsh Coast' in *Harper's* magazine in 1883.
6 It was in Norman times that churches were first dedicated to biblical figures in Wales. Whereas they were previously named after Welsh saints, we now begin to see dedications to St Mary, St Peter, St Stephen *et al.*

Chapter IV
The Beginning of the Modern Age

WITH the Act of Union of 1536,[1] Wales became an indissoluble part of England. The country was made into 13 shires with Llanelli finding itself almost on the eastern border of Carmarthenshire. There the town has remained to this day with the exception of a brief period as part of Dyfed between 1974 and 1996. At the same time, the church was being reformed in the reign of Henry VIII with the King replacing the Pope as Head of the Church. Wales, of course, had been a Catholic country for hundreds of years and, as Giraldus Cambrensis had observed, was steadfast in the old faith. It is amazing that there was virtually no opposition to this revolutionary change. There were violent protests in the North of England and in Cornwall, but Wales appeared willing to accept the change.[2] No doubt, the main reason for conforming was Wales's unswerving loyalty to the Tudor dynasty. In 1485, the Welsh had supported Henry Tudor (later Henry VII) when he landed in Pembrokeshire from Brittany. Henry marched through west and mid-Wales gathering an army of Welshmen as he progressed. The Welsh firmly believed that the old prophecy, of a Welshman again becoming King of Britain, had come true when Henry claimed the victory over Richard III at Bosworth under

Court farm, Pembrey, about 1900. An example of a house dating back to the Middle Ages. (Llanelli Library)

24

the banner of the Red Dragon. The native-born leaders of Wales now saw that their future would be much more secure under the patronage of the King of England in both political and ecclesiastical affairs. In fact, for Henry, the one was dependent on the other. By the time of Elizabeth, the Church of England was wholly Protestant and the country pursued an anti-Catholic policy at home and abroad.

Following the Chantries Act of 1547, commissioners were despatched to tour the country and make a report on every church parish. It is certain that most of the precious relics of the old Catholic faith had vanished by this time, but this is what the report (1552) had to say about the church at Llanelli with its attendant chapels:

1. Two chalices (communion cups)
2. Four bells, great and small
3. A chalice in the possession of Henry Howell Nicholas bought by him 'to s've' the chapel of Saint John.[3]
4. A chalice in the chapel of St Dyddgu (Dyddgen)
5. A chalice in the chapel of St David
6. A chalice and a bell in the chapel of St Gwynllyw

During the reign of Elizabeth, in 1574, a chalice was given to the parish church with the words *Poculum ecclesie de Llanelly* (chalice of the church of Llanelli) inscribed on it. It is still kept in the parish church and used once a year for communion on Easter Sunday. It is the oldest relic in the church today.

By 1588 a Welsh translation of the Bible had been made by William Morgan and placed in all churches alongside the English version. The main purpose of the translation was to facilitate the better understanding of the English bible which, once again, fitted in with the Act of Union's intention of turning Welsh people into monoglot Englishmen. In spite of this, William Morgan's bible proved to be the most powerful weapon placed in the hands of the Welsh in the fight to preserve the language and, without it, it is probable that the language would not have survived.

We have a description of Llanelli by John Leland who travelled through Wales between 1536 and 1539.[4] Leland writes of Llanelli as a village in the lordship

A 16th century saucepan from Llanelli. The words say 'Pity the Pore'. (Carmarthen Museum)

of Kidwelly where the inhabitants dig for coal-that is bituminous coal which he contrasts with the anthracite of the Gwendraeth Valley. In his *History of Llanelly* (1886) J.L. Bowen says that coal was mined on Caecotton Isaf land as early as 1500 though his source is not stated. Despite this, it is clear that the coal industry was well established by the 1530s, and that, from mid-century onwards, coal was being exported from Llanelli to the West of England and to France. There was no harbour as such, but the ships would tie up in small creeks or along the shore in the Seaside area.

We get a fascinating glimpse of Llanelli in the Accounts of the Duchy of Lancaster for the years 1609 to 1613.[5] Under the heading 'Commote of Carnwallon' we find 'Borough of Llanelli'. The word 'borough' appears often in connection with Llanelli although there was never, before 1913, an official charter making it a borough, as was the case with Kidwelly in the 13th century. We sometimes come across the description 'borough by prescription' for a case like Llanelli. In the account book, there is reference to a corn mill and also to the ruins of an old woollen mill. A fair is said to be held 'within the borough on the 19th day of September formerly by farmers of Machynys and now by Harry Bowen, a farmer of Machynys.'[6] There is also evidence of 'a weekly market held every Thursday within the borough of Llanelli' and we find the names of two craftsmen: Ieuan Jenkin ap Owen, blacksmith, and Wyllim Griffiths, glove-maker. There are two long lists of freeholders within the borough including a knight, Sir John Vaughan, and four esquires, Ffrauncis Maunsell, Ffrances Lloyd, Phillip Bowen and Edward Cotten. It was the Cotten family, presumably, which owned the land at Caecotton. The rest are gentlemen and other freeholders.[7]

It is interesting to note that five of the top eight names in the first list are in

Machynys Farm (formerly Machynys House) with Gower in the background. (Painting from Trostre Museum)

the old Welsh style-Thomas ap Rhys, John ap John Richard, Thomas Davye ap Robert, Thomas ap Rees and Griffith ap Icuan. In the first list of about 40 people, it is said that they brought their deeds 'to be surveyed before Gerard Bromley, His Majesty's Surveyor for the South Parts.' Many of these names are also to be seen in the second list.

The Accounts also take notice of the appalling state of roads in the area, saying that the old Roman roads are still the main highways. It also tells of the erosion of coastal areas, the submerging of villages and forests, the flooding of marshland and changes in the shape of the coastline in the Llanelli-Kidwelly area between the 14th and 16th centuries. During this period, several places in eastern Gower disappeared under encroaching sand and this was the time when the same fate befell the old borough of Kenfig. It was only in the 16th century, according to the Accounts, that Caldy Island was separated from the mainland. While considering such catastrophes, we must also remember the Black Death which reached Weymouth in 1348. There is no record of the plague in our town but it is certainly recorded that it reached Carmarthen by the end of March 1349, and that, in the manor of Llanllwch, everyone died except one person.[8] One-third of the entire population of Wales and England was wiped out in this terrible visitation and it is unlikely that Llanelli escaped completely.

In 1566, according to the report of a Commission comprising the Bishop of St David's, Thomas Vaughan and Dafydd Morgan, Llanelli is described as 'a village of 12 houses on a creek of Burry.' Here there was one ship, the 'Jesus', with a crew of three seamen. Llanelli, under the name 'Burry', is described as a creek under the governance of John Vaughan as part of the Duchy of Lancaster. Through the 'port' of Llanelli, for example, on 9 November 1586, came a cargo from Bristol on its way to William Johnes of Llandeilo consisting of iron, cheese, soap and raisins. From Wexford, on 17 August 1599, came a ship carrying eight horses and two colts. Throughout the 16th and 17th centuries there is considerable traffic using Llanelli according to the Welsh Port Books.[9] We know from the will of John Howell ap Ieuan Thomas, of Llanelli, who died in 1604, that he owned a ship worth £3 6s 8d. In 1623, fishing and keelage rights in the Loughor, Lliedi and adjacent streams were granted to Walter Vaughan by James I. It is interesting to note that, in 1626, when Walter Vaughan was High Sheriff of Carmarthenshire, he refused a request from the impecunious Charles I for a ship of 30 tons. He said that Carmarthenshire was an inland county with only a few creeks in which there was no such ship.[10]

Walter Vaughan died in 1639. He came from the family which owned the great estate of Golden Grove, and married Anne Lewis, the daughter of Thomas Lewis, a wealthy Llanelli landowner, some time in 1605. For some years, they made their home at Talyclun, between Llangennech and Hendy. By 1616, they had moved to Llanelli, to a house opposite the church, which probably belonged to Anne's father, where Llanelli House stands today. At that time, it was a substantial stone-built house but smaller than the present building which dates from the 18th century but it is possible that parts of the older house still remain as out-buildings. According to Walter Vaughan's will, he left 'the mansion house wherein I dwell in Llanelly' to his wife during her lifetime. His property was divided among his five children. John Vaughan, his second son, succeeded his elder brother and it was he who safeguarded the estate during the Civil War – a difficult time for Royalists. As a Royalist, he was fined £227 13s 4d yet managed to play an active part in public life. He was High Sheriff in 1659 and a Deputy Lord Lieutenant in 1663 after the restoration of the monarchy.

There is an echo of the Civil War in Llanelli in 1644. In March of that year, the town of Tenby was under siege by Cromwell's troops as well as by three warships. A ship, having sailed from Bristol, was attempting to bring ammunition for the Royalists when it was intercepted by one of the warships.[11] It managed to escape, however, and despite being pursued, found shelter in one of the creeks of Llanelli, also loyal to the King. The fact that the gun-runner was a Bristol ship may be significant because her captain was more likely to be acquainted with the river and its dangerous sandbanks than the warship's commander. Again, on 13 April 1648, we have evidence of a skirmish between Parliamentary troops and Royalist cavalry just outside Llanelli.[12] The Roundheads won the day and took 12 Cavaliers prisoner together with their horses. The site of the skirmish was Talsarnau, on the Swansea Road near to where Bryntirion Hospital and the Star Hotel now stand.

There is evidence that another plague struck Carmarthen in 1652, once again wreaking great havoc. It reached Llanelli in 1653 although, once again, we know very little about its effects here. The hope is that there were few victims because of the care taken to keep the plague at bay. On the Felinfoel road, men were posted to keep watch and stop strangers from entering the town. Traders left their goods at the same place and money used in transactions was passed through a stone vessel filled with salt-water. This place was called Cae Watch or Cae'r Halen and is the field on which Capel Newydd was built. John Innes speaks of a similar vessel seen near Dr Cooke's house, which is where the Library now stands. This site is right in the middle of town and the vessel would serve no purpose there. Perhaps it was the vessel used at Cae'r Halen or at some other spot just outside the town.

Among the prominent Royalists in the Llanelli area during the Civil War was Francis Howell. He was Deputy Sheriff of Carmarthenshire in 1644. He lived in a sizeable house in Cwm Llethri, above Felinfoel, a house which is now Cwm

Llethri Farm. What is unique about the house is that it is the oldest externally-dated building in the county. The inscription is difficult to read today since it is covered by whitewash but, by careful study, we can make out the following inscription: F.H. (Francis Howell) E. (his wife) and M.H. (his son) Anno Dom 1665.[13]

By 1676, the number of houses in Llanelli had increased to 188. At the time, houses were taxed according to the number of hearths they contained. Henry Mansel, for example, was taxed on 15 hearths and Henry Vaughan on 12. The number of hearths was not only a measure of the size of the house, but also of the size of the estate. There was an obvious correlation between the size of the house and the owner's wealth. It is possible that more than one house was involved in this survey. Vaughan owned Llanelli House, opposite the church, and Machynys House. Mansel owned Trimsaran Mansion and also, perhaps, a house on Stradey land, near the sea, by this time. Mansel's land, of course, developed into the Stradey estate and Vaughan's into the Stepney estate.

Another four persons were taxed on 10 hearths, one on six, one on five, one on four and 12 on three.[14] These returns reflect the growth of a middle class in Llanelli. Some of the houses would perhaps have three floors while others would be solid two-floor buildings with bedrooms upstairs. The majority of these houses would be clustered around the church with the exception of Machynys House (owned by Vaughan) and one or two others.

To end this housing survey, we have 164 houses with one hearth. Some of these would be in the town centre and others in the Seaside area. They would be single-storey houses with beaten earth floors, tiny windows no more than holes in the walls, and covered with thatched roofs.[15] According to statistics of the period, 20 percent of Carmarthenshire people were too poor to pay hearth tax and we can be fairly certain that this figure was true for Llanelli also.

Llanelli was literally put on the map in the 16th century. The town appeared on Leland's map between 1536 and 1539. It subsequently appeared on Saxton's map in 1579, Camden's in 1586 and Speed's in 1611.

Although William Morgan's Bible was published in 1588, it was a large expensive book and, generally, confined to churches. By 1630, the Little Bible had appeared, a smaller and comparatively inexpensive edition. Although most of the population was still illiterate, educated people were able to buy it and read it at home. This period in history saw the rise of independent sects throughout the land whose faith was wholly based on the word of God as revealed in the Bible. Once again, we see religion and politics walking hand in hand with the 'Rule of the Saints' during the period of the Republican Commonwealth between 1643 and 1660.

A detail from Saxton's Map showing Llanelli and surrounding area.

By 1650, a group of Baptists were meeting at the house of Jennet Jones, Berwig.[16] Llanelli Baptists were nominally members of Ilston Church in Gower and they would cross the river Loughor to attend services there. John Myles was the minister at Ilston and was also responsible for organising the sect in South Wales, covering a vast area from Hay-on-Wye to Carmarthen. He was paid a salary of £40 for preaching at Llanelli Parish Church. The money was paid by Cromwell's government which used the post of Public Preacher to spread its Puritan propaganda.[17]

It was in ordinary dwelling-houses that the majority of meetings were held at this time. Since 1653, the house of Hugh Matthews at Lower Mill in Llanelli was used as a place of worship and, from 1567 onwards, services were being held at the house of Jenkin Franklyn in Llangennech.[18] After the restoration of the monarchy in 1660, nonconformists suffered persecution. At the height of this persecution, the church at Ilston was destroyed and John Myles, together with many of the followers, emigrated to Swanzey, Massachusetts, in 1663.

The state of the church, physically and spiritually, had deteriorated badly by the end of the 17th century. From time to time the Bishop or the Archdeacon would send churches a questionnaire to ascertain their condition. The replies would come in the form of a Presentment. According to the Presentment from Llanelli Parish Church made in 1684, these were some of the answers.[19] There was no carpet in front of the altar and no linen cloth on it. There was no up-to-date Bible either in Welsh or English. There was no chest with locks to keep the silver plate (one wonders where the Elizabethan silver chalice was kept). There was no bier to carry the coffin for funerals. The doors were defective and locks didn't work. The great tower was in a dangerous state and had no bells. The floors were in a bad state and the windows defective. The report was signed by Rawleigh Mansel.

From the spiritual point of view, the parish had only a curate to minister to its needs and he also had care of Llangennech. He was criticised for not teaching the Catechism to the children. There were members of the church who never took communion and failed to have their children baptised. The sexton was suspected of sheep-stealing. The majority of the population paid little heed to Sunday as a holy day and one side of the great tower was used to play ball games and was known as Cwrt y Bêl – the Ball-Court. Indeed, it seemed that Sunday was given over almost to pagan enjoyment and licentious behaviour.

Listen to the words of Rhys Prichard, Vicar of Llandovery, in his Cannwyll y Cymry (The Welsh People's Candle) about 1630. I translate literally:

'A day to get drunk, a day to swagger,
A day to dance, a day to loiter,
A day for bullying and for fighting;
That's the Lord's Day for the Welsh.'

Notes to Chapter IV

1 See Ivor Bowen: *The Statutes of Wales* (London, 1905).

2 For a classic study, read Glanmor Williams: *Wales and the Reformation* (University of Wales Press, 1970).

3 'to s've the chapel of St John' may mean to save expense. It is more likely, however, that it means 'to serve'.

4 L. Toulmin Smith (ed.): *The Itinerary in Wales of John Leland* (1906).

5 Williams Rees (ed.): *A Survey of the Duchy of Lancaster Lordships in Wales* (1609-1613) Cardiff (1953).

6 'Farmer' here means tax-farmer, responsible for collecting rents due to the Duchy.

7 Spellings vary. It was not until the publication of Samuel Johnson's *Dictionary* in 1755 that spelling became standardised.

8 William Rees 'The Black Death in Wales' in R.W. Southern (ed) *Essays in Medieval History* (London, 1968).

9 E.A. Lewis (ed.): *Welsh Port Books* (London, 1927).

10 Essay by Moelwyn Williams: 'Carmarthenshire's Maritime Trade in the 16th and 17th Centuries'. In *Carmarthenshire Antiquary* (1978).

11 Lyn John (video): *Take another Look* has a reconstruction of this event. Available at Llanelli Public Library.

12 J.F. Rees: *Studies in Welsh History*. (University of Wales Press, 1947). Article on the Second Civil War in Wales. See also Lyn John video op. cit.

13 The inscription is computer enhanced in the above video.

14 For Housing Statistics see: *Carmarthenshire Historian (Vol. XIV,* 1977). Article by Moelwyn Williams: 'Life in 17th Century Carmarthenshire'. See also article in *Llanelli Miscellany* (1977) by Dr Ilid Anthony: 'Social Life in Llanelli in the 18th century.'

15 Some of these were one-roomed houses but, usually, there were two rooms with partitions of wattle and clay on either side of the entrance passage. It was in a cottage of this type that I was born at Gatygarn, at the top end of Penyfai Lane, in 1927. By that time, corrugated zinc sheets had replaced the thatched roof.

16 John Edwards (ed.): *Footprints of Faith: Aspects of the Origin and Growth of Christianity in the Llanelli Area*. (Workers Education Association Llanelli) contributions by J. Wyn Evans, Noel Gibbard and Maurice Loader (W.E.A. Llanelli, 1992).

17 Lambeth Palace Library. M.S. Vol. 1004. April 21st, 1657. Ilston. Ordered that the yearly sum of £40 be granted to and for the increase of the maintenance of the minister of Ilston, in the county of Glamorgan. And that the same be, from time to time, paid unto Mr John Myles, the present minister there, approved according to the Ordinance for Approbation of Public Preachers. The said £40 a year to be in lieu of so much to him formerly granted as Minister of Llanelly in the county of Carmarthen.

18 *Footprints of Faith* op. cit. P. 30.

19 *Footprints of Faith* op. cit. P. 17.

Chapter V
The 18th century

IN 1700, Llanelli was still a small town, rather more like a village today, with one grand mansion, Llanelli House, and about 55 buildings comprising houses, shops and taverns clustered around the parish church. Some distance away, there were other dwellings in the Seaside and Machynys areas. John Innes tells of a small brewhouse being set up, at about the same time, on the present site of the late-lamented Buckley's Brewery. There were vast gardens attached to Llanelli House and it is on these gardens that the main streets of the town were subsequently built. The present Llanelly House was erected by Sir John Stepney on the site of an older mansion belonging to Thomas Lewis. The work was completed in 1714 when the family moved in. The date can still be seen on the cast-iron down-pipes on the front of the house.[1]

Llanelli House. (J.E.)

The Stepney family originally came from Aldenham in Hertfordshire. Alban Stepneth was offered a position under the diocese of St David's in 1559. Stepneth moved to Pembrokeshire and a branch of the family found itself in Prendergast, near Haverfordwest. It was from this place that the family came to Llanelli. Sir Thomas Stepney was a Member of Parliament in Carmarthenshire between 1717 and 1722 and he played a prominent part in the life of the town.

It is apparent that there was quite a surge of social activity in the town during the first half of the 18th century. Bridget Price was born in 1713 and her father's name is given in the Parish Register as William Price, Gentleman. He was the younger son of the Dyffryn estate in Llandybie and had moved to Llanelli to start up a business and marry Margaret Jones. Incidentally, many names in the Register are described as Gentlemen and Esquires which points to the rise of a fairly wealthy middle-class in the town. At the age of 24, Bridget Price, who had grown into a very beautiful young lady, was married to Thomas Jones who, unfortunately, died two years later. Bridget now became a much sought-after widow.[2]

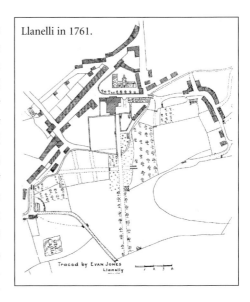

Llanelli in 1761.

Traced by Evan Jones
Llanelly

Richard Savage arrived in Swansea in 1739. He was a poet and counted among his friends literary figures such as Samuel Johnson, Alexander Pope, Henry Fielding and many others. However, as befitted a poet perhaps, he was not well-versed in composing his finances and had fallen into serious debt. Swansea was, in fact, a place of exile away from his creditors in London. Arthur Mee remarks: 'For all his genius, he was a mere babe in money matters and continually getting into trouble. To such a pitch had things arrived that, at length, his friends advised him to retire for a period to Swansea which would be equivalent today (1902) to a voyage to Timbuctu!'[3] Among Savage's friends in the London litterati was John Dyer who was at Westminster School with William Rees of Cilymaenllwyd. Perhaps it was to visit Rees that Savage first came to Llanelli. But, be that as it may, he fell headlong in love with the beautiful Bridget Jones and pursued her with unabated zeal. His muse did not desert him in the town and he wrote an epitaph on the death of Bridget's grandmother and three poems addressed to Bridget herself. His ardour may have been spurred by the hope of getting his hands on Bridget's money, but she was wise enough to reject him. A couplet from a poem written on St Valentine's Day reads:

'Cambria farewell! My Chloe's charms no more
Invite my steps along Llanelly's shore.'

In January 1745, Savage was arrested for debt in Bristol and thrown into jail there. He died in jail seven months later. Bridget Jones made another two successful marriages. She buried her second husband then married a cousin,

William Jones of Dyffryn, Llandybie, and thus she came to live in her father's family home. She lies buried in Llandybie Church.

Sir Thomas Stepney's wife (née Margaret Vaughan) died in 1733 and Sir Thomas himself died in 1744. He was followed by Sir John Stepney who died within four years in 1748. Then came another Sir Thomas (the 7th baronet) and, although he was only 23 at the time, he showed a great interest in the estate, especially in the development of its coal resources. He was also a shipowner and he successfully exported coal to France, Portugal and Ireland. Following his death in 1772, the Stepney interest in the family home came to an end. The next Sir John was a politician and his life was spent away from Llanelli. He had been Member of Parliament for Monmouth since 1767 when he was only 24. He moved from politics to pursue a career in the diplomatic service and, in 1775, was appointed envoy to the Elector of Saxony in Dresden. In 1782, he was appointed ambassador to Berlin. After retirement he went to live in London. So, just two years after the death of Sir Thomas Stepney, Llanelli House was put up for sale but did not attract a buyer. Subsequently, part of the house was on the market in 1787 and the whole in 1791. Still there were no buyers and the fine house continued to deteriorate from one year to the next. Thus it was only for 60 years that Llanelli House was occupied by the Stepney family. Despite the fact that (with the exception of the Chambers' occupancy) this noble house has been neglected over the centuries and put to many purposes, most of them totally unsuitable, its outward appearance is still impressive.

Frances Stepney married Henry Mansel of the Stradey estate. After Henry's death in 1673, he was succeeded by his son Edward who married Dorothy Lloyd, widow, the daughter of Philip Vaughan of Trimsaran.[4] She had recently inherited the Trimsaran estate on the death of her father. In 1696 Edward Mansel was created a baronet (of Trimsaran). Between his estate and that of his wife, Sir Edward held a vast amount of land in the area. Another Sir Edward succeeded his father in 1721 and from here on the family fortune dwindled.

Edward Mansel was married three times and his last wife was Mary Bayley of Hereford. On his death, in 1752, with no heir, the title passed to Edward Vaughan Mansel, son of Rawleigh, his late brother. According to his uncle's will, however, he inherited only the Stradey estate, the Trimsaran estate going to his aunt Mary Mansel. This was a cause of great contention between them and involved lengthy and expensive litigation.

By 1754, Edward Vaughan Mansel had incurred enormous debts because of his extravagant lifestyle. He became friendly with Daniel Shewen, a Swansea solicitor. Shewen took advantage of this friendship to make money for himself out of the estate's coal resources. Shewen's wife died in 1757 and, within six months, he had married Mansel's sister Bridget. Two years later his brother, Joseph Shewen, married another sister, Anne Mansel. Shewen would bleed him dry. At one time, Mansel found himself £12,000 in debt, an enormous sum in those days. He was imprisoned in The Fleet in London for nine months and when he was released, he went to live with Joseph Shewen in Buckingham.

Edward Vaughan was a widower by this time and he married Mary, Shewen's daughter from his first marriage. Joseph Shewen was now both his brother-in-law and his father-in-law. Daniel Shewen died in 1770 and Mansel and his wife, together with Joseph Shewen came to live at Stradey which, by this time, was in the hands of trustees.[5] Joseph Shewen died in 1788, and Edward Vaughan died a week later. Edward Joseph Shewen Mansel then became the fourth and last baronet. Dame Mary succeeded in regaining the estate and began to put its affairs in order by developing the coal interests at a time when great changes were afoot in the town's history. The fourth baronet died in 1789, childless and intestate, and thus the title came to an end.

In 1709, the Baptists started building Adulam chapel in Felinfoel, the first Nonconformist meeting-place in the area.[6] Following the destruction of the Baptist cause at Ilston, Swansea became the headquarters of the South Wales Baptists and Adulam came under the control of Swansea before becoming independent in 1735. The first ministers were members of Adulam, the very first was David Owen assisted by Evan Thomas, Morgan David, John Duckfield and Morgan Rees. In 1761, John Duckfield and Morgan Rees were actually ordained to the ministry. In 1777, ministers preached in other places locally on Sundays apart from Adulam and all the small congregations came together to the chapel, once a month for a communion service. A group of Baptists attached to Adulam met in Llanelli at the Tŷ Cwrdd (meeting-place) near the Steam Mill at David Robert's house in Spring Gardens (opposite where the Town Hall stands today).

The beginnings of the Independent cause at Llanelli is rather more obscure. We know that the Revd Thomas Morgan, minister at Henllan, made preaching visits to Llanelli in the 1740s although no meeting-places are mentioned. In the Carmarthenshire Quarter Sessions of 1748 a place called Pentref, on

Gelli Onn, 1900. (Sgt Dunn). The Calvinistic Methodists' first place of worship.

the west side of the parish, was registered as a place of worship. This reference is difficult to identify but I believe it could possibly be Pentre-iago farm to the west of Llanelli, near Cwmbach on the Trimsaran road. More secure is the registration of Llwynwhilwg, another farm on the south side of Llanelli and the home of Thomas Howell. Llanelli Independents had, however, for many years travelled to the Hen Gapel (Old Chapel) in Llanedi parish for Sunday worship. Yr Hen Gapel was the mother-church of the Independents of East Carmarthenshire and, in 1745, the children of William Thomas, Llanelli, were baptised there. According to registers kept at the Public Record Office, other Llanelli members are listed but there is only one mention of a place name, Capel (presumably Capel Farm on the Swansea road) the home of John Francis.[7]

It was during the ministry of Evan Davies (his home was Gelli Farm near Llanelli) that the first Independent Chapel was established in 1780. That chapel was Capel Als. It is claimed that the name, derives from a cottage called Tŷ Alys which previously stood on the spot where the chapel was built. Alys apparently sold water from a well which was still there until 1852 when it was filled in during the building of an extension to the chapel. The word 'als' in Welsh means rock cliff (compare the Gaelic, Ailsa Craig) and if one ventures to the vestry behind the chapel one is faced by a steep rock face. The chapel could conceivably have been named after this feature. That is my own personal theory for what it is worth, but I have never known the word Alys or Alice shortened to Als.

The seeds of Methodism were sown in Llanelli by no less a person than Howel Harries, the acknowledged leader of the Welsh Methodists. Between 1738 and 1766, he visited Llanelli on several occasions. He was a friend of a Mr Dalton of Pembrey who was a devout Anglican. At this time, of course, the Methodists still adhered to the Church of England and were trying to reform it from within. They were finding this a difficult task, however, and were gradually setting up congregations of their own, though it was not until 1811 that they severed all connection with the church. Places visited by Howel Harris in the area were Cwmblawd and Pentref near Llannon, Ffoi near Pontyates and Maesarddafen on the south side of Llanelli. All these are farms and it will already have been noticed that farms were also prominent as meeting-places in early Baptist and Independent history. Farmhouses were generally of generous size and their barns also proved useful as congregations increased. They were also found in fairly isolated parts and during times of persecution had provided safe hiding-places, though persecution had ended by the end of the 17th century.

Strangely enough, the Methodist cause in Llanelli had its origins in the desertion of Baptists from Adulam who went to hear the famous David Jones, Llangan, preaching at Goppa, Pontarddulais. Walter Bowen and Henry Rees had attended service at Adulam, but left before taking communion and, for this, they were expelled. They joined the Methodist congregation at Goppa but also held services in Llanelli at the house of an Adulam widow named Martha. They preached a mixture of Baptist and Methodist teaching and the house became too small for the growing congregation. Bowen and Rees then leased premises at Gelli Onn[8] which were demolished when the new road was built between West End and Thomas Street. The congregation, however, was still known as Teulu Martha (Martha's family) and Gelli Onn can claim to have been the first Sunday School in Llanelli and was visited by Thomas Charles of Bala, the founder of the Sunday School movement in Wales. Land was purchased from the Stradey estate on Felinfoel Road; it was Cae Halen (the Salt Field) previously mentioned in connection with the plague and Teulu Martha, (now all convinced Calvinistic Methodists) put their hands to building Capel Newydd which was opened in 1809.

John Wesley preached in Llanelli on eight occasions between 1768 and 1790.[9] He visited Robert and John Deer on his earliest journeys. The Deer brothers lived in Church Street (now demolished – behind the Parish Church) and he would have just had to walk a short distance down the street to preach in the open-air in the market-place in front of the church lychgate.

The principal Wesleyan Methodist in Llanelli was Wilfred Colley who was butler to Sir Thomas Stepney and he seems to have converted a number of the Stepney servants to the cause. Wesley invariably came to Llanelli in the month of August, and always on horseback, either on his way to and from Ireland or to oversee the work of the Glamorgan Wesleyan Circuit. Llanelli was the most westerly part of the Glamorgan Circuit which stretched east as far as Gloucestershire.[10] In 1774 he was saddened by the death of Sir Thomas Stepney: 'I went on to Llanelly but what a change was there. Sir Thomas Stepney, father of the poor was dead… the family (the Wesleyan group) was broken up and Wilfred Colley, his butler, the father of the society, obliged to remove.[11] Soon after, John Deer who was next in usefulness to him, was taken into Abraham's Bosom.' Only once was he allowed to preach in the church itself and that was in 1771: 'I rode to Llanelly… and read prayers in another large church almost as ruinous as that of Pembroke! (He had travelled from there.)'

After John Deer's death, Wesley visited Henry Child's house in Thomas Street.[12] Child had come to Llanelli from Pembroke at the age of 18 to become agent to Sir Thomas Stepney and, under the influence of Wilfred Colley, he joined the Methodists in 1769. He was an astute man of business and brought up several licensed premises in Llanelli including the Falcon Inn at the bottom of Thomas Street. He also bought a malt-house and leased farms to grow his own barley. He also leased a mill to grind flour to make bread for a growing population. He also had interests in coal, shipping and many other concerns. Perhaps he will be best remembered for the purchase of land, again at the bottom of Thomas Street, where he set up a brewery. By 1790, on the occasion of Wesley's last visit, Henry Child told him of his plan to build a Wesleyan Chapel at the bottom of his large garden. Wesley took a guinea from his pocket and gave it to Mrs Child as a first contribution to the building fund. The chapel was built in 1792. Mrs Child, incidentally, was the local-born Mary Jones who was Welsh-speaking. She had nine children, one of whom, Maria, became the wife of the Revd James Buckley who took over the brewery business.

Coal-mining, at the beginning of the 18th century, continued on a small scale with both the Stepney and Mansel estates granting leases to local operators. Coal had been mined at Caeswddi (Bigyn) and other places since early in the previous century. One is reminded of the couplet 'Ceffyle Pwll y Bigyn, dim ond esgyrn, croen a blew' – 'Bigyn Pit horses, only skin and bone and hair.' There was further activity in the Bynea-Pencoed area after 1750 involving the use of steam engines, primitive railroads, small canals and shipping places on the river Loughor. In 1752, the Stepney and Mansel estates granted most unleased coal under their lands to a Londoner named Chauncey Townsend in the hope of seeing great developments. They were disappointed, however, and although a start was made, there was no real progress. Townsend died in 1770 and the work was taken up by his son-in-law, John Smith, who was just as reluctant to move forward. Smith, in fact, gave up a good many of the Mansel leases. Perhaps the main reason for their lassitude was that both Townsend and Smith had considerable mining interests in Glamorgan, especially in the Swansea and Llansamlet areas and they feared that a glut of coal might push down the price. There were also, of course, the usual financial difficulties. In any case, their inactivity held back the development of the Llanelli coalfield until the end of the century. By 1795, William Roderick, Margaret Griffiths and Thomas Bowen had opened the Bres Pit (the site of the present Asda supermarket) and had constructed a canal to connect with their shipping-place at Seaside.

At the beginning of the 18th century coal was used, almost exclusively, for domestic use but, by the end of the century, there was a demand for industrial purposes, especially in the iron industry. Steam was replacing water as the motive power of industry and coal was needed, in increasing quantities, to fuel steam engines. The very first uses of steam-engines, in fact, was to pump water out of mines and this meant that coal mines could be sunk ever deeper and thus increase production.

Sir Thomas Stepney attempted to link up coal with metal smelting and, as early at 1755, had built a lead-smelting works at Pencoed,[13] near Bynea. This was, in fact, the first metal works to be set up on the Llanelli coalfield. Arthur Mee stated that a small iron foundry, run by William Yalden, was working on the Wern in 1784 but no documentary record of it has yet been found. Alexander Raby first showed an interest in the Llanelli coalfield in 1893 and was in touch with the Stepney estate but nothing came of it. John Givers and Thomas Ingman arrived in Llanelli in 1894 and started making iron at Cwmddyche. There may well have been an existing iron furnace here built by Daniel Shewen in the late 1850's. In 1762, he wrote to his brother Joseph: 'We have had a bad time of it, the furnace being idle for two years.'[14] Givers and Ingman certainly came here on Raby's recommendation and Raby may also have had a financial interest in the venture from the start. In any event, he took over the furnace in 1796 with Givers still on the pay-roll. From now on, Cwmddyche would be no more and the nearby village would be known simply as Furnace!

Notes to Chapter V

1 A list of the contents of Llanelli House was made for sale purposes in 1776. Details may be found in an appendix to the book.
2 Article in *Carmarthenshire Antiquary* (1996) by Conway Davies entitled 'Mrs Bridget Jones, Widow Lady of Llanelly.'
3 John Innes, *Old Llanelly* (1902). Article on Savage by Arthur Mee.
4 Three great Llanelli families are here seen together, Vaughan, Stepney and Mansel.
5 The trustees were Thomas Price, Alexander Swail and Gabriel Powell.
6 See *Footprints of Faith* op. cit. for a summary of Nonconformist history in Llanelli.
7 Registers RG/4/3919 and 3772 in National Archive, London.
8 It is the *road* which bears the name Gelli Onn (Ash Grove) today.
9 *Carmarthenshire Antiquary* (1973). Article by W.K. Buckley on 'Wesley in Carmarthenshire, 1763-1790.'
10 See A.H. Williams, *Wesley and West Wales* (Cardiff, 1990).
11 Wilfred Colley moved to Cardiff where he became a shopkeeper. See W.K. Buckley's article above.
12 Wesley would often visit and move on after preaching. His movements can be read in detail in his diary, *Wesley's Journal.*
13 Remains of this old works can still be seen.
14 See M.V. Symons, *Coal Mining in the Llanelli Area, Volume I* (Llanelli Borough Council, 1979) This is the standard book on early industry in the Llanelli area even though its emphasis is on coal. Shewen's letter can be seen in Mansel Lewis, *London Collection*. The date is 14 February 1762.

Chapter VI
Transport, Industry and Religion

THE expansion of the Llanelli coalfield in the early 19th century led to a quickening of maritime activity to cope with the export of coal. Shipping places were nothing more than the most rudimentary quays and larger ships had to stand off and load coal from barges. There were several of these in the area including Pwll Quay, set up by John Rees, Cilymaenllwyd; Banc y Llong in the Old Castle area used by the Mansels, Givers and Ingman, and by Raby; Penrhyngwyn, Machynys; and several others in Pencoed, Bynea and Llangennech.[1] The first recognisable dock was that of Roderick and Bowen, called Lead Works Dock or Pemberton Dock, at Seaside, on the site later occupied by the Pemberton tinworks.[2] As we have already seen, Raby's dock was built in 1799 and was later improved by the Carmarthenshire Railway Company. The Copperworks Dock had become a floating dock in the early 1820s. All these docks were connected to the collieries by short canals or railroads. Coal exports increased almost fourfold between 1807 and 1815 to 71,000 tons.[3] We even see the beginnings of ship-owning in Llanelli; Sir Thomas Stepney, the seventh Baronet, had owned two ships around 1750 while Thomas Harries was part-owner and master of the 'Speedwell', a sloop of 29 tons, towards the end of the 18th century. Raby owned four ships while Nevill owned two. Apart from iron-ore imported by Raby and copper-ore imported by Nevill, most of the shipping arriving in Llanelli was ballasted and this gave rise to the famous Ballast Bank at Seaside, remains of which could be seen until recently from the Swansea-Llanelli coast road.

The New Dock was built in 1834 on a site between Seaside and Machynys and provided Llanelli's second floating dock. The Llanelly Railway and Dock Company which built the line to Llandeilo via Pontarddulais, controlled this dock. On one day, in May 1836, according to the *Cambrian* newspaper, this dock held upward of 5,000 tons of shipping. Three ships, of over 400 tons each, were bound for Bombay and the others were loading coal for ports on both east and west coasts of Africa as well as for Mediterranean ports. Most of the cargoes were intended for the East India Company. It must have been a wondrous sight with the harbour a forest of masts.

Although efforts were made, almost from the beginning of the century, to place buoys marking the river channel and make the approaches safe for navigation, the work was largely unco-ordinated because the docks were in different hands and often in competition. An Act for the Improvement of the Estuary was passed in 1813 and a Harbour Commission was in place from this time onward. The 'Great Embankment' or Bulwarks was started in 1808 to protect Machynys from flooding and the course of the Dafen river was diverted to enter Machynys Pool, later the New Dock.

The first railways in Llanelli were primitive horse-drawn freight carriers. The famous Ffordd Wagen (Waggon Way) ran from the Box Colliery past Capel Als, down to what is now Murray Street and through the Erw to Seaside. As we know, Raby had tramroads connecting his iron-furnace and forge with his collieries which were later taken over by the Carmarthenshire Railway Company whose line reached Gorslas.[4] In turn, this line was taken over by the Mynydd Mawr Railway. In 1835 the Llanelly Railway and Dock Company was running passenger trains as well as coal trains. By 1840, this line was using two steam locomotives and two carriages to carry 2,500 passengers a month. The main line passed through Llanelli in 1852 when the South Wales Railway opened the section between Swansea and Carmarthen to connect with the Great Western Railway's main line from London. Catching the 11:15 a.m. express train at Llanelli would now get a traveller to Paddington by 5:25 p.m.

There was some improvement in the state of the roads due to the development of Turnpike Trusts. A group of gentlemen would get together and put in money to repair stretches of road. They would recoup the money invested by setting up toll-gates to collect money from travellers. Tolls varied but the following may be taken as average. Pedestrians, of course, went free; a man on horseback would pay a penny or two; a coach, a cart or a wagon would pay sixpence; cattle would pass through at a shilling for 20 with half that amount for pigs, calves and sheep. It is well known that drovers would find ways around a toll-gate and so would horsemen, so we are left only with coaches and carts to be concerned with. The mail-coach was allowed through at no expense and with no delay, hence the horn which gave the gatekeeper ample warning to open up. Tolls were a burden on the

Llanelli in 1821. (Llanelli Library)

backs of coach operators and, in our part of the world, farmers found it a real hardship to send their produce to market or to cart lime, the only fertilizer used, from the outlying quarries.

Llanelli was ringed around with tollgates owned by the Kidwelly Trust. There was the Capel gate on the Swansea road; the Tŷ'rfran gate on the Felinfoel road; the Sandy gate on the Pembrey road and the

Llanelli House, 1900. (Sgt. Dunn)

Furnace gate to control the traffic on both the Five Roads and Trimsaran roads. There were also scores of barriers guarding the surrounding countryside. The Trusts let out the gates to agents who, in turn, employed people to man the gates for a pittance of a weekly wage.

In 1842, William Lewis of Swansea had bought up all the gates of the Kidwelly Trust and he was nothing less than a cheating rogue.[5] Some of the toll-keepers employed by Lewis were paid as little as 2s a week and, as there was no accounting system, it was not surprising that they siphoned off some of the takings. Meanwhile the agents were more interested in toll-money and neglected the upkeep of roads. For this greed, there would soon be a price to pay.

Llanelli House took on a new lease of life in 1827 after having lain empty for 60 years. The new tenants were William Chambers and his son of the same name from Bicknor, near Sittingbourne in Kent. William Chambers, senior, had inherited the Stepney estate in a seemingly bizarre fashion. Sir John Stepney had made a will which completely ignored his immediate family.[6] He made over the estate to three close friends and then to three others if the first three died without heirs. William Chambers's name was among the second group and it was to him that the inheritance fell. Sir John and Chambers had been prisoners together in 1803, during the Napoleonic War at Valenciennces, near the Belgian border today. Sir John was released early through the influence of the diplomatic service but Chambers remained a prisoner until 1815, by which time Sir John had died. It must have been a fairly lenient kind of custody for William Chambers because he became friendly with a lady named Emma

Photograph showing rear of Llanelli House. (T. Ace)

William Chambers, junior.
(National Library of Wales)

Maria Adams who bore him a son called William in 1809. After the victory at Waterloo, Chambers returned to Kent with Emma Maria and William, then aged six. In 1816 another child was born, a girl named after her mother. Chambers's marriage was not recognised at the time since, according to Hardwicke's Act of 1754, marriages had to be performed by Anglican clergy to be deemed lawful.

John Stepney Cowell (a nephew) went to the courts to establish the illegitimacy of William Chambers, Junior, which made it impossible for him to inherit the Stepney estate on the death of his father and William Chambers, Senior, was deemed to be 'tenant for life'. William, Junior, like his father, was educated at Eton and St John's College, Cambridge.[7] He married Joanna Payne at Llanelli Parish Church in 1835 where six children were subsequently baptized.[8] Both father and son were magistrates in Llanelli. William Chambers, Junior, was a radical in politics and was the founder of the Llanelli Reform Society. He played an active part in the life of the town and, when the corrupt local government was re-organised in 1850, he became the first Chairman of the Board of Health which today would be the equivalent of Mayor. It was a post he held until he left the town in 1855. Chambers even made a brave attempt at making the town more attractive by planting trees on its streets.

William Chambers, Junior, is also important in the industrial development of the town for it was he who established the Pottery. He took an active interest in its construction, which began in 1839, and he also made sure that there were good homes for his workers by building substantial houses for them in Pottery

A collection of Llanelli Pottery. (Llanelli Library)

Street and Pottery Row (later Pottery Place). Many Staffordshire potters lived in these houses, some of whom had previously worked at Swansea's Glamorgan Pottery which closed in 1835. When cholera struck Llanelli in 1849, a subsequent report stated that its primary cause was poor housing and that its effects would have been minimal if housing, generally, had been of the standard set by Chambers.

Vicar Ebenezer Morris. (Llanelli Library)

Production at the pottery was begun in 1840 under the management of William Bryant. There was a report in the *Cambrian* newspaper of February 1842, describing a dinner given to his employees by Chambers at the Ship and Castle, now the Stepney Hotel. William Bryant presided over two groups sitting at separate tables, with punch for the drinkers served at one and lemonade for the teetotallers at the other. Bryant urged the workers to save all they could so that they could purchase their own houses eventually, which was the 'firm determination of Mr Chambers'. Until he gave up his interest in 1855, William Chambers, Junior, remained actively involved with the Pottery which was Llanelli's first and rare example of light industry which provided work for artists, craftsmen and general labourers until its closure in 1923.

In 1819, the Revd Ebenezer Morris was a curate at Llanelli. In 1820, at the age of 30, he succeeded Jeremiah Davies as vicar.[9] Morris had a rival in the Revd Thomas Clement who was also a candidate for the post of Vicar. The living was in the gift of Rees Goring Thomas of Llannon, the patron and lay impropriator of the tithes of the parish. Goring Thomas could have decided the issue himself, without reference to anyone else, but he gave the parishioners the choice and they chose Morris. Clement then went off in a huff and built his own chapel about half a mile outside Five Roads. He lived at Bryngroes Fach nearby and was minister of the chapel, called Capel Clement, which was run on Independent lines. Clement lived to be 76 and was buried in a coffin made of Mynyddygarreg limestone. When the chapel was closed, his body was removed to Rehoboth chapel, Five Roads.[10]

Ebenezer Morris was a tall and handsome man with a fine physique. He was also a very

Drawing showing the church's second tower.

good preacher both in Welsh and English and drew large congregations. Indeed, so many people had crowded into the gallery on one occasion that it cracked under their weight. It was probably from this time that thought was given to church repairs and, indeed, it was during the twenties that the second steeple was taken down. It was considered to be unsafe but its demolition was not universally popular. Not many churches could boast of two towers. The tower which was removed was almost as high as the battlement tower and had contained a sanctus bell, rung at the elevation of the host in Catholic times when the bread and wine was believed to turn into the body and blood of Christ.[11] Morris was a staunch and uncompromising Anglican who strongly resented the rising tide of Nonconformity in Llanelli.

The Church Rate was levied for the upkeep of the fabric of the church and this was agreed at Vestry meetings. These meetings were fairly uneventful when the majority of parishioners were Anglicans, but now that Nonconformists were in the majority, matters were very different. A Vestry was held in 1836 to raise £45 and it was decided to do so by voluntary subscription. Nonconformists were willing to contribute to the Church Rate out of affection for the old church, which, after all, was the town's cradle of Christianity. Morris flew into a temper at the meeting and insisted that the Church Rate should still be compulsory even though the Vestry had voted for voluntary payment.

Vestry meetings also elected churchwardens and it was at such a meeting in 1837 that John James of Cilaugwyn Farm was elected as warden. James was a member at Capel Als and Morris wrote to him to request his attendance at church. James paid no attention to the vicar's request and was consequently summoned to appear before the archdeacon's court at Carmarthen where be was admonished and ordered to pay costs. James refused to pay and soon found himself in Carmarthen Jail. His friends rallied to his cause, paid the costs which had now reached £20 and secured his release.

Morris tried to argue that James had been jailed not for refusing to attend church but for contempt of court in refusing to pay costs. There was also talk of collusion between John James and his minister, David Rees, to the effect that Rees had put him up for election in the first place and advised him not to attend church. David Rees, as well as being minister of Capel Als, was also the editor of *Y Diwygiwr* (The Reformer) the organ of the Independent cause and John James was able to put his case in its columns in February 1839. He wrote that he had never sought office and was unaware of the Vestry meeting. When elected he said he did not think he would have to attend church because his predecessor had not done so. He denied that David Rees had put him up for election and said that he had actually advised him to attend church occasionally. A similar case involved

Llanelli in 1854. Painting by Mrs Havard (Llanelli Library)

David Jones of Llannon, also under Morris's care. Jones, a weaver, was prosecuted by Morris and ended up spending seven months in Carmarthen Jail. A circuit judge ordered him to be freed and awarded him £40 costs. Soon after, Morris once again threatened Jones with prosecution and the poor man left home in a state of great agitation and died at Gorseinon in a house where he had sought shelter. These two cases were given great importance in the press at the time.

Rees Goring Thomas built the Thomas Arms and leased it to Vicar Morris. At its grand opening in 1830, the vicar invited all the county magistrates to dinner. After dinner, the discussion turned to the etiquette of singing during which the Vicar got very angry before standing on a chair and assaulting John Edward Saunders of Glanrhydw, Llandyfaelog, himself a big man and wont to be aggressive. He struck Saunders repeatedly until he lay senseless on the floor and attempted to walk over the table to continue the attack. His friends then carried Saunders into a bedroom and prudently stayed there with him. The place was in uproar, when Morris stormed into the bedroom and threw everybody out, including Saunders who, by this time, had recovered consciousness. According to Innes, the Vicar then threw Chambers through the window, but there is, unfortunately, no evidence of this in the case brought by Chambers against the Vicar in 1832.

It was in 1832, that the Bostock and Wombell Menagerie came to Parc Eynon and William Chambers and a group of friends were invited to a private viewing prior to the opening. A drunken Vicar Morris appeared on the scene and demanded admittance. When the showman refused to let him through, Morris, true to his customary method of settling arguments, knocked him senseless and walked through the entrance, taking with him a crowd of people waiting to pay to go in. The vicar then proceeded to lecture the crowd, comparing Chambers and his friends to some of the animals. As if this were not enough, Morris followed Chambers home and, when he reached the front door of Llanelli House, the Vicar demanded that Chambers move out of his way. Chambers refused, saying he was on his own doorstep, whereupon the vicar repeatedly kicked him. This time, the vicar was arrested, handcuffed and brought to court. He was fined £20 and bound over to keep the peace.[12] The Vicar was really living up to his description as a 'fighting parson'. In his less ill-tempered role, he was a staunch Churchman and a great champion of education and set up the first National (Church of England) school on the Wern.[13] He was also a great supporter of the Mechanics' Institute whose library subsequently became the foundation of Llanelli's Public Library.

By 1844, another church restoration had become necessary. This was carried out by Edward Bagot who, in turn had been a surveyor, a tinplate manufacturer and, presumably in retirement, a clergyman. John Innes wryly states: 'He restored the Parish church as a bull restores a china-shop…he removed the ancient south porch, took away the oak beams of the roof …removed the wonderful old three-decker pulpit and was stopped in his career of destruction only by lack of funds.' The 'restored' church was reopened in 1845. St Paul's church was consecrated in 1850[14] to serve the people of the Wern, and Capel Ifan, Pontyberem, which had become a Methodist chapel, was rescued for the church by Morris. He was vicar of Llanelli for 47 years until 1867 although his last years were rather sad, being paralysed and confined to a wheelchair. He was also heavily in debt to his patron, Rees Goring Thomas, and was declared a bankrupt. One of the young curates who helped him greatly during this time was A.J.M. Green. Green married the vicar's granddaughter and they became the parents of Charles Green, the second Archbishop of Wales.

Nonconformist chapels began springing up all over the town. Zion was built in 1823 and became independent of Adulam by 1831.[15] By 1840 it had 400 members, and in the following year it released 45 of those to start the cause at Bethel, Seaside, with Zion contributing half the building costs of £800. Not to be out-done by the Baptists, the Independent cause built a new chapel at Capel Als in 1831 and, a decade later, sent 116 members to start Siloa, almost next door to Bethel, and 40 members to Bryn Chapel. In 1839, Capel Als sent out 80 of its members to set up an English-language congregation at Park Church. Capel Newydd was rebuilt in 1828-9 and again in 1840 but the Calvinistic Methodists built no more chapels until the second half of the 19th century. The Wesleyan Methodists extended their chapel in Wind Street with the Revd James Buckley preaching on its opening in 1828. Buckley was unsympathetic to Welsh speakers and the Welsh-language congregation had to be content with a very small meeting-place in Marine Street, Seaside. When the English Wesleyans moved to a new chapel in Hall Street, the Welsh congregation came to Wind Street and called it Jerusalem.

The Mormons came to town in 1847 and, in the next two years, built up a congregation of 180, worshipping in Island Place, by 1849.[16] They attracted members from both Zion and Capel Newydd which caused much concern in Noncomformist circles. Many Llanelli Mormons subsequently emigrated to Salt Lake City, Utah, USA.

An interesting literary work was published in London in 1847 called 'Mary de Clifford' by Madeline Jones.[17] It was a work of fiction centred on Llanelli which was described as Melton (a town where metals were melted?) 'A vile place, the streets always dirty and full of black coal-dust from the neighbouring collieries, and the houses small and ill-built.' The author is kinder concerning the surrounding countryside and writes of 'Swiss Valley – a very pretty valley.' Was this, perhaps the first time that Cwmlliedi was so described? Another document, which throws light on the first half of the 19th century, is a series of letters written by an employee to James Buckley of Bryncaerau between 1887 and 1888.[18] The unidentified servant describes what he remembers as a boy and what he heard from older people, having been born fairly early in the century. His English is often poor and his spelling worse but he writes, in a good style, a mixture of sound history and dubious gossip. For example, he starts with: 'The Mansels of Trumsaran could hunt a fox from Spuder's Bridge to Lougher ford on their own property.' As a piece of gossip he tells of the transfer of Stradey lands from Mary Mansel to Thomas Lewis of Llandeilo: 'He made the will for himself. After she expired, he put a fly in her throat to prove there was life in her when she signed the will.' Thomas Lewis was not even present at the signing of the will before witnesses, but why let the facts get in the way of a good story?

Notes to Chapter VI

1 See list of shipping places in John Innes: *Old Llanelly* (1902).
2 Later known as Middle Dock (Doc Canol) because it lay between the Carmarthenshire Dock and the Copperworks Dock. It was taken over from Roderick and Bowen by the Pemberton coal interest.
3 Malcolm Symons: *Coal Mining in Llanelli Area. Vol. I*, (Llanelli Borough Council) p.260.
4 The projected destination, Castell y Garreg, was not reached.
5 He was convicted of malpractice in the Porthyrhyd area but got away with a fine of £50 because six of the nine magistrates present were members of the Kidwelly Trust. D. Williams: *The Rebecca Riots*. (University Press, 1954.) Professor Williams remarks: 'Many a man had been transported for less'. He was said to have owned gates worth £6,000 in South Wales.
6 Recent evidence points to the fact that William Chambers was, in fact, the illegitimate son of Sir John Stepney, resulting from a liaison with Mrs Ann Chambers. Two other persons named in the succession, Orlando Williams and Richard Falkland, were also illegitimate sons of Sir John's. See article in *Llanelli Miscellany No.17*, 'The Stepney/Chambers Inheritance' by Dr J.D. Davies.
7 Chambers does not appear to have graduated at Cambridge. Howard Jones, of Hendy, has

acquired a copy of the registration of the birth of William Chambers, Junior. On it, Emma Maria Adams is described as his father's wife. His book, *Llanelli Lives*, was published in 2000.

8   There were 14 children in all. Two, at least, died in infancy. Charles Campbell Chambers was a steel-merchant in Swansea, played cricket for Glamorgan, was captain of Swansea RFC and was the first President of the Welsh Rugby Union. See Gareth Hughes and Robert Pugh: *Llanelly Pottery* (Llanelli Borough Council, 1990) for further biographical details and involvement with the Pottery.

9   A CD-ROM has recently been researched by K.M. Jones, a descendant of Ebenezer Morris, and edited by William and Benita Rees of Meiros Publications, Llanelli. Other valuable CD-ROMs of local interest produced by Meiros Publications are, *Llanelli – Birth of a Town, Parc Howard – from Mansion to Museum* and *Old Llanelly and John Innes*.

10   Clement was actually buried in three coffins, one of wood, one of lead and one of stone. All these were reinterred in Rehoboth. A year after Clement's death, with the chapel willed to the Revd David Davies, the will was challenged and the chapel closed as a place of worship. A rough translation of an epitaph reputedly inscribed on Clement's coffin is:
'Clement's coffin made of stone
Will keep its colour, that we know,
And when the world shall end in flames,
It will be white as snow.'

11   See Arthur Mee: *History of Llanelly Parish Church.* op. cit.
John Innes: *Old Llanelly*, op.cit. and article by J.Wyn Evans in *Footprints of Faith*, op. cit.

12   The case for the prosecution may be found in Document LC7116 at Llanelli Public Library. The case does not contain the charge of throwing Chambers out of the window as quoted by John Innes. Vicar Morris is, however, much condemned for putting up posters and inciting Welsh-speaking workers against Chambers.

13   There had previously been a small schoolroom attached to the church since 1806.

14   St Paul's later became a parish of its own. It cost £2,300 to build, a sum which came from a Government grant and a Church Building Society grant in addition to voluntary subscriptions. It seated 500 people. The church was closed in 1980 and demolished in 1987.

15   Zion's request for release from Adulam is a veritable epistle written on 4 February 1831. For those who read Welsh, it is to be found in *Hanes Sïon, Llanelli* by E.T. Jones and R.T. Jones (Llanelli, 1931). There are many histories of individual Llanelli chapels, Welsh and English, for those who require further information.

16   The original Mormon temple stood, until quite recently, opposite the Island House. It was latterly known as Elim Gospel Hall. A new temple has been built at Llwynwhilwg.

17   The work was published by J.S. Pratt, London, 1847, and is 300 pages long, containing 14 chapters. It had previously appeared as a serial in *World of Fashion*, a London monthly magazine under the name Mary Mortimer. Local places are easily identified such as Belinda-Felinfoel, Bryncariad-Bryncaerau, Stanmore-Stradey, Cathwelly-Kidwelly and Merlin's Carr-Carmarthen. Dundas Cottage is Aelybryn and Welsh Chapel is Adulam. Characters readily recognisable include The Roomys – Chambers Family, The Lewishams-Lewis (Stradey) Family, The Y-Bars-Raby Family, Sir John Stepwell-Sir John Stepney and Mr Machiavel-Vicar Morris. A transcript is available at Llanelli Public Library. It is not a good read.

18   These letters were found in an old desk at Buckley's Brewery in 1985. I have copies in my possession given to me at the time by Jack Morgan, ex-secretary of the Brewery. See W.K. Buckley: 'Memoirs of an Old Retainer', *Carmarthenshire Antiquary* (1986). The article contains an explanatory note by Francis Jones on 'The Legacy of Mary Anne Mansel'.

Chapter VII
Industrial Pioneers
– Raby and Nevill

IN 1807, E.H. Malkin described the town as follows: 'Llanelly is a small, irregular, dirty town, nor does the appearance of its inhabitants, chiefly miners and sailors, render it more inviting' – a severe criticism of the town and its workers.[1] A similar observation was made by Henry Scrine towards the end of the previous century who complained of 'the miserable village of Llanelly…famous for nothing but a deserted seat of the Stepneys.'[2] Iolo Morgannwg's description in 1796[3] was more dispassionate when he wrote of a good trade in coal leading to an increase in the population with better houses being built even though there were still very many one-floor cottages still to be seen. He also mentioned the unique church with its two towers. Richard Fenton's factual report said that Llanelly was a small town of 51 houses, governed by a Portreeve and that the parish was seven miles long from the river Loughor to Pontyberem and about three miles wide from the Lliedi to Llannon.[4]

One of the reasons why tourists took a jaundiced view of Llanelli was that the approach roads to the town were in such a bad state. The main road between Swansea and Carmarthen lay through Pontarddulais and Llannon. A subsidiary road between Pontarddulais, Llanelli, and thence on to Kidwelly, was described as the worst stretch on the Gloucester to Milford road.[5] Some tourists, however, preferred this route for its scenery as compared with the Llannon road. Although the advent of Turnpike Trusts had seen a general improvement in the state of the highways by this time, many were more concerned with the collection of tolls than with the upkeep of roads. Frequently there

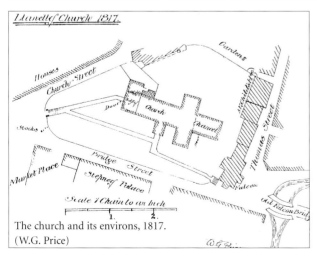

The church and its environs, 1817.
(W.G. Price)

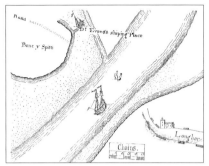

The Spitty Ferry, 1772. (W.G. Price)

were roads which raised clouds of dust in summer and notorious potholes deteriorated into muddy quagmires in winter.

The main road westward lay through Trimsaran and was the old Roman road. Another road to Carmarthen was via Penyfai Lane, Five Roads and Meinciau. Penyfai Lane is a good example of an ancient trackway in that it is very narrow, has twists and turns and has the characteristic sunken-hollow appearance in its upper section.[6] Travellers approaching from the east could save time by crossing the river from Loughor at low water. Although quicker, saving 10 miles, it could sometimes be quite hazardous, especially on foot, as the Revd James Buckley, among many others, found out on his way to Llanelli. There was also a ferry crossing between Loughor and Spitty Bank which was operated between 1782 and 1827 by William Hopkins using two boats and paying a rental of £2 10s 0d per annum to the Vaughans of Golden Grove.[7] The ferry came to an end in 1834 when the first Loughor Bridge was built and, by this time, there was also a general improvement in the state of the roads.

It was along the rutted roads of 1796 that Alexander Raby came to the approaches of Llanelli, reputedly crossing Falcon bridge with a wagon containing £175,000. Whether the figure is correct or not, Raby was certainly a wealthy man. He was born in Smithfield in 1747 and was a Freeman of the City of London as well as being a member of the prestigious Drapers' Company of which Lord Horatio Nelson was a contemporary member.[8] Raby carried on business at five different London addresses and worked iron and copper at Cobham, Surrey. He also had interest in copper and coal in the Neath area. His main concern in Llanelli was with coal, not only for making iron but also for export.

The coal was mined on Stradey estate land and included Caebad, near Sandy Bridge; Caemain, near the present Caemain Centre; Cilfig, between Old Road and New Road; and the Slip collieries on the Parc Howard slope facing Pentrepoeth Road. In connection with the iron furnace, he built a forge just to the north of Sandy Bridge in an area then called Morfa Bychan. He had built houses for his workers at Cobham and now proceeded to build almost 100 houses in Forge Row, Caerelms and Pentrepoeth. This was probably the first housing development of any size in the newly industrial Llanelli.

Raby amassed a great deal of money making cannon and shot during the early years of the Napoleonic Wars, with the furnace working at full tilt by day and by

The Carmarthenshire Dock in 1969. (Llanelli Library)

night. He built a house opposite the furnace with a commanding view of the works and called it, appropriately, Furnace House. The house was subsequently named The Dell when the Stepneys lived there, but it was demolished some years ago to make way for housing. Raby had two daughters and two sons. Alexander, Junior, lived at Bryn-ar-y-Môr where the present Stradey Park Hotel stands, and Arthur lived at Caemawr, latterly known as Glyncoed which burned down in its days as a country club and now has a housing estate built in its grounds. These two houses were immediately to the north and south of the furnace and, with their father's house in the middle, the family had perfect oversight of all the work that went on there. Raby also built Cilfig House, near the colliery, as a house for his coal-agent.

Raby built a tramroad connecting his furnace with the forge and collieries in the Morfa Bychan area and leading down to his shipping place at Seaside, later known as Squire Raby's Dock and, later still, as the Carmarthenshire Dock, immediately to the north of the present North Dock. After such a promising start, however, Raby eventually ran into deep financial trouble.

In some years between 1796 and 1804, the furnace alone was making £2,000.[9] In 1804, he extended his enterprises to the Box Colliery, opposite the present Star Hotel, where he worked a 9 foot seam and, in three years, between 1802 and 1805, his collieries raised an amazing 66,000 tons of coal.[10] Yet, Raby had seriously overstretched his resources. His downfall was occasioned by his eager participation in the Carmarthenshire Railway set up by an Act of Parliament of 1802. Raby was the major shareholder in this venture which was to run a railway-line between Llanelli and Castell-y-Garreg, near Llandybie, a source of ironstone and limestone. The company agreed to purchase Raby's own railroad system for

Cwmddyche Farm, 1880. (Llanelli Library). At the western end of Cwm Terrace, Furnace, today.

a sum of £3,117, a railway which has been recognised by CADW as the oldest public railway in Britain. Raby's shipping place was to be developed into a major dock and he stood to do well out of making iron rails and wheels for the horse-drawn railway. Raby, himself, made improvements to the existing wheels making them run more smoothly. One of his employees, Charles Le Caan, who lived at Cwmddyche Farm, invented a braking system and L-shaped rail-plates. The prospects for Raby looked very bright indeed at this time.

Alexander Raby was virtually in control of the Carmarthenshire Railway but he was soon being accused of looking after his own interest to the detriment of the company. He had run unauthorised branch lines to his own works and collieries and had avoided paying the necessary tolls. It was found that the capital assets of the company had all been used up and no dividends had been paid. On top of all this, Thomas Lewis was pressing Raby for arrears of rent owing to the Stradey Estate, amounting to £1,000. Lewis, a Llandeilo solicitor, had inherited the estate on the death of Mary Mansel. In 1806 a general meeting of the Carmarthenshire Railway Company was convened and a sub-committee set up to survey progress on the line.

The committee found that Raby had been borrowing money, using his land and property as security and, during the next two years, he was forced to assign all his possessions into the hands of trustees. These soon found that there were not sufficient funds to discharge his debts. The situation worsened from year to year but somehow Raby still survived. In 1819, Charles Nevill, of the Copperworks, came to his rescue by advancing him a loan of £5,000. This meant that all Raby's concerns were now effectively under Nevill's control although Raby was still managing them. The furnace was blown out by 1818 and Raby concentrated on the coal industry. In 1823, he handed over the management of his collieries to his son Arthur[11] and returned to live in Wells in Somerset where he died, aged 88 years, in 1835. During his 27 years in

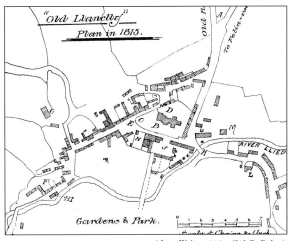

Llanelli in 1815. (W.G. Price)

Llanelli, Raby laid the foundations of the town's industrial future. He played a prominent part in the civic life of Llanelli and was a benevolent man, in many ways. On a visit to Carmarthen Jail, for example, he secured the release of a prisoner in whom he saw some potential and gave him employment as a clerk. He was obviously unwise in his financial dealings but his greatest contribution to the history of our town was the fact that he was prepared to stake his entire wealth on developing its industrial resources. This encouraged other industrialists, with more acute financial acumen, to come in to Llanelli and set up their own works. Alexander Raby had led the way in which others were to follow.

The first to tread Raby's footsteps, and by far the most influential, were the Nevills. Charles Nevill had managed a copper works in Birmingham and had been Mayor of the city before coming to Wales to manage a copper works in Swansea just before the turn of the century.[12] He turned his sights on Llanelli and formed a consortium with John Guest, another Birmingham industrialist and William Savill, a London copper merchant, with the purpose of building a copper works on the Llanelli coalfield.

The company went through several changes of name in the ensuing years

but it was generally known as the Copperworks Company although it was also concerned with the smelting of silver and lead. After exploring the possibilities, Charles

Glanmor or Field House. Nevill's Llanelli home. (Llanelli Library)

Nevill wrote to Guest and Savill in 1804: 'The result of our enquiries are that it will be most to the interest of the company to erect our works at Llanelly…Our reasons for this determination were the very superior quality of coal in that neighbourhood and the abundant resources which surround it.'[13] Sites surveyed for the copper works included Machynys and Spitty Bank but Nevill settled on Penrhos in Seaside. Work began on the buildings and the dock in 1805 and production started in the same year. Charles's son, Richard Janion Nevill, was assigned a share in his father's partnership in 1807. The Nevills played a large part in improving the safety of the approaches to the dock where copper-ore was unloaded and coal exported. In time, they came to own most of the Llanelli coalfield. Charles Nevill died in 1873, at his home, Vauxhall House, where the Grange now stands, and Richard Janion became a full partner in 1876.[14] He lived at Field House, or Glanmor House, near the site of St Peter's church today.

R.J. Nevill was a man of imposing stature, standing over 6ft tall. The success of the Copperworks was due, largely, to his astute management over a period of almost half a century. He was a man of wide interests, acted as French consul in Llanelli, and was a member of many learned societies. He travelled abroad extensively and had agricultural as well as industrial interests which he put to good use after moving from Field House to the magnificent mansion of Llangennech Park.[15]

Richard Janion Nevill.
(National Library of Wales)

He was very much involved in the civic life of Llanelli and was High Sheriff of Carmarthenshire in 1836. He was a Justice of the Peace and, at the height of the Rebecca Riots locally in the summer 1843. It is indicative of the respect shown towards him that he travelled every day by horse and carriage between Llanelli and Llangennech without being molested in any way. In winter, Nevill travelled by train on a railway which he had been instrumental in building between Llanelli and Llandybie by way of Pontarddulais. A story is told of a train kept waiting at Llanelli because Nevill was late arriving. A messenger was sent to the Copper Works to enquire when the train should leave and was met by the response: 'The train will leave when I come.' Another tale is told of one of his captains rushing out of Nevill's office to

A drawing of the Copperworks in 1848. (Llanelli Library)

be warned by the harbourmaster: 'Don't sail on this tide, there's a storm coming up.' The captain replied: ' That's nothing compared to the storm in the office.' In spite of his short temper at times, R.J. Nevill showed great concern for his employees and provided them with housing, health-care and education for their children. A report of 1818 describes a school being held in a storeroom at the Copper Works known as the Barracks. There were 59 pupils on the roll – the children of workers at the Copper Works and Caemain and Box collieries. In 1846, Nevill leased land from William Chambers and built Copperworks School for boys and infants to which children of all working-class parents were admitted.[16] A girls' school was added in 1852 and a row of teachers' houses built, called Heol Fawr, which stood between the school and the Western Tinplate works until comparatively recent times although teachers no longer lived in them. Nevill was of the opinion that workers would be convinced of the value of education if they could be persuaded to pay to have their children educated. His workmen paid contributions from their wages to maintain the school and the children were asked to bring 'school pence'. Fees were graded for members of the same family and the children of non-employees paid a penny extra per week.

The company bore the cost of any deficit for the first few years but, after that, the school was self- supporting. In addition to the normal syllabus of Reading, Writing and Arithmetic, there were classes in Navigation and older Llanelli inhabitants still remember a compass set into the floor of one of the classrooms.

There was genuine mourning in Llanelli when R.J. Nevill died in 1856. Among lines written in his honour by Titus Lewis at Llanelli Eisteddfod in 1856 were:

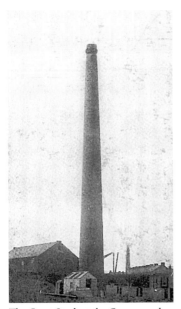

The Great Stack at the Copperworks.
(Llanelli Library)

Dark is the cloud, appalling is the gloom,
Llanelly weeps and sighs o'er Nevill's tomb;
All shed alike the sympathising tear,
Alike all sob: 'A friend lies buried here.'

He lies buried at Llangennech churchyard. A testimonial fund was set up and the Nevill Memorial Hall was added to the Atheneum, the present Public Library, in memory of Llanelli's foremost industrialist. In a tribute paid to Nevill at its opening, the following words appear: 'He elevated his workpeople, socially and morally, and liberally supported all institutions tending to improve the conditions of the masses.' There is only a very slight exaggeration in the old saying: 'Nevill made the Copperworks and the Copperworks made Llanelli.'

In 1839, Nevill had built a square stack, 272ft high, allegedly to carry fumes from the works over the top of Bigyn Hill borne by the prevailing southwesterly winds, even though the fumes were claimed to be 'disinfectant and salutary.' It was not until 1861, however, that the famous round Stac Fawr (Great Stack) was built under the management of his son Charles W. Nevill. This huge stack was originally 320ft high but was shortened to just over 300ft subsequently. The base was 33ft across, narrowing to 10ft at the top; it used up more than 700,000 bricks and cost £2,300, the same amount as the original square stack.[17] It was the giant among Llanelli's future forest of stacks and acted as a landmark for incoming ships. Until its final demolition in 1966, the Stac Fawr was a proud symbol of Llanelli's industrial history. The Copper Works, although under different management, is still in existence and some of its production of copper wire takes place in the original buildings, now almost 200 years old.

The period between 1795 and 1855 must have been the most exciting time ever in the whole history of Llanelli. So many events, so many changes and so many colourful characters conspire together to make it a centrepiece of the town's historical tapestry. In 1795, Innes tells us that John Wedge[18] made a wager that there were not 500 people living in Llanelli, a bet which he apparently won. Certainly, the population could not have been much above 1,000 at that time. By the time of the first official census in 1801, Llanelli's population was 2,972, including the hamlets of Borough, Berwig, Glyn, Hengoed and Westfa. These hamlets were administrative units of land; Borough was the town area, Berwig stretched through Llwynhendy and Bynea to the Loughor river, Glyn lay between Felinfoel and Pontyberem, Hengoed was the area between Felinfoel and Pwll, and Westfa lay between Felinfoel and Machynys. In fact, the borders of Glyn, Hengoed and Westfa all converged within half a mile of Felinfoel. The population at the beginning of the century, was engaged mainly in agriculture, coal-mining and in Raby's iron-making enterprises. By 1811, the population increased by almost 1,000 to 3,891 and, by 1821, it had reached 5,649, showing the influence of the Copper Works and the increased mining activities of Nevill and other operators in the coal industry.

Further industrial and maritime activity is indicated by a 2,000 increase during the following decade to 7,646 by 1831[19] and, in 1841, the population reached five-figures for the first time at 11,155. In 1851, the figure was 13,663, by which time the first tinworks with its attendant iron-forge (1846) was built at Dafen and the Llanelli Tinplate Works (later renamed Morfa) was in the process of being built. These latter developments would herald a new and significant era in Llanelli's history.

The 1830s saw the beginning of a period of great social unrest. The Great Reform Act of 1832 had promised much but ended in disappointment when the franchise was extended only to 40-shilling freeholders and Llanelli was to share an MP with Carmarthen. The Poor Law Amendment Act of 1834 provided for the building of Workhouses to house paupers whereas, before this time, they had been entitled to outdoor parish relief in their own homes. We have already seen how the Church Rate was causing concern and, now, the growing Nonconformist population was also objecting to the payment of tithes to the church, especially as these had fallen into lay hands whose main concern was to squeeze as much profit as possible from them. Tithes had been easier to pay in kind but, from 1836 onwards, they had been commuted to money payments which poorer tenants found difficult to find. After the end of the Napoleonic War, the Corn Law was introduced which kept the price of corn artificially high in the interests of great landowners who formed the majority in Parliament.[20] The period after 1815 saw a great increase in the price of food generally as well as a steep rise in unemployment. All these factors were fairly general throughout Wales but what brought matters to a dramatic head were the tollgates of the Turnpike Trusts in south-west Wales.

Notes to Chapter VII

1 E.H. Malkin: *Scenery of South Wales* (1807).
2 Henry Scrine: *Tours through Wales* (1795).
3 Iolo Morgannwg: *Travels in Carmarthenshire* (1796).
4 Richard Fenton, *Tours in Wales* (1804-1811). There are many more descriptions, mainly

derogatory in nature, such as:

William Mavor: *British Tourist* (1798). 'The miserable village of Llanelly, close to the coast at which is a deserted seat of the Stepneys.'

Revd J. Evans: 'A poor small town inhabited principally by fishermen and colliers.' (1803).

5 South Wales Association for the Improvement of Roads report. The association was founded in 1789 and comprised landed and commercial interests in South Wales. See also article on 'Carmarthenshire Roads' by A.H.T. Lewis in *Carmarthenshire Antiquary* (1971).

6 See article by Michael C. Evans in *Carmarthenshire Antiquary* (1988).

7 Buckley was almost drowned while attempting to ford the river. Ferry charges were: Carriages – 6d per wheel; horses and cows – 1d; calves, sheep and pigs – ½d; foot-passengers – ½d.

8 Lyn John has pursued valuable original research concerning Raby's life in London and Cobham. This appears in his video *The Raby Heritage. Part II*. Both Parts I and II are rich sources of information on Raby and his contribution to Llanelli's industrial development.

9 Research by Dr J.D. Davies at the Ministry of Defence (ex-War Office) WO 48.270-1796/1797 and WO 274-1803-04 showing payments made to Raby for the supply of cannon and shot.

10 More detailed information on the collieries and on Raby's subsequent financial troubles may be found in Malcolm Symons: *Coal Mining in the Llanelli Area. Vol. I* (L.B.C., 1979).

11 More interesting research by Dr J.D. Davies shows that Arthur Turnour Raby joined the Consular Service in 1846, serving in Italy, Bulgaria, Turkey, the Middle East and the United States before retiring in 1889 as Consul to the Baltic States of Russia.

12 The *Llanelly Guardian* (14 June 1888) states that Nevill came to Swansea in 1795 but Nevill MS III suggests 1797.

13 Nevill MS IV. Copy of a letter of 1 November, 1804.

14 Charles Nevill's widow was killed when crossing a railroad in May 1821. She was run over by a truck. It was one of the earliest of many such accidents in Llanelli where railways ran along the streets.

15 For details of R.J. Nevill's residence in Llangennech, see Alwyn C. Charles: *History of Llangennech* (Llangennech Community Council, 1997).

16 See Isobel Sadler: *Cradled in Copper*. Copperworks Infant/Nursery School 1847-1997 (Carmarthenshire County Council, 1997).

17 The stack was designed and built by John Bowen, engineer at the works. I have in my possession a copy of notes made by Thomas Evans, Siop Newydd, Pwll, of 'The New Round Stack. Built 1861 at the Llanelly Copper Works':

Opening on Top Stack 10ft

Thickness on Top 1 foot 2 inches

Diameter at Bottom 33ft

Thickness at Bottom 3ft

Height from Base 320ft

Bricks in Stack 717,383

The original notes are in the possession of Miss Eluned Jones, Pwll.

18 Wedge was a surveyor who drew a chart of the Loughor estuary in 1805.

19 In 1831, there were 802 houses in Llanelli. By 1848, there were 1,552, almost twice as many. 143 houses were rated as £10 or more; 152 between £5 and £10; 1,236 under £5; and 21 empty. Of these houses, 562 were in the town, 452 in Seaside and 448 on the Wern. *Borough Rate Book*, 1848.

20 No corn to be imported until the price of home-grown corn reached 80s a quarter. The Corn Laws were not repealed until 1846.

Chapter VIII
Rebecca and Her Children

TURNPIKE Trusts had laid the foundations of a good system of main roads in the country over a period of 100 years since individual parishes had no longer been responsible for their upkeep. In the 19th century, however, by the end of the 1830s, the Trusts found themselves financially exhausted, failed to maintain the roads, and farmed out their tolls to rather unsavoury entrepreneurs. Llanelli town itself was ringed around by gates belonging to the Kidwelly Trust but rented out to William Lewis, a Swansea businessman who attracted almost universal hatred. Llandafen Gate guarded the Swansea road on the Llanelli side of the Dafen river. The Llannon road was barred by the Tŷrfran Gate near the present Parc Howard. Furnace Gate collected tolls on the Carmarthen roads via Trimsaran and Five Roads while the Sandy Gate covered the newly built road to Pembrey and lay just under the present Sandy Bridge.

The first incident of the Rebecca Riots took place at Efailwen tollgate on the Carmarthenshire-Pembrokeshire border in the Summer of 1839.[1] Nothing more was heard of Rebecca until three years had passed and the tollgate at nearby St Clears was smashed to pieces in 1842. This was a place well-known to Hugh Williams, a solicitor and a Chartist who had lived at Ferryside and Kidwelly and had set up a branch of the Working Men's Association at Carmarthen. The first two Rebecca attacks, in 1839 and 1842, had coincided with the first two Chartist National Conventions at which Hugh Williams was a delegate.[2]

Also, in 1839, Williams had defended workers accused after a Chartist uprising at Llanidloes and there is reason to believe that he had foreseen a coming together of the two movements in the cause of securing voting rights for all workers. His sister had married Richard Cobden who was secretary of the Anti-Corn Law League and was the man mainly responsible for the repeal of that law in 1846. The house where Williams lived at Ferryside was, in fact, called Cobden Villa. Hugh Williams has been suspected of being the mastermind behind the Rebecca Riots, as had David Rees of Llanelli, but there never was a chief Rebecca. The term refers only to the leader of a local group; the Rebecca movement was never organised as Chartism was.

The Rebecca storm reached its climax in 1843 and by this time, it is estimated that 2,000 troops were stationed in west Wales, consisting of both cavalry and infantry units. The most spectacular event was the attack on Carmarthen Workhouse in June. Threats were also made towards the workhouse in Llanelli and, early in July, tollgates were attacked at Kidwelly, Mynyddygarreg, Meinciau, Pontyates and Bolgoed, Pontarddulais. Llanelli was being encircled by a ring of fire and, early in the morning of 3 August, that fire burned into the very heart of the town. At the toll-house of Sandy Gate, Jenkin Hugh was asleep on the settle downstairs while his wife, Catherine, and the children were in bed upstairs. At 1.45a.m. Jenkin Hugh heard a commotion outside and knelt on a table to peer out through the window. He saw that the tollgate was being attacked in torchlight by a group of people in white gowns. This was followed by hammering on the door and two shotgun blasts at the window. Soon, the door crashed in and a group of Rebecca's black-faced 'daughters' burst into the toll-house. Hugh was ordered out of the house and his wife and children escaped through the back window while the roof was being torn down. Jenkin Hugh ran back into the house again to rescue the clock while the gang completed their task of destruction.[3] Hugh then heard them go, cheering and firing on their way along the railway line, to the Furnace tollgate where a similar attack was made on the gate and the toll-house, perhaps with even more severity including physical violence vented on the gate-keeper.[4]

The following morning Jenkin Hugh, with his arm in a sling following a blow from the butt of a gun, walked into town with his wife. They found a magistrate and told him what had happened during the night. Hugh named three persons: Francis McKiernon, landlord of the Tŷ Melyn Hotel and coach proprietor; George Laing, publican and haulage contractor; and John Phillips, all of Llanelli town. The magistrates' clerk wrote down their sworn statements and issued three warrants of arrest. McKiernon was a man who had and would still play an active part in the life of Llanelli. He was a popular publican and owned two stage-coaches, one travelling regularly to Swansea and the other to Carmarthen. He was a surveyor who drew up the plans for Commissioners' Bridge near Kidwelly. He was also a keen sportsman and played cricket for Llanelli where he was known as 'a demon bowler'.[5] On the morning of 14 August, McKiernon found himself facing William Chambers, junior, a magistrate and founding member of the Llanelli Cricket Club, with soldiers of the 73rd Regiment surrounding the building. Also present were the other two accused men together with Jenkin and Catherine Hugh and a neighbour named Edward Chalinder.

The story which unfolded was quite an incredible one. Jenkin Hugh said that on 2 August, the Llanelli letter-carrier delivered a letter to him. It was a warning from Rebecca and he had previously received many others, but this one worried him. After paying two pence for the letter at the Ship Inn in Church Street, he went on to the Tŷ Melyn and showed it to Francis McKiernon.[6] While drinking three half-pints of beer together, Hugh asked McKiernon what he thought of the letter and whether he should take his wife and children out of the house. McKiernon said: 'Never mind, Jenkin, if the gate is broken, I will take care that neither your wife nor your children will be hurt.' In fairness, when the attack took place that night, and the roof was being torn, McKiernon was heard telling the rioters to stop and let Hugh get his wife and children out of the house. George Laing, however, was heard to shout: 'Don't stop. Take it down. To hell with them!' Three or four men took the tiles off the roof, one of the group helped Hugh take a damaged clock out while others pulled down the dresser with all the dishes on it. McKiernon had nothing on his face but he had a long white shirt over his clothes. Laing had something like a handkerchief around his face but Hugh recognised his voice.

Catherine Hugh gave much the same story, adding that her husband had been drinking but was sober at the time and had no liquor in the house. When her husband named McKiernon and Laing to her, she told him to hold his tongue. Edward Chalinder said that the crowd numbered between 15 and 20 and they were at their work for half-an-hour on a dark and rainy night.

The three accused were released on bail to await trial at Carmarthen Assizes. A guard of policemen and soldiers saw the witnesses safely through a hostile crowd and back to Sandy. Late that night, someone brought an important message to Jenkin Hugh. It was a message that sent him hurrying into town again the next morning. He came, breathless, to the magistrates' clerk blurting out that he had lied under oath the previous day, that he was drunk when he'd made his first statement and that he definitely had not seen McKiernon nor Laing nor Phillips among the mob at Sandy Gate.

Williams Chambers, junior, realised that Jenkin Hugh had received a serious threat which had deprived him of a prime witness. He knew that McKiernon and Laing had sound business reasons for the attack as well as the fact that McKiernon owned land in the Sandy area which involved frequent travelling to and fro. He decided to charge Hugh with perjury and send him to Carmarthen Assizes as well. In the event, all prosecutions were dropped. Rebecca had got away with it again.

On Wednesday, 23 August, a raiding group numbering at least 100 was organised in Llannon for a march to Gelliwernen, halfway to Llanelli. Gelliwernen was the home of John Edwards, agent to Rees Goring Thomas, owner of the tithes of Llanelli, Llannon and many other parishes. The original group congregated at Llannon and were augmented, at the lower end of the village, by a contingent from Hendy. About a mile down the road, at Pontmorlais, they joined up with another group from Five Roads. There was a great tumult when they arrived at their destination to find the agent in bed due to illness. Mrs Catherine Edwards came to the window and narrowly escaped being shot[7] but the daughter, Hannah, was brave enough to go outside to speak to the rioters and to appeal to them to stay calm and do no violence. A spokesman for the party said that she and her mother had nothing to fear but that 'they would not set a greater value on her father's life than a feather thrown before the wind.' To demonstrate their hatred for the man, they proceeded to trample his fine gardens, smashed his many glass-houses and cut down his fruit trees. In a final blaze of fury, they attacked the gamekeeper's cottage, ransacking it completely.[8] Then, firing shots into the air, they returned home. Subsequently a reward of £500, put up by Goring Thomas and the government, was offered for information. It was an enormous sum, but it met with no response.[9]

More than likely, as a response to the attack on Gelliwernen, on Friday, 25 August, a great meeting was called to fields at Ystodwen Farm, halfway between Five Roads and Pontyberem on Mynydd Sylen. Its object was to put an end to the nightly exploits of Rebecca by organising a petition to the young Queen Victoria setting out the grievances and suffering of the populace. In a way, this was seen as appealing to the monarch over the heads of uncaring government ministers. Over 3,000 turned up on the day, both farmers and industrial workers giving up a whole day's work for the purpose. A farm-cart was pressed into use as a platform and William Chambers, junior, was unanimously elected chairman. The main speaker was none other than Hugh Williams who read out a list of grievances included in the petition. A translation in Welsh was read out by Stephen Evans of Cilcarw, himself a well-known Rebecca leader. David Rees, the minister of Capel Als, made a long impassioned speech, condemning nightly outrages and claimed that orderly meetings by day, as this one was, could be much more effective. Other speakers came to the platform and tributes were paid to the Chambers family while Rees Goring Thomas was roundly condemned as were the majority of local magistrates for their total lack of sympathy. The meeting concluded with Hugh Williams speaking again, stressing the need for all men to be in possession of the vote in order to deliver good government 'to protect the people from local oppression.'

The centre of Rebecca's activity in the Llanelli area was the village of Five Roads with its unofficial headquarters located at the Stag and Pheasant inn. The Rebecca group at Five Roads was led by two men with the prosaic names of John Jones and David Davies who were known to all and sundry as Shoni Sguborfawr and Dai'r Cantwr. Shoni had probably worked as a servant at

Sguborfawr Farm, Penderyn, Merthyr, and had been a soldier and a prize-fighter. With the decline of the iron industry, he had decided to move westward and sought work in Swansea before arriving in Llanelli where he found employment at the Copperworks. He was 32 years of age in 1843. Dai'r Cantwr was two years younger and was the son of a farmer from Llancarfan in the Vale of Glamorgan. He had been employed in the iron-works at Tredegar before finding recent employment as a carter at Pontyberem. It seems that he had, at one time, been a Wesleyan lay-preacher as well as being a precentor. He was also a country bard.

It was at the Farmers' Arms in Five Roads that a meeting was held on 5 September to consider a request for help from the pilots of Llanelli harbour.[10] They were in dispute with the harbour-master, John Paisley Luckraft, RN, who had ordered that no pilot should be a publican at the same time. Two pilots came to the Farmers' Arms to represent their colleagues and, after discussions with Shoni and Dai, together with seven other villagers, it was decided to pay half-a-crown to each member of the group to put pressure on the harbour-master. The deed was to be done that very night and the company set off from Five Roads, with Shoni leading on horseback, down Penyfai Lane, past Furnace, then along the railway through Sandy to Seaside.[11] When they got to Luckraft's house at about one o'clock in the morning, they demanded that he come down to speak to them. It was Shoni who spoke: 'We have come about those poor people you're sending to the Workhouse. You'll have to leave.' 'Do you mean leave this house?', asked Luckraft. 'No! We mean leave this place altogether. Before you came, those men were earning £40 a year, now they've got to go on the parish. You must promise to leave this place in a week or, by God almighty, you're a dead man.' Luckraft was in no position to refuse such a demand and shots were fired at the windows as the group moved away. Llanelli had a vacancy for a harbour-master within a week. Luckraft moved on to a similar position at Burry Port.

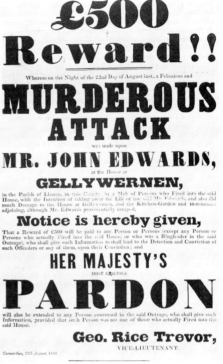

Reward poster issued after the assault on Gelliwernen. (original in the possession of the family of the late Mr D.J. Daniel, Five Roads)

On Wednesday morning, 6 September, a message came to John Edwards of Gelliwernen from Cefnybryn Farm in Five Roads. It said that a raid was planned on Hendy and Pontarddulais gates that night. William Chambers, junior, was informed and he sent a message to Captain Napier, the Chief Constable of Glamorgan as Pontarddulais lay within his jurisdiction. Chambers also sent to Carmarthen to call out the Light Dragoons and made plans to mobilise 40 soldiers of the 76th Regiment of Foot stationed at Llanelli. Chambers anticipated that the Hendy gate would be reached first as the attackers were due to come from Llannon. As it happened, it was Pontarddulais which was attacked, defended by Captain Napier with seven other police officers accompanied by three magistrates including John Dillwyn Llewellyn and Lewis Llewellyn Dillwyn of Penllergaer. All were armed with pistols.

The Rebecca party, numbering more than 100, arrived just before one o'clock in the morning led by John Hughes of Tŷ Isha Farm (known as Jac Tŷisha), riding a white horse, wearing a white gown, his face blackened – and carrying a pistol. The police lay silently in ambush until the men started tearing down the gate and then they pounced. John Hughes wheeled his horse and galloped straight at the police, firing at Napier. His shot missed and his horse was shot from under him. A short sharp fight ensued on foot and on horseback, John Hughes was wounded and both he and two others were captured before the hosts of Rebecca retreated.

Meanwhile, Chambers and his men were just across the river in Hendy and could hear the sounds of battle clearly. Then they almost clashed with a body of dragoons from Swansea sent up to support Captain Napier at Pontarddulais – they had arrived at the wrong bridge and they were too late in any case. Chambers accompanied the soldiers to Pontarddulais when he realised that there would be no attack at Hendy that night. He saw the three captured prisoners, John Hughes, David Jones and John Hugh. Chambers knelt beside John Hughes to offer him a drink of water before all three were taken away to Swansea jail.[12]

On the night following the Battle of the Bont, the Five Roads group decided to attack the gate at Spudder's Bridge, halfway between Trimsaran and Kidwelly. They met at the Stag and Pheasant and drank beer paid for by the Revd David Jones. As the group was about to leave, the Revd Jones said: 'Wait. I'll give you another shilling's worth to make you strong.' He then told them to return to the Stag when their work was done and he would see to it that they would have white bread and butter for breakfast. Shoni and Dai led a party of eight over the mountain road and called at Topsail Farm to collect Thomas Phillips and three others.[13] They went on to smash the gate at Spudders Bridge and then handed two letters to the gatekeeper, one of which was addressed to William Chambers, junior. This letter was probably the first indication that feelings were turning against him as a result of the rumour, which had spread from Pontarddulais, that he had shot John Hughes. The fighting, of course, was finished long before Chambers reached Pontarddulais.

Sarah Williams had been at the toll-house at Hendy for less than a week when Rebecca struck only two nights after Pontarddulais. Sarah Williams was known as a strict toll-collector even though she was 75 years of age and had been placed at Hendy by William Lewis to replace a gatekeeper who had proved rather lax in enforcing tolls. She had received several warnings to get out of Hendy in the space of a few days. Early in the morning of Saturday, 9 September, about a dozen daughters of Rebecca arrived in Hendy and set fire to the toll-house. Sarah Williams ran to a house across the road before returning to try and save a few belongings. There were three or four shots before she reappeared at the neighbour's door, bleeding profusely. She died soon afterwards. Rebecca had caused much damage to property but this was the first time that a life had been taken.[14]

Neither Shoni nor Dai were present at Hendy because, with others of the Stag brigade, they were setting fire to William Chambers' farms: Shoni, with eight helpers fired hay-ricks at Tŷ'nywern and Dai, with others, carried out a similar task at Gelligylwnog. Thomas Morris shot a white horse at Gelligylwnog and the company dipped their fingers in its blood as a kind of sacrament. On Sunday, another of Chambers' farms was set on fire at Maensant, near Pontyates. There was much talk in the Stag of killing Chambers, with David Thomas pleading the cause with vehemence and Thomas Phillips, Topsail, offering £5 to anyone who would do the deed.

The last major operation of the Five Roads group took place on Saturday night, 23 September, when Shoni and Dai led them to the Gwendraeth Ironworks at Pontyberem. The manager, a man named Slocombe, lived in a house on the premises and was intensely disliked by the workers. As the group surrounded the house, Shoni called out for Slocombe. Mrs Slocombe appeared at a window and said her husband was not at home whereupon Shoni told her: 'Tell him, if he does not leave within a week, we will make him a head shorter. We'll have no more English managers in Wales.' Then, firing guns at the house, the group vanished into the night. For David Lewis, a collier living on Trimsaran mountain, it had been a journey too far. He claimed that Shoni had forced him to march to Pontyberem, and on Tuesday morning, he walked into Llanelli to see a magistrate, R.J. Nevill.

Now that he had an eye-witness, at last, Nevill immediately issued warrants for the arrests of Shoni and Dai. Dai was arrested at the Plough and Harrow[15] on Thursday night and Shoni was captured at Tumble on the following day. They were taken to Carmarthen Jail and at the subsequent trial in that town, held on 27 December, both were found guilty. Shoni was sentenced to transportation for life and Dai for 20 years.

Thus came to an end one of the most turbulent years of our history. In Llanelli we saw an alliance between Rebecca and the Physical Force aspects of Chartism.[16] Events in Llanelli can also be explained as an urban extension of the Ceffyl Pren (Wooden Horse) tradition in the countryside where Rebecca took the law into her own hands by shaming people accused of wrong-going.[17] The attacks on the harbour-master and Pontyberem Ironworks can also be seen in this light. At Pontyberem, too, there is a flash of nationalism – a very rare event in those days – as a reflection of growing industrialisation fuelled by English capitalism. By and large, however, there is no escaping the fact that Shoni and Dai were a pair of renegades who, albeit with willing accomplices, terrorised the locality. There is evidence that they forced themselves on local residents, demanding free bed and board for days on end. They were thugs who were always willing to frighten people as long as they were paid to do so and they were adept at forcing people to join them. The Five Roads farmers certainly had real grievances against landlords and employers, but when they allowed themselves to be led by Shoni and Dai, they degenerated into drunken desperadoes. Rebecca's final act in Llanelli was the removal of the Tŷ'rfran gate on 30 September. The following morning, 40 farmers came together, retrieved the gate from a mine shaft and replaced it. This act, more clearly than any other, showed that Llanelli was finished with Rebecca.

Notes to Chapter VIII

1 The authoritative work on this subject is D. Williams: *The Rebecca Riots*, (UWP, 1955) but for sheer enjoyment read Pat Molloy: *And They Blessed Rebecca* (Gomer, 1983). A special edition of the *Carmarthen Antiquary* was published to celebrate the centenary and was dated 1943-4.

2 Hugh Williams was born in Machynlleth in 1796 and led a colourful personal life. He married a wealthy lady from St Clears and is said to have fathered 100 children, none by his wife. Two months after his wife died in 1861, he was married for a second time to a lady almost 40 years younger who bore him four more children. One of these children was the father of Hugh Williams the famous West End actor and the grandfather of Simon Williams, also an actor who took a leading role in the TV series *Upstairs Downstairs* some years ago. Our Hugh Williams died in 1874 and is buried in St Ishmael's Church near Ferryside.

3 The clock was the most prized possession in the house and was probably the possession of the Kidwelly Trust.

4 Some of the group, in fact, went on to town. The fact that others went to Furnace seems to point to the fact that they were returning to Five Roads. Professor David Williams states that the group attacked the gate and not the house 'because there were children inside and they were frightened'. He quotes no authority for this statement.

5 At that time the club was playing on one of McKiernon's fields at Waunybont between the Tŷ

Melyn and Falcon Bridge. The Tŷ Melyn has been renamed Circles. Much of our heritage is being lost by such mindless re-naming.

6   Letters were charged by weight and distance and payment was made by the receiver, not the sender. This had changed by the introduction of the Penny Post in 1840 but it was possible to send a letter to a collecting place to be picked up for double the price.

7   A grandfather clock from Gelliwernen, containing bullet-holes is now at Mount Farm, Five Roads.

8   The gamekeeper had fled, leaving his wife and child in the cottage!

9   The original reward poster is in the possession of the family of the late Mr James Daniel, Llandre, Five Roads, whose relative was present at Gelliwernen that night.

10   The Farmers' Arms is now a private house – the last on the left, leaving Five Roads on the road to Carmarthen.

11   Those present were Shoni and Dai, Thomas Morris and William James from the village; Charles Edmunds, Crosnant; Evan Jenkins, Gellihir; David Thomas, Cilferi Uchaf; Evan Hugh, Cilferi Isaf; and the publican William Jenkins to whom the pilots' request had been made.

12   The three were sentenced to transportation to Tasmania, John Hughes for 20 years, and David Jones and John Hugh for seven years each. The Tŷ Isha family are still in contact with their Australian relatives. The case for the defence was prepared by Hugh Williams. The trial was held in Cardiff.

13   Apart from Shoni and Dai, the group consisted of Thomas Morris and Charles Edmunds, as above, John Daniels from the village, William Walters the landlord of the Stag and two farm-servants, David Howells, Pantygwenith and David Vaughan, Soho. Thomas Phillips brought his servant, Josuah Thomas and boys Jonah and Tom. When a boy I was familiar with the name Twm o'r Top (Thomas Phillips, Topsail).

14   The coroner's verdict was that Sarah Williams had suffocated from an effusion of blood into the chest but 'from a cause to us unknown.' The man suspected of the shooting was John the Shoemaker of Horeb.

15   Not a public house today but still standing half a mile out of Five Roads on the Trimsaran road.

16   Feargus O'Connor was the leader of the Physical Force wing of Chartism with William Lovett advocating Moral Force. David Rees, Capel Als, was a great admirer of Lovett.

17   For example, making a man confess that he was the father of an illegitimate child.

Chapter IX
Religion and Politics: Education and Society

ONE of the outstanding characters of this period was the Revd David Rees who became the minister of Capel Als in 1829. He was a giant of the pulpit and even something of a giant in the physical sense of the word although rather short in stature. His tailor told John Innes that he had never in his life measured a man broader in the shoulders. He was a native of Trelech and came to Capel Als almost immediately after leaving Newtown Theological College at the age of 28, having turned down invitations to churches in Caernarfon and London.[1] When he first arrived, he was put up at the Mansel Hotel near the parish church. It was there, too, that his deacons met. Before long, he had established Saturday evening services at Capel Als in an attempt to put an end to gatherings at the tavern and he came to establish temperance as one of the pillars of his faith. In 1832, he married Sarah Roberts, the daughter of a wealthy deacon of Adulam, Felinfoel, and the marriage produced five children.[2] In the words of Iorwerth Jones: 'For many-sided activities, energy, persistence and courage, David Rees stands alongside the greatest Welshmen of the century.' As well as being a minister, he was a political radical, an educator, a businessman and editor and owner of the popular and influential magazine *Y Diwygiwr* (The Reformer).

David Rees's character is rather complicated. He had a lofty view of the status of a minister of religion, insisting that 'Christ himself gave him authority to stand in his place'. He once urged his deacons to go around collecting money from the members and one of them had the temerity to tell him: 'Go yourself, you've got more time.' The deacon was expelled on the spot. Although he claimed

Painting of Revd David Rees.
(Llanelli Library)

The original Park Church (J.E.). Now Iceland store.

that the Welsh language was 'as worthy as any to survive in the world', the language of his own hearth was English. He foresaw its decline and saw English bound to replace it with the coming of the railways.[3]

He started English services at Capel Als and said he was 'prouder of them than anything else I have accomplished.' When Park English Congregational Church was built in 1839, his wife was one of its first members and, by its establishment, he initiated a movement for setting up English Nonconformist chapels throughout Wales.[4]

David Rees became famous throughout the whole of Wales as the editor of *Y Diwygiwr*,[5] an Independent denominational journal which also became a political mouthpiece. He was a staunch Whig (Liberal) and an implacable enemy of the Tories. This led to fierce debates between him and Brutus,[6] editor of *Yr Haul* (The Sun), an Anglican Tory publication and their heated exchanges shed much light on the religious and political life of the period. *Y Diwygiwr*'s motto was 'Agitate, Agitate, Agitate' borrowed from Daniel O'Connell[7] and we see the Independents emerge as the most radical of all the Nonconformist denominations. Space does not permit an examination of all David Rees's crusades but he was suspected, of course, of supporting the Rebecca rioters and, indeed, it was reputed by some that he himself was Rebecca. He was severely criticised by English journalists and his name often appeared in English newspapers.

The *Times* accused him of inciting riot and its special correspondent, T.C. Foster, was especially hostile towards him although he was sympathetic to the Rebecca rioters as a whole. Foster quoted some rather provocative words written by Rees in the *Diwygiwr*: 'If you meet with an occasional Tory …tell him that you are Becca and that your profession is an opener of closed toll-gates or a destroyer of the same.' 'This,' he wrote 'from the organ of the Dissenters. Is it difficult to see the result?'

William Chambers, Junior, wrote a letter to the *Times* defending David Rees. Foster's last report was damning: 'Before leaving Llanelly … this town is a kind of Dissenter's stronghold. Here the chapels abound. Here the people are blessed with the ministrations of the Reverend Mr Rees. Here the Dissenting magazine, the *Diwygiwr*, is printed and extensively circulated in this town and the neighbourhood. There is not a district in all South Wales more disturbed.'

David Rees was described as 'a sort of bishop in his dirty diocese of colliers and coppermen' in *Blackwood's Magazine*.[8] His name was brought to the attention of the Home Secretary and questions were asked about him in the House of Commons. David Rees denied that his agitation was excessive or that he was 'disturbing the peace' but, at times, his rhetoric was extreme and could be construed as incitement to violence. As T.H. Lewis said: 'His writing is full of rhetoric which meant next to nothing to him, but which was dangerous in the turbulent spirit of the period.'

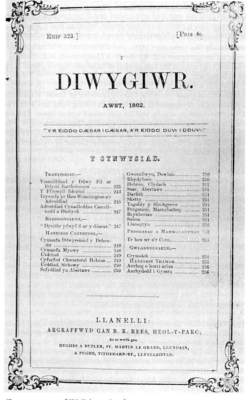

Cover-page of 'Y Diwygiwr'.

One is struck by a measure of inconsistency on reading *Y Diwygiwr*. In the very first publication, in 1835, he wrote 'Whoever urges you to take up any weapon, apart from the weapon of reason, to gain your rights, consider him your enemy.' In 1841, in an article on the Corn Laws we read: 'Put yourself in array against Babylon round about. All ye that bend the bow, shoot at her, spare no arrows.'[9] At times, he appears to be a staunch nationalist: 'Let us be nationalistic and independent …we know that Wales could take care of her own business …there is no part of the earth which could live better on its own than Wales.' Yet he was a great admirer of the British Empire and extolled the blessings it bestowed on its colonies. He was a fervent royalist 'enthusiastic towards our dearest queen Victoria. May heaven defend her.' He had an almost sickly interest in the royal family and its weddings and connections.

On the other hand, he was a great admirer of the United States and loud in his praise of its republican system of government. Indeed, he was very keen to get people to emigrate and, in 1854, when 80 people went from Llanelli to the USA, 55 of them were members of Capel Als. He was in favour of the Crimean

War at the beginning but against it before the end, mainly on the grounds of cost. He was always cost-conscious and stressed the importance of frugality and economy. He once said:[10] 'You can boil a bone ten times and still get something out of it.' The following morning, and for some days afterwards, he found the lawn in front of his grand residence, 'Goring Villa', littered with bones and his house acquired the name 'Plas Yr Esgyrn' (Bone Mansion). He preached self-reliance and quoted the saying: 'Heaven helps those who help themselves.' To this end, in 1847, along with C.W. and R.J. Nevill and the two Chambers, David Rees started a Savings Bank in Llanelli and, of the first five names registered, four were those of his children.

One of his consuming interests was education and, in addition to his successful Sunday School at Capel Als, he was foremost in setting up Market Street School in 1848 with the help of R.J. Nevill and William Chambers, junior.[11] From the £800 cost of building, £700 was collected from the pennies of Llanelli workers. David Rees was the first secretary of the board of management, a post he held until 1867. He also had a great interest in the Mechanics' Institute which he helped to set up in 1840. He was a vice-president of the organisation and urged employers to release their workers by 8 p.m. so that they could attend classes in English, French and Mathematics. It was the Institute's library which was the foundation of Llanelli's Public Library. David Rees had financial interests in collieries and was prominent in the formation of the Llanelli Gas Company. He was a member of the town's Chamber of Trade and collected rents from houses he owned in Oxen Street.[12]

It is, therefore, clear that he was heavily involved in the everyday life of the town but his main work, of course, was his ministry at Capel Als over a period of 40 years. By 1850, the membership stood at 580 in spite of losing 24 members to establish Park Church in 1839, 116 to Siloa in 1841 and 30 to Bryn in 1842. The chapel was extended twice during his ministry and, at times there would be 800 present to hear his eloquent preaching. He was an Independent to his fingertips and displayed great hostility towards the established church. As for other nonconformists, he was hostile to the Baptists because of their doctrines of adult baptism and closed communion. Lleurwg (Dr J.R. Morgan of Zion) penned the following ironic lines (in loose translation)

> *Baptists are godless, Priests are false,*
> *Truth is found nowhere, except in Capel Als.*

Iorwerth Jones says of him: 'He was a strange amalgam of despot and democrat'. David Rees was a very complicated character indeed.

Gradually, people became aware of the importance of education during the 19th century. The public schools of England were available for the sons of the

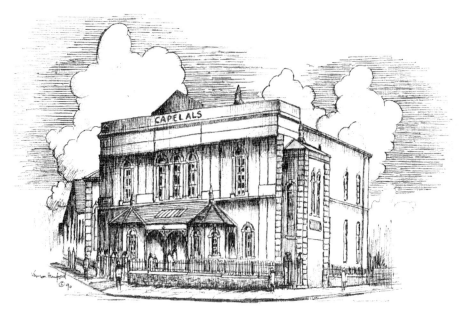

Capel Als (Independent) by Vernon Hurford who has spent a lifetime sketching in and around the town.

gentry but the provision of education for the children of the masses was thinly spread. As we saw in Sunday Schools, religion was the driving force behind education and, as early as 1675, there was a Welch Trust School in Llanelli and Circulating Schools[13] visited the town in the following century. In 1846, a

Greenfield Chapel (English Baptist) drawn by Vernon Hurford.

Commission was set up to inquire into the state of education in Wales.[14] The driving force behind the inquiry was a Carmarthenshire man, William Williams, MP for Coventry, who demanded to know what steps were being taken to teach English to Welsh children. Three commissioners were appointed, all young English barristers and Anglicans and this at a time when the majority of the population were Welsh-speaking and Nonconformist. They were helped by eight assistants chosen from among young men training for the Anglican priesthood at Saint David's College, Lampeter. The commissioner for our area was R.R.W. Lingen and his assistant was William Morris.

A National School (Church of England) was built on the Wern about 1827 and it is this school which takes up most space in the report on the Llanelli area. The building was dilapidated and the master of the boys' department was in poor health; he was from Somerset, was 33 years old and had previously been a druggist. He understood no Welsh but said he found no difficulty in this and used his senior pupils as interpreters when the need arose. The master's wife conducted the girls' department. She had been trained for six weeks at Cheltenham Normal College and had taught for a year at a Cheltenham school. Her sister was mistress of the Workhouse School. The commissioner also attended a lesson in the Infants' School built in Prospect Place in 1841. The master, Mr Boulter, asked questions and the mistress, his wife, stood in front of the class 'conducting' the answers. The children seemed 'uninterested and were very inattentive and restless.' The lesson, incredibly for infants, was on Sodom and Gomorrah!

William Morris was responsible for inspecting the remainder of Llanelli's schools. He started with the Sunday schools which, generally, came out well in the report. In Zion Chapel, he examined a class of six and found that three of them could read English with ease. In Capel Als, he found that David Rees taught a class of 15 in Welsh to become teachers themselves. There were 72 classes in all and two-thirds of the females were reading English. Capel Newydd held 33 classes starting at 10.30 a.m., after morning service, and finishing at 12.15. The most glowing report was reserved for the English Wesleyan Church which was 'conducted on a good system and everything carried on with regularity.'

William Morris then went on to list 16 smaller schools carried on as private concerns. Some of these schools were held in small single rooms and were of variable quality. Miss Brebyn's school in Seaside was held in a room measuring 10ft by 8ft with an 8ft headroom and taught reading only. When asked about numbers at the school she replied: 'They comes and goes.' She taught only reading and her annual income was £5 10s 0d. At the top end of the range, Captain Phillips of Seaside was a mariner who had been a prisoner of war in

France for seven years. He spoke English and French (no mention of Welsh) and taught navigation, among other subjects, for a respectable £52 a year. Two Baptist schools, one at Adulam, Felinfoel, and the other at Horeb, Five Roads, came in for special praise while that run by the famous Billy Williams, was housed in a room in Oxen Street specifically set out as a school. All in all though, the picture was fairly dismal with instruction given only in reading, some writing and simple arithmetic, with needlework sometimes offered as an additional subject for girls. The average annual income earned from these schools was about £22 per person for there were sometimes two or three people involved in a school. In comparison, the master and mistress of the National School earned £60 each. The situation was soon to improve with the opening of Copperworks School in 1847 and Market Street in 1848, both being supported by the nonconformist British and Foreign Society. When the report was published in 1847, it seriously over-stepped its terms of reference and blamed the Welsh language for all kinds of ills ranging from ignorance to violence and loose morals. The report which was published in three volumes of blue books provoked a backlash from enlightened Welsh opinion and was known, thereafter, as the Treachery of the Blue Books.

Sessions of the Court Leet of the Lordship of Kidwelly had been held at Llanelli from about the end of the 17th century. [15] As a result of the Enclosure Act of 1807, the town was governed by a Portreeve and 13 burgesses acting as Trustees in an uneasy partnership with the Court Leet at first but becoming the sole authority from 1813.

Irregular meetings were held at the Falcon Inn at the bottom of Thomas Street and these were often adjourned because too few burgesses turned up. The building of a Town Hall was first discussed in 1813 but it was not built for another decade and more. This was indicative of the lethargy of Llanelli's local government. Thomas Lewis of Stradey leased for 500 years a piece of land on the newly constructed Pembrey road. There is no record of its official opening but the initial building was not very satisfactory and tiling and other extensive repairs were necessary in 1826.

Alexander Raby, junior, was Portreeve in 1827 and it was he who assumed responsibility for the Town Hall at an annual rent of £5 13s 4d. There was a corn-market on the ground floor with a meeting-room and courtroom on the first floor. The street which developed alongside the Town Hall was appropriately named Hall Street. [16] The first meeting was held at the new Town Hall on 19 October 1827. It was immediately clear that a new building would not necessarily mean better local government. One of the first directives made was: 'A dinner for the burgesses with a quart of ale for each person to be provided at the Town Hall on Friday next, 26 October, not later than 2 o'clock.' There were, in fact, 50 burgesses in 1827 but, from then on, we find their numbers decreasing. The custom was to share any surplus income over expenditure among the burgesses so that fewer burgesses meant more money for each individual. By 1832 the number of burgesses was down to 37 and these shared a surplus of £222 between them. That year, out of an expenditure of £149 10s 0d, £35 was spent on a grand dinner. The Municipal Corporation Act of 1835 attempted to make local government more effective by creating elected councils in specific boroughs. There were 22 of these named in Wales and Llanelli was one of them. The topic of incorporation was discussed in the House of Commons on 5 July 1835. Suddenly Llanelli was withdrawn from the list after Alexander Raby, junior, had been despatched to London to oppose the measure on behalf of the majority of the burgesses.

Local government carried on in Llanelli in the same desultory fashion as before. The burgesses seemed more concerned with cutting costs than with improving standards. They had a contract, in 1835, with the Llanelli Gas Company for 45 street lamps for 179 nights at a cost of £94 10s 0d. In 1848, in spite of an increased population, a new agreement was made providing for the service for 135 nights only at a cost of £65. In 1847 the report of an inquiry into sanitation complained of neglected drains, open gutters and stagnant water in the streets. Five doctors responsible for the report urged that 'the poorer part of inhabitants be made aware of the importance of individual cleanliness in their own persons and the interior of houses.' In 1849, Benjamin Thomas, the district Medical Officer, complained about skinners' yards, tanneries, slaughterhouses and pigsties in the town. Roads lacked solid foundations and paving was poor. Houses and public buildings were damp and badly ventilated because windows were not made to open. There was inadequate drinking water with fresh water being sold for ½ d per two gallons. This was a fertile breeding ground for disease and outbreaks of cholera were frequent. In the same year, an inquiry was directed by G.T. Clarke[17] who stated that Llanelli was deficient in everything usually considered necessary for the good government of a town and the health and comfort of its inhabitants. 'It has a worse government than that of an ordinary rural parish since those who administer its funds are irresponsible.' G.T. Clarke maintained that the application of the Public Health Act would go far towards remedying matters since it would provide for an elected local government with authority to carry out improvements. This became reality in 1850 when the Llanelly Board of Health was set up consisting of 12 members to be elected from the whole district, the Town, the Wern and Seaside. It was foreseen that 'since each of these three dimensions are increasing, the whole will, one day, become one large town.'

The first Chairman of the Board of Health was William Chambers, junior, a man who had long since agitated for a better form of local government and gave up the post only when he left the town in 1855. In 1853 Chambers had bought the Hafod Estate in Ceredigion. Chambers, senior, died in February 1855,[18] and his son moved into Hafod before the end of the year. The Pottery was leased to the partnership of Coombs and Holland. Chambers was presented with a silver salver by the people of Llanelli in a ceremony in the Town Hall in November 1855, in testimony of their respect and esteem and of regret at his leaving the town. Noting his death in 1882, the *Llanelly Guardian* remarked: 'The older inhabitants of Llanelly can well remember Mr Chambers's handsome presence and manly address. He loved Llanelly dearly …and it is a pity his successors in the estate (the Stepneys) did not follow in his wake.'[19] This observation is very acute and applies equally to both father and son. Both were educated at Eton and St John's College, Cambridge. William Chambers, senior, could easily have been an absentee landlord, as indeed was his benefactor Sir John Stepney. He could have lived well off the profits of the estate without once setting foot in Llanelli. He left his estate in Kent, however, and brought his family to live in our town. He restored Llanelli House to its former grandeur after it had been abandoned by the Stepneys for 60 years and he and his son threw themselves into the life of the town with the greatest enthusiasm. The Stepney estate was well-managed under their care and they treated their tenants well. They were concerned with ameliorating the lives of ordinary working people particularly through education and were to the fore in the establishment of Market Street School, the Mechanics' Institute and the Savings Bank. Although they were churchmen, they opposed the Church Rate and sought to work alongside Nonconformists like David Rees. They were radical in politics and were strongly in favour of adopting the secret ballot for elections. William Chambers, junior, formed a Reform Society in the town.

The South Wales Pottery was also his brainchild, the only substantial light industry in a town dependent on iron, copper and coal. He built good houses for his employees, setting an example which others would follow. The two Chambers were the only magistrates in town during the height of the Rebecca Riots since R.J. Nevill lived in Llangennech. The son incurred the wrath of his fellow landowners by chairing the great open-air Rebecca meeting at Sylen which condemned the majority of landlords for their insensitivity to the suffering of their tenants. There is no doubt that Llanelli benefited generally from the family's sojourn in the town and it is true to say that they did more good here than almost all the Stepneys put together.

When William Chambers, senior, began putting Llanelli House in order he cleared out a number of people who were using parts of the building as workplaces and shops. To compensate for this, he built a market to the side of the building between Llanelli House and where the Library stands today. When this proved too small, he built a larger market near Falcon bridge where the Tinopolis TV building now stands. The Trustees had talked about building a market since 1813, linked with a Town Hall and lock-up. When the Town Hall and lock-up were finally built, there was room only for a corn-market where official weights and measures were strictly enforced. David Lewis, squire of Stradey, then set up a rival market to Chambers on his own land opposite the Town Hall. He was aided and abetted in this venture by disgruntled tradesmen who had been evicted from Llanelli House. This market was taken over by the Trustees in 1830 in a deal which involved an exchange of land, with David Lewis being granted ownership of Trustee land in the Sandy area. Before this time, goods were bought and sold in the churchyard and the vicar took a share of the tolls.

John Innes tells us that people still alive in 1902 remembered cockles being sold around the cross and butter under the sycamore near Raby's tomb – flat gravestones made perfect stalls. Church Street had so many boot and shoe stalls that the street was known as Heol y Sgidie (Boot Street). Other stalls (called 'standings') were set up in the streets around the church. This is confirmed in the famous portrait by Mrs Harvard of a market outside the Parish Church which was painted in 1854. In addition, there was a pig market at the junction of Wind Street and Thomas Street, a cattle fair in Oxen Street, and a horse fair at Caeffair near the Thomas Arms.

Among its other tenants, Llanelli House was the home of Llanelli's first Post office in 1811.[20] It was managed by Jane Griffiths at Cwrt y Plas (Mansion Court). It subsequently moved to various inns including the Ship, the Falcon and the Thomas Arms mainly in hands of two postmasters, J.B. Morgan and Captain Eynon. The mail coach left the Ship and Castle (Stepney Hotel) at 4.15 a.m. for Haverfordwest, returning at 8 p.m. and at 8 a.m. for Swansea, returning at 5 p.m. Another mail service used the Falcon Inn. When the South Wales Railway first came through Llanelli, it marked the beginning of the end for mail coaches. On 21 August 1852, the great engineer Isambard Kingdom Brunel found himself travelling on the train with David Lewis of Stradey, through whose land the train passed, on the journey between Swansea and Carmarthen. It was not only mail coaches which were affected by the railway for, by building the embankment along the shoreline, it proved a valuable sea-defence. This, combined with the diversion of the river Lliedi, in 1834, towards the Carmarthenshire Dock instead of the Sandy, went a long way towards drying out a large tract of land between Llanelli and Pwll.

The number of houses, according to the Rate Book of 1849, had now grown to 1,552, almost twice as many as the 802 recorded in 1831. There was, consequently, a much heavier demand for water. Water was taken from the River Lliedi and from several wells in the area, one of these was Ffynon Alys (Alice's well) which lay perilously close to the cemetery at Capel Als.[21] Other wells were near coal pits and were seriously polluted. In 1854, it was decided to build a reservoir in Trebeddod, above Furnace, to serve the needs of the town. With an earth dam and a clay core, Trebeddod was 24ft deep with a surface area of three acres and held 5 million gallons of water.

Alas, water was not the only liquid that Llanelli people craved. In spite of the efforts of David Rees, the teetotal movement and the claim that Llanelli had become a much more sober place towards mid-century,[22] it was still a hard-drinking town. According to the Rate Book, there were 89 licensed premises in the town in 1849, a staggering figure of one for every 17 houses. Drunkenness was not confined to the working classes and Dr Benjamin Thomas told John Innes that, as a young doctor, he was often called out to minor injuries late at night caused by drink. He solved the problem by charging half a guinea instead of his normal 1s 6d.[23] Young bucks were fond of the Ship and Castle, known as the Slaughterhouse while, for a cosy evening, the Parlwr Bach (Little Parlour) in the Mansel was recommended.

The Chamber of Trade was a powerful force for change in the town and, as well as being in the forefront of local government reform, was supportive of educational projects such as the Mechanics' Institute and the Reform Reading Room. There were signs that the old enmity between church and chapel was becoming less bitter with the abolition of the Church Rate. Chapels were now free to baptise, marry and bury their members.

Church and chapel were also coming together for purposes of local government and in the establishment of schools like Copperworks and Market Street as well as co-operating in adult education. David Rees spoke highly of the Anglican Nevill and Chambers families and said he would never have got anywhere near to the achievement of his goals were it not for their generosity and co-operation.[24] Bishop Thirlwall of St David's preached a powerful sermon at the consecration of St Paul's church, on the Wern, in 1850 which was indicative of the change in attitudes. David Rees was present and was so impressed that he sought a printed version. The bishop took his text from Corinthians: 'For by one Spirit are we all baptized into one body...' The following is an extract: 'The centre of unity is Christ. As long as we hold steadfastly to Him we need not be disheartened because others differ from us in some particulars ...Let us be more willing to see and own and honour and love whatever is good in the work even of those who differ from us most widely…' The sermon was extensively quoted in the press.

By 1855, Llanelli had become 'one large town', as forecast a few years earlier. The three wards, Town, Wern and Seaside now sent six members each to represent them on the local authority, the Llanelli Board of Health. Between 1795 and 1855 the town had passed through the most turbulent and exciting period of its history which saw it grow from an insignificant little village into a sizeable industrial town.

Notes to Chapter IX

1 Welsh-readers should consult Iorwerth Jones. *David Rees y Cynhyrfwr* (Swansea, 1970) for a detailed survey. The history of the chapel can be found in concise form in Maurice Loader (ed) *Capel Als: 1780-1980* (Swansea, 1980) – also written in Welsh.

2 The two were married in the Parish Church by the Revd Ebenezer Morris. Chapel marriages were not recognised until 1836. Bernard (named after David Rees's father) was born in 1833, Elizabeth in 1834, John Calvin in 1836 (died at 18 months), Luther in 1839 and Frederic in 1840 (the last two were drowned off Llanelli beach in 1851).

3 David Rees claimed it was he who had coined the word 'rheilffyrdd' for railways. *Y Diwygiwr*, 1848.

4 Her son Bernard was treasurer of Park Church for 40 years. David Rees was one of the trustees. He was also a trustee of the English church at Castle Street, Swansea.

5 David Rees founded the journal in 1835.

6 Brutus was the pseudonym of David Owen, a former Nonconformist minister turned Anglican. *Yr Haul* was printed at Llandovery.

7 A popular Irish politician of the period.

8 Joseph Downes 'Touring in the Disturbed Districts', 1843. *Blackwood's Magazine* was printed in Edinburgh.

9 A text from the *Book of Jeremiah, Chapter 50, Verse 14*.

10 In a lecture to the Mechanics' Institute in 1859.

11 See Eluned Jones: *Their Hard-earned Pennies* (Llanelli Borough Council, 1990).

12 A row of little houses (later named Edgar Street) behind the top end of Thomas Street. Now a car park.

13 Thomas Gouge was the pioneer of the Welch Trust, founded to teach children to read the Bible in English. Gruffydd Jones, Vicar of Llanddowror, was the founder of the Circulating Schools. There were also private schools which used literature provided by the SPCK (Society for the Promotion of Christian Knowledge). One of the oldest private schoolteachers was William Morris, or Maurice. Arthur Mee says that he taught boys and girls in Wind Street over a period of 50 years. He died in 1793. Billy Williams started teaching in Oxen Street in 1814 when he was 19. See article by Noel Gibbard; 'Llanelli Schools 1800-1870' in the *Carmarthenshire Historian*, 1968.

14 See the *Report of the Commission of Inquiry into the State of Education in Wales*, 1847. It is available in the Public Library. For a concise survey see John Edwards: 'Llanelli and the Blue Books' in *Llanelli Miscellany, No. 12*, 1998.

15 A meeting was held in the house of Alice Daniel in 1687.

16 The building stood at the bottom of Gelli Onn Road.

17 Superintendent Inspector of the Board of Public Health. There was an outbreak of cholera in 1849.

18 He was succeeded by Sir John Stepney's nephew who adopted the family name and was known as John Stepney Cowell-Stepney.

19 William Chambers, Jr. had 14 children. He suffered a stroke at the home of his son, Charles Campbell, at Swansea in 1878. (C.C. Chambers was captain of Swansea RFC and was the first president of the Welsh Rugby Union.) He died in sad and straitened circumstances. Hafod was sold in 1871 and he had been admitted to a mental hospital in Briton Ferry by 1882. For interesting details about his children, read *Llanelly Pottery* by Gareth Hughes and Robert Pugh (Llanelli B.C. 1990).

20 For a detailed survey see article by Brian Cripps: 'Postal History of Llanelli', *Carmarthenshire Antiquary*, 1976.

21 Ffynon Alys was sealed during the extension of Capel Als in 1852. Some of the others were the Bres Well in the town and, a little further distant, the Llanerch Well, Furnace Well and Tyisha Well.

22 In answer to the Commissioner of the Education Inquiry of 1847 both William Chambers, junior, and R.J. Nevill expressed this opinion.

23 Half a guinea was 10s 6d. The difference today would be 52p and 7p.

24 He said of Chambers, before he left the town in 1855: 'He is a churchman but too much of a gentleman to expect anyone to sacrifice his principles in order to please him. He and I always agreed on political matters and no one did more for free education.' He preached a laudatory sermon when Nevill died in 1856.

Chapter X
An Industrial Town

THE second half of the 19th century saw Llanelli becoming almost totally dependent on heavy industry. The Dafen Tinplate works was built in 1846[1] and was followed, five years later by the establishment of the Morfa works, the first tinplate works in the town of Llanelli. Both of these works had their own iron forges attached to them, and both were financed by English capital.[2] In the case of Dafen, Thomas and James Motley were from Leeds and John Winkworth was a Bath dentist. The partnership of Motley and Winkworth, however, was not destined to last very long and, in 1848, the works was sold to Phillips, Nunes and Smith.[3] The owner of the Morfa works was John Simmons Tregoning, a Cornishman who had interests in a tin-smelting company in Cornwall as well as being a partner in the Liverpool firm of Clint, Tregoning and Company. When this partnership broke up, Clint took the shipping interest and Tregoning the metal side. Although Tregoning built the Morfa works, he stayed firmly rooted in Liverpool. It was his son, of the same name, who came to Llanelli to play such a large part in the life of the town. He arrived in 1865 and stayed with Octavius Williams, the works manager, at his home at Highfield. When Williams moved to Hendy to build a tinworks there, Tregoning took over the house and the managership of the works at the age of 23. He married when he took possession of Highfield in 1866 and lived there for six years before moving to Iscoed mansion in Ferryside.[4]

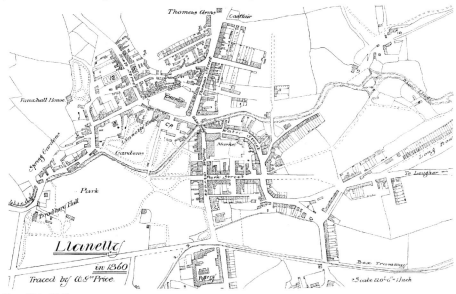

Llanelli in 1860.

The Whitford Lighthouse. (Garret Howells). Built in 1866 to plans drawn up by John Bowen, engineer at Copperworks.

John Simmons Tregoning II was a generous man who had a genuine regard for his workers. He built 50 solid houses for his workers at a cost of over £9,000, charging a rent of 12 shillings a week.[5] He was also influential in supporting the building of New Dock School to cater for his workers' children.

He built a Reading Room and a Library in Cornish Place,[6] employing a librarian at four shillings a week to serve the needs of the workers and their families.[7] He retained the services of Doctor Buckley to treat accidents and illness and organised a Sickness and Disability Fund for the workforce. Deductions from pay were made to support these benefits and Tregoning himself also contributed. His paternalistic approach can be clearly seen in a statement he made during the recession of 1868: 'We must work as well as we can. Our people have stuck with us in good times and it would be uncharitable to reduce their wages or work short-time.' When matters failed to improve in the following year, he said: 'We must not look for profit in these times but consider ourselves fortunate if we manage to feed and clothe our people without sacrificing capital.'[8] Tregoning was an able negotiator and was mainly responsible, in 1874, for drawing up a scale of tinplaters' wages for the whole of South Wales with the co-operation of the union leader, Lewis Afan.[9] It was a scale which remained virtually unchanged throughout the hand-mill period of the tinplate industry. Tregoning played an important part in the public life of Llanelli and Carmarthenshire. He was a wizard at figures and it was said that he could make a balance-sheet sound like poetry, so he was in great demand on all kinds of financial committees. He was a County Councillor and took a great interest in all spheres of local government and public education. He was a Conservative in a Radical county and unsuccessfully fought the Parliamentary seat in 1866. In 1896 he was made Chairman of the County Council, the first non-Liberal ever to hold the post. He was a respected Justice of the Peace and was one of the founders of Christ Church, New Dock. He died, in retirement in 1900.[10]

The 1860s were the most enterprising years in the history of shipping, ship-construction and seaborne trade in the whole history of the town. A peak of maritime activity was reached which was never to be surpassed.[11] The Llanelly Railway and Dock Company, through its links with the Vale of Towy Railway, was able to reach markets as far as the English Midlands. By 1867, the export trade, still mainly coal, had grown to 15,904 tons.[12] Imports were mainly metal-ores and timber. Timber was required for building purposes to house a growing population as well as for railway sleepers, pit props and boxes for packing tinplate. Ships carrying timber were quite sizeable vessels, nearing almost 600 tons and those sailing from North America often carried emigrants on the return voyage.[13] The Burry Harbour Commissioners controlled only the Carmarthenshire Dock and its limited income was largely spent on improving the harbour approaches.[14] There was little co-operation with the other three docks[15] and this, combined with shifting sands and treacherous channels meant that Llanelli fell behind Swansea, Port Talbot and Cardiff as ships increased in size towards the end of the century. As early as 1857, I.K. Brunel, in a report to the Commissioners, had stated: 'Nature has not done much to fit Llanelly for a port'.

Smaller ships from Llanelli often voyaged only as far as Bristol and Liverpool where they discharged their cargoes to larger vessels for shipment all over the world as tinplate gradually overtook coal as the main export. In spite of the failure to make major improvements to Llanelli's docks, local ship-owners expanded their fleets. By 1868, vessels registered in the port numbered 90 sailing ships and six steamships with a total tonnage of 11,668 tons. Changes in the law

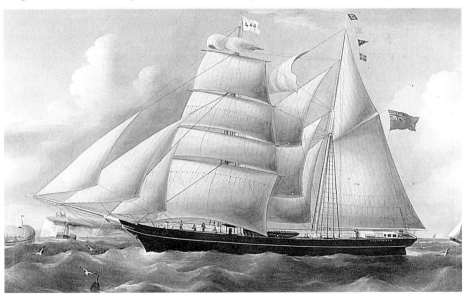

The 'Fanny Alice' (196 tons) owned by Henry Rees of Llanelli. Lost in the West Indies, 1872. (Robin Craig collection)

meant that limited liability companies could now be set up and this led to the establishment of the Llanelly Steam Navigation Company in 1862 with a capital of £21,000 made up of shares of £30 each. The following year saw the formation of the Llanelly Iron and Shipping Company with a capital of £25,000 consisting of 500 shares of £5 each. One of the company's aims was 'the affording of the means of a safe and profitable investment to tradesmen, workmen and others…'

W.H. Nevill took 254 shares and others included rollermen, fitters, masons, grocers and shipping agents. Of new vessels owned by local people in the 1860s, a considerable number came from local shipyards. Nevill had a yard alongside the Carmarthenshire Dock and, between 1864 and 1867, all these berths were continuously occupied. Wooden ships were built by the brothers John and James Bevan on Llanelli Flats between the Copperworks Dock and the Pemberton Dock. During the decade, 22 ships were built at Llanelli, 17 by the Iron Shipping Company and 5 by the Bevan brothers.

The first SS *Llanelly*, built by the Iron Shipbuilding Company in 1867 at a cost of £8,000, was lost off Bishop Rocks in 1873 and a second ship of the same name was registered two years later. This was only one of a number of shipping disasters which can be catalogued along the years along with those in the local coal-mines and metal industries. January 1868 saw the Broughton Bay disaster when about 20 vessels left Llanelli on the evening tide, being towed by steamtugs. There had been a recent storm and there were heavy seas on the bar when the tow ropes broke. The wind had dropped by this time and when the ships hoisted sails, they failed to make it out to sea. Some of the ships collided and others were driven on to the sands of north-west Gower. Four Llanelli vessels were totally wrecked along with four others registered elsewhere. Two ships limped back into Llanelli and one French vessel made it to France carrying with

Llanelli from the Bigyn, 1821. (Llanelli Library)

Painting of a tinworks mill by Jacqui Murphy. Furnaceman (right), Rollerman (left) and Doubler (centre).

it one of the local pilots, Daniel Rees. There was much loss of life but the crews of three Llanelli ships were saved along with five men from the Llanelli ship 'Onward'.[16] Captain Clement of the 'Onward' was lost, along with his son as well as Christopher Lewis, the pilot, and an unnamed apprentice. Many local seamen died within sight of their homes just an hour or so after leaving harbour and coal is still washed up on the shores of Broughton Bay after stormy weather.

In 1831, the population of Llanelli was just over 17,000. This number almost doubled over the next 20 years and the next 30 years would see it double again.[17] The primary reason for this increase was the building of tinplate works with their attendant iron forges as well as foundries which supplied the tinworks with their manifold requirements. By 1880, seven tinplate works were in operation in the town of Llanelli itself.[18] So famed was Llanelli for its tinplate that the town became known as Tinopolis. The work involved rolling bar-iron (averaging 20 inches by 14 and about ½ inch thick) to finish up with a pack of eight thin sheets measuring about 5ft by 2½ft. In the finishing process, these sheets were cut in half, coated with a thin layer of tin, and packed into boxes – 112 sheets to a box.[19]

This was the kind of work experienced by a growing number of Llanelli's population in the second half of the 19th century. Coal was in decline

The Tinworks and its Product. One of the mills of the Old Castle Works. (Llanelli Library)

within the town limits and shipping would be unable to compete in the long run because of inadequate port facilities. Llanelli could no longer be described as 'a town of sailors and colliers'; it was now a town of workers mainly involved in heavy industry. For the next hundred years, Llanelli's future lay with iron-workers, steel-workers, tinplate-workers and foundry-workers. These were all heroes in their own way and their work was physically hard in dangerous conditions. They came from the countryside around and were well used to hard work though it yielded little profit. Although they exchanged the open-air for the suffocating atmosphere of heavy industry, there were certainly advantages. Their wages improved and, as they saved money, they bought well-built stone houses with running water and upstairs bedrooms. They found shops, within walking distance, offering an ever-increasing variety of food and a large market in the middle of town. They brought their countryside values with them and were always ready to help and support each other in and out of work. They freed themselves from the tyranny of the land and became used to the idea of self-reliance.

During the same period, the town saw an increase in chapel-building financed by the workers themselves. They soon became prominent as members, deacons and officers, taking full responsibility in the running of their placcs of worship, and sharing that responsibility, on equal terms, with people perceived to be of a different class. In the democratic structures of Nonconformity, the vote of even the humblest member counted equally with that of the most prosperous. It was in the chapels that they safeguarded the language and they took it even to their place of work. Although management was predominantly English, as were the technical terms of their new industry, they persisted in working in Welsh. In the mills they adapted words for rolling (rowlo) and shearing (shero) for example. In the iron industry they spoke of tapo (tapping) and timo (teeming) while in the foundry they were engaged in sanding (sando) and moulding (mowldo). They made free use of English words where there were no equivalents in Welsh – a practice well-known to other languages, especially English! It was thus that Welsh was preserved as the language of work as well as the language of home and chapel.

The chapels themselves had spread out to other parts of the town by this time with the Independents colonising the Seaside and New Dock areas by establishing Siloa in 1841 and Bethania in 1870. The Calvinistic Methodists reached only the edge of these areas by building Trinity, just past the station gates in 1858.[20] The provision of chapels also meant the extension of Sunday Schools, virtually the only means of education for children and adults before the setting-up of state schools in 1870. It should be stated also that the two main Nonconformist denominations had established English churches in the town by a very early date; Park (Independent), 1839 and Greenfield (Baptist),

Painting of Dock Chapel by John Bowen, doyen of Llanelli Art Society.

A striking picture of Park Church, about 1900.
(Llanelli Library)

1858. The Methodists came along later with the opening of the Presbyterian Church in 1870, suggesting that some Welsh Nonconformists were more concerned with the saving of souls than with the preservation of the language. It is fair to say, also, that the Anglicans were not inactive in this context, setting up St Paul's in 1850 and St Peter's in 1869.

With new works, new houses, new chapels and new churches in the industrial areas and new streets with new shops in the centre of town, this was an exciting time in the history of Llanelli. The main thoroughfares of Stepney Street, Vaughan Street and Cowell Street were developed, as their names suggest, on the extensive grounds of Llanelli House. This was why the original Park Church was abandoned and a new building erected in Murray Street. David Rees was firmly against the idea of a spire for the new church but, on being persuaded, primarily by his wife and son, Bernard, he relented and said; 'If you must have a spire, make it the tallest spire in town.' Some of the Llanelly House land was developed as a private park by E.H. Douglas, a future town surveyor. Here, gentlemen would take their ladies and promenade. The new park was also the home, for a time, of the Llanelli Cricket Club of which Douglas was a prominent member. The club played on this ground between 1856 and 1861 when it was sold for development.

The Cricket Club is the oldest of all our sporting organisations. Thomas Mainwaring,[21] a cricketer himself, tells us that it was established at Llanelli in 1839 by William Chambers,

St Paul's Church. (Brian Cripps collection)

junior, and four other gentlemen. The club played on Upper Cilwrfa Field and Cae Isa'r Afon – the Lower River Field. Fixtures were limited at first owing to travelling difficulties. The journey to Carmarthen, for example, would take three hours in Francis McKiernan's coaches. With the arrival of the railway in 1852, this time was cut to three-quarters of an hour. The club was reorganised at this time and regular fixtures were played against teams as far afield as Haverfordwest and Neath. Meetings were held at McKiernan's hotel, the Tŷ Melyn, and McKiernan also provided the club with a new ground at Waunbont, alongside the river Lliedi, near Falcon Bridge. It was a gentleman's club and consisted of many people who were active in the life of the rapidly expanding town. An early player was Bernard Rees,[22] an accountant and the son of David Rees of Capel Als.

Bernard Rees was treasurer of Park Church and he brought with him Henry Howell, the church Secretary,

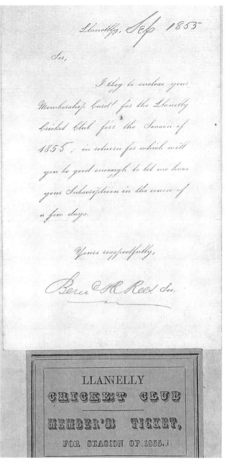

Cricket Club Season Ticket, 1855. Signed by Bernard Rees, Secretary. (Llanelli Cricket Club)

who was a member of the local Board of Health. After 1855, both the new owners of the Llanelli Pottery, C.W. Coombs and W.T. Holland played for the side. By 1856 the club was playing on the new park created by E.H. Douglas. John Dillwyn Llewellyn[23] of Penllergaer played for the club. He had industrial interests in the town. In 1863, Ernest Trubshaw,[24] manager of the Marshfield Tinplate Works, was a prominent member of the side. That the club was not quite exclusively for gentlemen is shown by the inclusion of Ben Arthur,[25] a legendary batsman, bowler and wicket-keeper. He was a butcher. His brother William also played, and he was a fishmonger. In this connection it is interesting to note that when the Carmarthenshire Cricket Club was formed in 1864, it was clearly stated; 'The club is strictly exclusive and no tradesmen or any of the working class are admitted.' Mercifully its existence was short-lived. After being forced to leave Llanelli Park in the early 1960s, the club played at various unsatisfactory venues

Mrs Havard's painting of the Parish Church and Market. Mid 19th century. (Llanelli Library)

until it settled at Stradey in 1877. Immediately before moving to Stradey they had played at the new public People's Park. They had to leave this ground because the Board of Health considered the game dangerous to the park users.

Llanelli's first hospital, according to John Innes, was a Fever Hospital set up on the Wern, next to the National School Building. It was probably opened during the cholera outbreak which swept South Wales in 1849. In 1866, 186 people died from cholera in the Llanelli area during a two-month period between July and September. Every week, the *Llanelly and County Guardian* reported the death totals and one of the most harrowing reports was of a young mother and child in Felinfoel dying within hours of each other. On the same day, when family mourners returned to the home, they found that the father, too, was dead. These reports and the appalling death-toll led to demands for a hospital in the town.

In 1867, three houses were leased on Bigyn Hill and converted into a hospital.[26] The work was largely financed by contributions from Llanelli's growing number of tradesmen and was managed by a Hospital Committee which found itself in financial difficulties within a year. It was regularly rescued by music concerts held annually in the town between 1868 and 1874 in addition to bazaars and voluntary contributions. In 1873, when there was a real threat of closure, a Hospital Sunday was arranged with collections made at churches and chapels. By this time, the number of beds had increased, from the original four, to ten. The hospital's future, however, was secured when Llanelli's working-men agreed to the placing of collecting-boxes in their places of employment. Many serious accidents sustained at the works were, of course, treated at the hospital.

In 1864 it was decided to take up three acres of the old Llanelli Park as a site to build a new market for the growing population. On a rainy day in September a great procession walked from the Town Hall, up Goring Road, down Thomas Street and along Stepney Street to the market site where the foundation stone was laid by R.T. Howell, the Chairman of the Board of Health. Colonel Stepney said a few words and explained that his lady could not be present because of the heavy rain. It would have been wiser if the Member of Parliament, Mr D. Morris, had stayed away too because he got soaking wet, caught a chill and died a fortnight later.[27] The market was opened for business by June 1866. It was well supplied with stalls selling, among other items, fruit and vegetables, poultry, butter, cheese, flannel, hosiery and shoes. No fewer than 35 stalls were occupied by butchers. By this time, Thursday and Saturday were the market days with Thursday being the more important of the two.

The Ivorites Friendly Society organised an important Eisteddfod at Llanelli in 1856 which was held in the grounds of Llanelli House. It was a one-day affair during which many works and shops were closed. Deheufardd and Mathetes shared the essay prize for a History of Llanelli.[28]

In 1857 the Athenaeum, next to Llanelli House, was opened and provided a centre for all kinds of cultural activities in the town. The Mechanics' Institute made its home there, providing a basis for higher education including a valuable library and a Reading Room. There was a hall for lectures and public concerts and a geological museum which had been presented by the Earl of Cawdor. On the subject of the American Civil War, one memorable public debate at the Athenaeum lasted for three nights and was reported in the London papers.

There were calls for beautifying the centre of the town by deepening the bed of the river Lliedi and planting trees along its banks. What a difference it would have made if this scheme had been carried out and we found ourselves today with a tree-lined river running through the centre of town. Nowadays, the Lliedi disappears from view at the bottom of Thomas Street, not to emerge again until Old Castle Road. The need for open spaces was well appreciated, however, and, in 1864, a 15-acre site, designated as the People's Park, was earmarked to compensate for the loss of the old Llanelli Park.

In 1872, there appeared a Llanelly Directory compiled by James Jenkins Chalinder,[29] who, curiously, in his first sentence wrote; 'Llanelly is a seaport and market town in the county of Carmarthen.' The MP by this time was Sir John Stepney, popularly known as 'the Old Colonel', who had been elected in 1868.[30]

London House – the old 'Falcon' at the bottom of Thomas Street. (Llanelli Library)

The parish is described as an area of 18,075 acres with a population of 21,483 at the census of the previous year. It still included the hamlets of Borough, Glyn, Berwig, Hengoed and Westfa, virtually unchanged since the Middle Ages. Chalinder describes Llanelli as 'a town of comparatively recent origin, old inhabitants now living remember it as a small, straggling village. Its rapid progress from an insignificant place to a town of commercial and manufacturing importance is remarkable… The newer portions of the town are well planned and built, and the shops in the principal streets are large and in the most modern style.' Chalinder computes the annual export of coal from the port at about 850,000 tons although, most of it was now mined outside the town. The average annual number of tinplate boxes produced is estimated at 350,000 with all of these, with the exception of Dafen, coming from the town itself. The 72 vessels registered at the port represented a carrying capacity of 20,000 tons. The Directory lists, 51 Llanelli master mariners together with 39 pilots. Consular agents are named for France, Portugal, Sweden, Norway and the USA.

As early as 1835, coal-miners had emigrated to the USA and, in the following year, about 100 local miners, including families, sailed from Liverpool to New York to work under the West Columbia Mining Company. Periodic waves of emigration followed in subsequent years. Now that the Civil War was over, with the country peaceful and offering employment and opportunity, we find five emigration agents with offices in Llanelli, including J.J. Chalinder himself. Lest we get carried away with the idea of Llanelli as a town devoted to religion with the frantic building of places of worship, Chalinder lists 128 taverns, all within the limits of the town. Many of them offered accommodation for ships' captains and crewmen. At no time, in fact, were more than 50 percent of the population chapel-goers or church goers, and, in spite of a vociferous teetotal movement, many happily combined chapel membership with the enjoyment of a pint or two of beer. Thirteen chapels are listed, three of them English, and three churches.

Chalinder's Directory is a veritable mine of information and provides a snapshot of the town at that particular time. It is a gem of a little book containing 90 detailed pages containing residents' names and addresses and a gazetteer of all trades carried on in the town in alphabetical order ranging from Arsenic Manufacturers to Watch and Clock makers. It also has 80 pages of advertisements which are informative, illuminating and sometimes amusing. One of the full-page advertisements is for the iron steamer 'Cambria' which took freight and passengers to and from Bristol. A good story is told about this boat. Captain William Thomas was in the habit of making small purchases in Bristol as favours for people. He soon found himself out of pocket as a result of non-payment. He solved this problem on his return one day by saying he had placed all his side-orders on the binnacle; those with money on them stayed but those without had been blown away in the wind!

Notes to Chapter X

1. See article on The Dafen Tinplate Works by Byron Davies in *Tinopolis – Aspects of Llanelli's Tinplate Trade* ed. John Edwards. (Llanelli Borough Council, 1995.) Also *Dafen Recollections* by Byron Davies. (LBC, 1996.) Recent research suggests that the works did not become operational until 1848.

2. Read 'Morfa and Tregoning', article by John Edwards in *Tinopolis* op. cit. The first works financed by local capital was the Old Castle Tinplate Works in 1866.

3. Byron Davies has made an investigation into the Nunes (Portuguese/Jewish) family which appears in *Llanelli Miscellany* No. 12, Llanelli W.E.A., 1998.

4. He travelled to and from Ferryside by train which became known as 'Trên Bach Tregoning' (Tregoning's Little Train) Like Nevill before him, he often made the train wait.

5. These are houses in Campbell Street and Cornish Place.

6. This building is now a private residence but can be easily recognised in the middle of the street by being taller than the other houses.

7. The librarian was Ann Evans. Two Tregoning wage-books are housed in the National Library of Wales, Aberystwyth. They cover the period from 1868 to 1875.

8. When his son came of age in 1889, a presentation was made to him of a silver tray weighing 60lbs. The sum was collected by 600 workers and ex-employees. Bethania chapel was packed and the son accepted the gift as a mark of esteem to his father.

9. Wages for the mill-team were agreed as follows in 1874; Rollerman – 3s 5d per dozen boxes. Doubler – 2s 9d per dozen boxes. Furnaceman – 2s 5d per dozen boxes. Behinder – 1s 3d per dozen boxes. A box contained 112 sheets.

10. He had retired to the family house at Landue in Cornwall but still retained a house,

Brynhafod, in Llanelli. He died, appropriately perhaps, on a train travelling between Chester and London.

11. See Robin Craig: 'The 1860s at Llanelli – a Dynamic Decade for Trade and Shipping'. *Carmarthenshire Antiquary*, 1987. An outstanding study.

12. *Official Trade and Navigation Accounts.*

13. The largest was probably the Charlotte Harrison, 578 tons, which arrived here from Quebec in July 1861.

14. The Whitford Lighthouse cost £1,680 and the pier and harbour lighthouse cost £2,758.

15. There were the two floating docks – Nevill's Dock and the Llanelly Railway Company Dock, and the Pemberton Dock on the site of the later Pemberton Tinplate Works

16. The others were 'Rocius', 'Water Lily' and 'Brothers'.

17. Official figures are 1831 – 7,646; 1851 – 13,663; 1881 – 27,779.

18. These were Morfa, 1851 (originally called Llanelly Tinplate Works); Cambrian 1860s; Marshfield, 1863; Old Castle, 1866; South Wales (Morewood), 1872; Burry, 1875 and Old Lodge, 1880. The Old Lodge was converted from the Glanmor Iron Works built by Nevill in 1854.

19. For a survey of the tinplate industry see *Tinopolis* op. cit. Also includes information on iron, steel and foundry works.

20. Nearby Capel y Bryn was established in 1841 and Tabernacle, in the town centre in 1875, both Independent. The Baptists built Moriah, in town in 1872. Siloh was built by the Calvinistic Methodists in 1876. The English Wesleyans moved to Hall Street in 1869 and the old church in Wind Street was occupied by a Welsh congregation (which had previously worshipped at Marine Street, Seaside) and renamed Jerusalem.

21. Thomas Mainwaring's manuscript *Common Place Book* is available at Llanelli Public Library. The four other founders were G.J. Webb, Samuel Price, B.W. Leighton and Harris Fowler.

22. There is in existence a season ticket signed by Bernard R. Rees, Secretary, 1855.

23. Afterwards, Sir John. He later created the Gnoll Ground, Neath.

24. He was also Chairman of the Welsh Steel and Plate Manufacturers' Association. A keen sportsman, he was a founding member of the Tennis Club in 1880 and was among the earliest members of Ashburnham Golf Club.

25. Ben Arthur later kept the Cricketers' Arms in Murray Street on the edge of the Llanelly Park ground.

26. The houses were leased for 21 years at £30 per annum. They still exist as Nos. 1, 2, and 3 Bigyn Park Terrace. The hospital was staffed by one nurse. Local doctors attended when necessary. There was also a group of voluntary lady-visitors.

27. John Innes states in *Old Llanelly* that he was standing near Mr Morris when the foundation stone was laid.

28. Deheufardd was David Bowen. Mathetes was the Revd John Jones (1821-78).

29. John Chalinder was, among other things, Assistant Postmaster, Bookseller and Travel Agent. He was probably the son of Edward Chalinder who was called as a witness during the wrecking of the Sandy toll-gate in 1843.

30. He was silent in Parliament but noisy in church. When Vicar Williams cut down the tall pews in the Parish Church, he moved to St Peter's. His performances there are said to have dismayed the older members but to have delighted the younger element. He had had a distinguished army career during the Peninsular Wars.

Chapter XI
Tinopolis

THE town's population doubled in the 30 years between 1851 and 1881 mainly as a result of the building of seven tinplate works within the town's limits in that period. The population growth and the increasing demands of the tinplate industry put a great strain on Llanelli's water supply and, by 1868, it was realised that a larger reservoir would have to be built. A site was selected at Cwmlliedi and the inauguration ceremony took place in January 1869. The occasion was marred by torrential rain but, in spite of this, the assembled dignitaries 'managed to crack a few bottles of port and claret before parting'.[1] The new reservoir took rather a long time to build and involved buying up the Felinfoel Mill along with the Upper and Lower Town Mills.[2] It was opened in September 1878, was three-quarters of a mile long and held 160 million gallons of water. Once again, rain marred the opening ceremony but, still, the Board of Health managed to arrange a banquet.[3] Cannons were fired and Board members and their friends were rowed up and down the lake in boats. Hundreds of people lined the banks, marvelling at the beauty of the site which was later to be called Swiss Valley.

The close connection between the town and the game of rugby has its beginnings in this period. Its exact beginning is in some doubt but there is no written evidence that the Llanelli Rugby Club was formed in 1872, in spite of the

Cwmlliedi Reservoir. Built in 1878. (Llanelli Library)

fact that its centenary was celebrated to coincide with the year of the famous All Blacks victory in 1972. The earliest report of a game is in 1875, found in the *Llanelly and County Guardian* under the heading 'Llanelly Football Club' – even then, football meant rugby in Llanelli. It was an account of a game played on 27 November 1875, between sides chosen by W.Y. Nevill and Arthur Buchanan at People's Park.

The first real match was played on the same ground on 6 January 1876, between Swansea (Cambria) and Llanelli. The game is reported to have been brought here direct from Rugby School by John D. Rogers,[4] who had been a pupil there. He was the son of J.H. Rogers, a partner in the Morewood Iron and Tinplate Works.

Andrews' Tramcar, 1880. (Llanelli Library)

Rogers captained the team for a short while before handing over to Arthur Buchanan. Buchanan was killed in an accident in November 1876[5] whereupon the captaincy fell to F.L. Margrave[6] who remained in that capacity for a number of years. The fixture list was extended to include Neath, Bridgend, Cardiff and Newport, in addition to the old enemy, Swansea. The club was playing at Stradey by 1879. The South Wales Challenge Cup had been introduced by 1877 and, by 1881, Llanelli were playing Cardiff in the Cup Final held at Neath. Cardiff won in extra time and it was Llanelli's first defeat of the season.[7] A year later the club celebrated its first international caps when Harry Bowen and Alfred Cattell[8] were chosen to represent Wales against England. In 1884, Llanelli won the South Wales Cup by beating Newport at Neath with Margrave still captaining the side. In this year, also, Llanelli adopted scarlet as their colours and would henceforth be known as 'The Scarlets'.[9] An Irish international team played against Llanelli on their return journey from the Wales match. Although the game was played on a Monday, it attracted a crown of 5,000. By 1885, Llanelli were playing against their first English opponents on a tour of Yorkshire, matched against teams like Dewsbury, Hull, Bradford and Halifax. In 1887 Wales played England at Stradey and in 1888, Llanelli beat the touring Maoris.[10] By this time 'scarlet fever' had really gripped the town – rugby had become an integral part of social life. 'Where', asked the *Guardian* in January of that year, 'has football found a more congenial soil than at Llanelly?' Where, indeed?

The demand for a better system of education was expressed by the *Llanelly and County Guardian* as early as 1867. 'The working classes of Wales are every bit as anxious as the more wealthy and powerful to improve the means of education.' In the same year, the old National (Church) School on the Wern was abandoned and a new one built on land on the

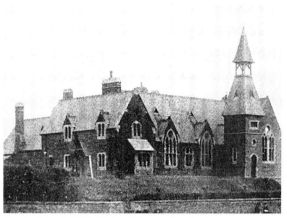

Pentip School, 1905. (Brian Cripps collection)

Pembrey Road given by David Lewis of Stradey. The land had once been the slag-heap of Raby's Caemain pit and the school became known as Pentip. In fact, the school had simply moved from one old colliery site to another. The existing British (Nonconformist) schools continued to prosper at this time, showing some innovative educational practices. For example, the principles of horticulture were taught at Market Street, music was on the time-table at Prospect Place, taught by William Williams, describing himself as a Professor of Music, while Sciences were introduced in Copperworks by the headmaster, J.E. Jones.[11] Also, there were still many good private schools in existence, offering classical, commercial and technical education.[12] In spite of all this, it was felt that an educational system relying on voluntary societies and private schools was inadequate and that the time had come for an increase of state control which powered education in France and Prussia. There had been, since 1833, a system of government grants to the voluntary school societies although the British

schools were more wary of accepting them that the National Society. The Education Act of 1870 created a network of elementary schools to be controlled by local school Boards. The Llanelli School Board was set up in 1871 under the chairmanship of James Buckley and, up to the turn of the century, the

Old Road School. A Victorian building. (J.E.)

Board gradually took over the British schools and set up new elementary Board Schools as the demand arose.[13]

The need for education suitable for a rapidly expanding industrial town was, at first, mainly catered for by the Mechanics' Institute which, apart from its evening classes at the Athenaeum, organised lectures on all kinds of topics. In 1865, for example, it had 534 members and its pride and joy was a library consisting of 1,651 books on subjects as diverse as history, religion, science, art, commerce, law, politics and literature, including Welsh literature. Its Reading Room also housed six daily newspapers, 24 weekly newspapers, six weekly Welsh publications and five monthly magazines, among others. Books could be borrowed from the library and reference books were available for study in the library from 8am until 10.30 p.m.[14] One of the leading lights of the Institute was Thomas Mainwaring. He was the author of the Commonplace Book, a fairly reliable source-book on the history of the period written in a copper-plate hand, which can be consulted at the Public Library to this day. Llanelli schools, both voluntary and private, also opened their doors to evening classes, the most prominent being Copperworks School. Here, science classes led to examinations conducted by the Kensington Science and Art Department while navigation was examined by the Royal Naval School of Architecture and Marine Engineering. All this activity led to a demand for higher education and it is not surprising, therefore, that a public meeting held at the Athenaeum in October 1864, was well supported. It was organised by a committee pledged to establish a University in Wales. When the University College of Wales, Aberystwyth, was eventually set up in 1872, it was destined to enjoy a long and fruitful relationship with Llanelli students.

Llanelli Intermediate School, about 1900. (Brian Cripps collection)

What we now call Secondary education was given a further boost in 1891 with the building of the Higher Grade School.[15] The aim of the school was to provide education for children beyond the elementary stage and the fee was 9d a week. Local industrialists and members of the Chamber of Trade took a great interest in the new school which was equipped with 'a plentiful supply of apparatus for technical instruction'. The first Headmaster was a Mr Major from London and the Headmistress was a Miss Redmayne from Halifax, both monoglot English. J.E. Jones of Copperworks School was appointed science master and he, himself, became Headmaster in 1894.

Following on the Welsh Intermediate Education Act of 1889, proposals were published in 1894 for the provision of Intermediate and Technical Education for the County of Carmarthen.[16] A list of 13 School Managers was drawn up for Llanelli, and they found temporary accommodation at the Athenaeum in 1895 while a new school was being built at the top of Marble Hall Road.[17] Fees were fixed at 1s 6d per week with 20 scholarships for free tuition to be offered in the first year. The Headmaster appointed was William Lewis of Lewis School, Gelligaer, and the Headmistress, Miss Catherine Davies who was teaching at a Secondary School in Chester.[18] The School Managers were insistent that the Headmaster should be interested in technical subjects and, once again, industrialists and members of the Chamber of Trade were among the school's supporters. The first pupil to be registered on the school roll was Thomas Campbell James, who came from the Higher Grade. He would later become Professor of Chemistry at Aberystwyth. It is thus clear that the drive for secondary education was fuelled principally by the need to produce students proficient in technical and scientific subjects. When the new school opened, in 1897, it was well endowed with physics and chemistry laboratories as well as with woodwork and metalwork shops. It is perhaps significant that the opening ceremony was performed by Mrs Maclaran, whose husband Rowland had been manager of Dafen Tinworks and a pioneer of the Works School 50 years since. Industry and education had long walked hand-in-hand in Llanelli.

By the 1880s, it was clear that Llanelli's little hospital on the Bigyn was totally inadequate and that a new building was urgently

Llanelli General Hospital, about 1925. (Brian Cripps collection)

The New Dock, 1896. (Llanelli Library)

required. In 1883, a Building Committee was set up, consisting mainly of local industrialists, under the chairmanship of Rowland Maclaran. Their brief was to choose a site and arrange for subscriptions. William Thomas, Cwmbach, provided a site of one acre at the top of Marble Hall Road plus a donation of £200.[19] The foundation stone was laid by Mrs William Thomas in October 1844. The new hospital, with accommodation for 20 patients and provided with the most up-to-date facilities, was opened by Mrs Rowland Maclaran in November 1885.[20] Most of the money required was raised from workers' contributions and from fund-raising activities including concerts, sports-days and bazaars. The Hospital Bazaar Fund, itself, raised an astonishing £1,111. The total cost of building the new hospital was £3,895 with £3,761 available at the time of the opening. By the following year, the debt was cleared. There was a financial crisis in 1898 when the hospital faced a deficiency of £400 and was forced to close its doors temporarily, admitting emergency cases only. The trustees, all wealthy men, were obviously not prepared to come to the hospital's rescue even though it would have meant only a contribution of £50 from each.[21] Salvation, however, came from a very unexpected source. Henry Studt, the fairground proprietor, said he would guarantee a sum of £500, from the profits of two fêtes, provided the working-men of Llanelli would increase their monthly subscriptions. The deal was struck, the hospital was saved and Mr Studt was made a Life Governor. No such honour was accorded the Llanelli workers who continued to support the hospital until it was taken over by the National Health Service almost half a century later.

In the latter part of the 18th century, the task of the local historian is made a lot easier because of the availability of local newspapers housed in the Public Library. Although a Llanelli correspondent contributed to Swansea's *Cambrian* as early as 1804, the first genuine local paper was the *Llanelly and County Guardian* which first appeared in 1863. It is true that a paper called the *Llanelly Advertiser* appeared in 1848. John Innes refers to it thus: 'It was given away gratis and was quite worth the sum charged for it.'

There was also a *Llanelly Telegraph* which appeared in 1857, but it was the appearance of the *Guardian* which marked the high point in local journalism. Strangely enough, it was anything but local in its early days, carrying barely one single page of Llanelli news and news of other Welsh industrial towns in its eight pages. It was obsessed with Royalty, London markets and London gossip. There were reports of other English provincial cities and an astonishing coverage of world news encompassing North and South America, India, Russia, China and most European countries. It clearly resembled the *Times* with the addition of a little local news and local advertisements which took another page. Its local news

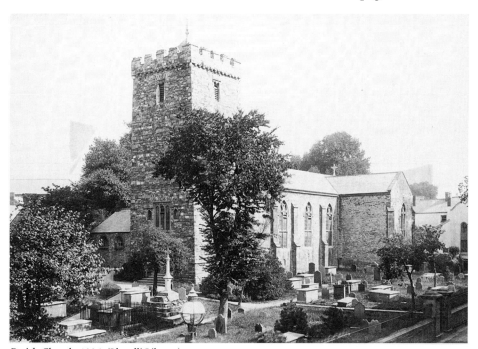

Parish Church, 1896. (Llanelli Library)

was mainly gleaned from Llanelli's Petty Sessions, reporting cases such as drunkenness, assault, paternity claims, breach of promise, furious driving and carts without names on them. The early advertisements are a good indicator of social history especially with regard to prices.

The Bwthyn on the Bigyn, about 1898. (Llanelli Library)

We see social mobility improving with the publication of railway time-tables and the offer of cheap Summer railway excursions to Llanwrtyd and Llandrindod and to Aberystwyth where one could enjoy an eight-hour stay before returning home. Llanelli's thirst for education was reflected in the 1860s with the offer of Cassell's Popular Educator at 7d each in a range of 56 different topics. Births, marriages and deaths command very little space in the early years, rarely more than three column inches. Gradually, local news increases as the century moves on and the *Guardian* takes its place as the foremost newspaper in a town so hungry for news that, at one time, there were five local newspapers in circulation at the same time.[22]

The Market Pavilion and its builders. (Llanelli Library)

Another valuable source of information for this period is the Llanelly Directory and Local Guide published in 1897. This, again, is available for study at the Public Library. There are extensive lists of local authority members and officials including their salaries. There are lists of schools and their head teachers, lists of chapels and their ministers, churches and their priests, and lists of surgeons and solicitors. The Directory contains all manner of information on contemporary Llanelli life. The most remarkable feature is a Street Directory which lists every house in every street together with the name of the householder. There is also a Commercial Directory listing trades and professions in alphabetical order. It was the work of James Davies, the editor of the *South Wales Press* in Murray Street, and it is a great pity that subsequent editions did not appear. It is probable that sales were insufficient and that not enough money was raised from its advertisements. Its most intriguing advertisement was for Franklyn's Tobacco 'as smoked by the Burry Port centenarian, Mrs Sarah Thomas, who lived 109 years!' Mrs Thomas is pictured sitting serenely in her armchair.

Towards the close of the century, Llanelli possessed all the trappings of a modern industrial town. There was an adequate police force and a fire-brigade. A horse-drawn tramway system was inaugurated in 1882, a telephone exchange installed in 1883 and a General Post Office was built in Cowell Street in 1885.[23] A new Market Hall appeared in 1888, and in 1895, a magnificent pavilion of glass and steel was added in the Victorian style best seen in London's main railway stations. In the end, it cost £5,000 and was used by the Eisteddfod in the same year at a charge of £1,000 for the week. It seated 9,300 people and, as a market, was Llanelli's pride and joy for 75 years. In the same year, an elegant arcade was built in Stepney Street. There was an air of supreme confidence in the town. When the Eisteddfod came

An impression of the Arcade. (*Llanelli Mercury*, 8 August, 1895)

The Old Town Hall in Hall Street. (Llanelli Library)

to Llanelli in 1895, the *Guardian* reported: 'It was a glorious success. Llanelly has covered itself with credit. It was essentially a Llanelly success, exceeding the hopes of the most roseate dreams.' Llanelli had famous choirs under the superb batons of John Thomas, R.C. Jenkins and Meudwy Davies. There were regular theatre shows at the Grand Theatre and at the Royalty.

In his introduction to the *Llanelly Directory*, James Davies had written: 'Llanelly has no rival as the chief town in Carmarthenshire and, excluding some great centres in Glamorgan, is the most considerable and important town in Wales.' Perhaps the ultimate expression of this pride and confidence is found in the building of the new Town Hall. The old Town Hall had become hopelessly inadequate for judicial and administrative purposes as early as 1870 and there was much talk of building a new one but very little action. It was not until September 1891 that the Board of Health decided on a site between Moriah and Tabernacle chapels. The new Town Hall was to house court facilities with seating for 300 members of the public and a Council Chamber for 30 members and officials. It was also to include a Public Hall to seat 2,000 people but this provision was withdrawn in March 1892 in spite of much public protest. This was a great pity because it deprived the town of a valuable asset. Charles Burny, a London architect, was asked to adjudicate on 25 plans for a building costing around £10,000. The winning design was submitted by an Edinburgh firm and William Griffiths of Falcon Chambers, Llanelli, was placed second. At a meeting

Llanelli Town Hall. (Llanelli Library)

soon afterwards, the Board of Health, in its wisdom, mercifully chose the design of William Griffiths.[24] Thirteen tenders for the building were obtained in January 1894 and the contract awarded to T.P. Jones of Station Road at a price of £11,000. By the time the building was completed, the Board of Health had been superseded by the Llanelly Urban District Council as a result of local government reorganisation in 1894. The magnificent new Town Hall was opened on 31 March 1896, by the wife of Dr J.A. Jones, Chairman of the Council, in the presence of thousands of spectators and to the accompaniment of the Town Band. The opening ceremony was followed by a banquet for distinguished guests at the Athenaeum at which an incredible number of toasts were drunk and 32 speeches made. In the evening, a free concert was held at the Market Hall when the Llanelly Choral Society performed under the baton of John Thomas. It was probably the most memorable and, certainly, the most exhausting day in the history of our town. It is true to say, however, that the Town Hall still stands, until this day, as Llanelli's most impressive building.

We have already seen emigration by colliers to the USA and now, towards the century's end we see an exodus of tinplate workers. The tinplate industry had been hit by tariffs on all plates entering the USA imposed by President McKinley. The largest single number of emigrants went to Gas City, Indiana, where J.H. Rogers

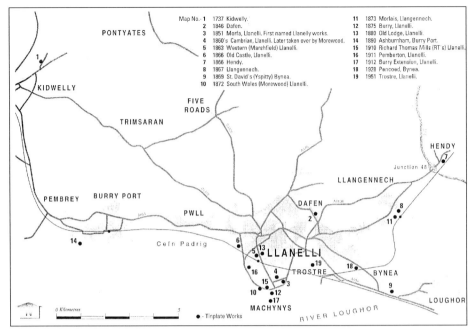

Map showing location of tinworks in the area. (Philip Fitzsimmons)

of Morewoods set up a works in 1892.[25] When it opened in 1893, it was the largest tinplate works in the world, employing 2,000 men. The attraction was natural gas found in the area which provided the works with free fuel. The venture crippled the works in Llanelli but came to an end 12 years later when the gas ran out. It was also in 1893 that Llanelli workers helped to set up and run a tinplate works in Piombino in Italy.[26] Piombino lay on the coast opposite the island of Elba and

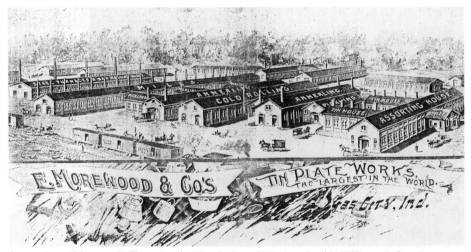

Impression of Morewood's Tinworks, Gas City, Indiana, USA. (sent by R.E. Williams, Indiana)

Llanelli Steelworks – the Klondike. (Llanelli Library)

must have been the most exotic location ever for a tinplate works, facing the blue Mediterranean on one side and hillside vineyards on the other. To the other extreme, William Thomas had taken a group of Llanelli workers to build a tinplate works at Hughesovka in the Ukraine in 1875 where John Hughes, of Merthyr, had set up an ironworks. They even tried to establish a works in the Urals but this had to be abandoned because of the severe weather conditions. Similar works were later set up by Llanelli workers in places as varied as Norway, Belgium, Spain and India.[27] That the tinplate trade was vulnerable to outside forces was experienced in Llanelli as early as the American Civil War, 1861-65, when valuable markets were lost. Trade was fairly good between 1870 and 1890 and three more tinplate works made their appearance in the town during this period, the South Wales Works (Morewoods) and Burry Works, both at Machynys, and the Old Lodge, converted from an ironworks, in Station Road.

The effects of the McKinley tariffs were not immediately felt but, by 1894, they were causing great hardship to the tinplate workers of Llanelli. The Burry works closed in 1896. Richard Thomas and Company took over the Morewood works in 1898 and the Burry Works in 1899. By this time, the Western Tinplate Company had taken over the Marshfield and Old Lodge Works. This company, together with the Old Castle Company and the Briton Ferry Steel Company formed the Llanelly Steel Company, in 1897, which built a new steelworks on the site of the present

Sandy Water Park. The enterprise of these new companies, coupled with new markets in the southern hemisphere, meant that Llanelli's tinplate industry reached the end of the century in a fairly healthy state [28]

Notes to Chapter XI

1   *Llanelly and County Guardian*, 7 January 1869.
2   The Upper Mill was near the site of Buckley's Brewery while the Lower Mill was near Moriah Chapel and was known as the Felin Dân – the Steam Mill.
3   It was clear that, by this time, that the Board of Health was developing an aptitude for spending ratepayers' money on occasions such as these. In fairness, of course, it was no different from other authorities in this respect.
4   Rogers was manager at the Marshfield Tinworks.
5   He fell over a wall while duck-shooting on the foreshore. He was aged 24 and was a cashier at the Marshfield Works.
6   Director of Margrave's Wine and Spirit Merchants trading from a shop at Llanelli House. Played twice for Wales in 1884. He retired, upon marriage, in 1885.
7   The result was disputed as the Cardiff team left the field after scoring some minutes before time.
8   Harry Bowen was the son of David Bowen (Deheufardd) who shared a prize at the Llanelli Eisteddfod in 1856 for a history of Llanelli. He was 18 when he was first capped. He was a school-teacher in Yorkshire before returning to Llanelli to become headmaster of Bynea School. Cattell was teaching at Pentip Church School at the time. He became a headmaster in Sheffield and was elected Lord Mayor of the city.
9   The team had worn a number of colours before this. They first played in blue, then black, black and red quarters, and primrose and rose (or yellow and pink!).
10   The Maoris were the first touring team ever to visit Britain. The match was won by the fabled goal dropped from the halfway line by Harry Bowen.
11   Copperworks School was particularly blessed with two good headmasters for the first half century of its existence. The first, David Williams, built up a library of 400 books and left in 1863 to become the South Wales agent of the British and Foreign School Society. In 1872, he became Vice-Principal of Swansea Teacher Training College. He was succeeded by John E. Jones who was headmaster until 1891. One of his most distinguished pupils was Alfred Daniell, FRS., an eminent chemist who was made Freeman of Llanelli. For a summary of the school's history, read Isobel Sadler: *Cradled in Copper* (Carmarthenshire County Council, 1997).
12   Among the better private schools were those of Captain Phillips of Seaside specialising in navigation, John Howell (took over William Morris' School in Wind Street) specialising in land-surveying, and John Evans' Classical and Commercial School in Park Street.
13   The first Board Schools were neither compulsory nor free. Two further Acts of 1876 and 1880 made education compulsory to the age of 10 and, in 1891, this education was provided free of charge. Market Street and Prospect Place Schools came under Board control in 1872. Copperworks School did not become a Board School until 1893. Following the Education Act of 1902, all schools were taken over by the Carmarthenshire Education Authority.
14   Details from *Llanelly and County Guardian* Report on Mechanics Institute AGM, 1866.
15   Constructed on a site at Coleshill purchased from C.W. Mansel Lewis for £1,500. Built by local builders Brown, Thomas and John. Later became Coleshill Central School and Secondary

110

Modern School. Now demolished. See Denver Phillips (ed) *End of an Era; Coleshill School 1891-1977* (Llanelli, 1977).

16 Read W. Gareth Evans: 'Education and the needs of an Industrial Community'. *Carmarthenshire Antiquary*, 1992 and A.H. Ward: 'The beginnings of Intermediate Technical Education for Boys in Llanelli.' *Carmarthenshire Antiquary*, 1972. Llanelli was one of the few towns in Wales to provide both a Higher Grade and an Intermediate School.

17 The local Board of Health charged £2 2s 0d for rooms at the Athenaeum. The managers were responsible for heating and lighting as well as cleaning and making good any damage. The site in Marble Hall Road was donated by Sir Arthur Stepney. The school was built by Edward Groom of Marble Hall Road.

18 William Lewis was one of the first students to enter University College, Cardiff, in 1883. In 1896 he undertook research into the education systems of France and Switzerland and gained an MA at Aberystwyth in 1912 for a thesis on education. Both Mr Lewis and Miss Davies proved to be inspired choices.

19 William Thomas was born at Penywern Farm, Stradey. The family moved to Cwmbach Farm and thence to Llanlliedi. He became a successful businessman. The Woolworth side of Vaughan Street was once known as Cwmbach Buildings. For a fuller account, read W.J. Griffiths: 'William Thomas, JP (Cwmbach)'. In *Llanelli Miscellany*, No. 12, 1992.

20 There was provision for a male and female ward with 8 beds in each. There was an emergency ward with 4 beds plus an operating theatre. The builder was George Mercer of New Road.

21 The eight trustees were Rowland Maclaran, J.S. Tregoning, Hugh Nevill, Richard Nevill, J.H. Rogers, Ernest Trubshaw, Henry Thomas and John Jennings. The first six were industrialists.

22 The *Llanelly Telegraph* changed its name to the *South Wales Press* in 1867 and became a substantial newspaper. Other local papers were the *Ariel* in 1875; the *Llanelly Echo* and the *Carmarthenshire and Llanelly Punch* in 1880; the *Llanelly Mercury* in 1891; the *Llanelly Star* in 1909; and the *Llanelly Argus* in 1911. Several other local papers appeared in the following years but all were short lived. The *Llanelli Star* is the sole survivor. In addition to the *Guardian*, the *South Wales Press*, *Mercury* and *Star* are preserved at the Public Library

23 The Post Office had moved around various places in Llanelli since the beginning of the century, including a long period at the Thomas Arms. The building in Cowell Street was opposite the junction with John Street and, after 1911, was occupied by the Westminster Bank until fairly recently. It is currently a hair-dressing establishment. A branch office was already in existence at Llanelli Docks since 1877. Half-a-dozen sub-post offices were scattered around the town. See Brian Cripps: 'Postal History of Llanelli', *Carmarthenshire Antiquary*, 1976.

24 For further information on the design of the building and details of the opening ceremony read David F. Griffiths: *A History of Llanelli Borough Council.* (Llanelli Borough Council, 1996).

25 Several existing Llanelli families have links with Gas City. I am in correspondence with Robert E. Williams, Goshen, Indiana, who has provided me with much information on its history. His grandfather emigrated from Furnace.

26 Tom Williams of Kidwelly and Loughor supervised the building of the works and became manager of the hot rolling-mill. His son John took over the Cold-Roll department. John emigrated to the USA in 1897 and became a millionaire. He was a great benefactor to Llanelli, Kidwelly and Loughor.

27 For more information read John Edwards (ed) *Tinopolis* (Llanelli Borough Council, 1995).

28 Oil and petrol were becoming important at this time and oil-drums and petrol-cans were in demand. There was a market for canning fruit from Australia, New Zealand and South Africa. Tinned corned beef from South America was also popular at the time.

Chapter XII
Into the 20th century

A century has just slipped by,
The long, long years we mourn;
But now the peoples of the world
Have seen a new one dawn,
To put aside their fears
That they may joyful be,
For faith now flies the banner
Of a Happy New Century.

THUS, in translation, was how the 20th century was greeted in the Welsh language columns of the *Llanelly Mercury*.[1] Most of the space in Llanelli newspapers, however, was taken up by reports of the South African War which included letters written by Llanelli soldiers. This imperial frenzy

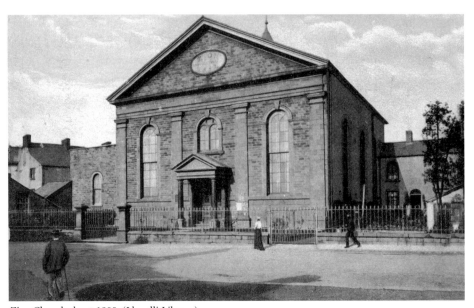

Zion Chapel, about 1900. (Llanelli Library)

Roll-turning in Glanmor Foundry, about 1900.

reached a crescendo with the relief of Mafeking in May 1900. March witnessed an outpouring of grief at the passing of Lleurwg who had been minister of Zion Baptist chapel since 1855. His ministry was indicative of the rise of Nonconformity in Llanelli in the latter half of the 19th century. When he arrived, the membership numbered 260, at his death it had reached 850 with the chapel well on its way to becoming 'the Jerusalem of the Welsh Baptists'.[2] Llanelli's newspapers had all their columns edged in black at the death of Queen Victoria in January 1901. She had reigned through the town's industrial expansion and most of the population had known no other monarch. She had given her name to a whole era and now the Victorian era had come to an end. Our majestic Queen Victoria Road was named after her as was the more modest Albert Street after the consort who had preceded her so many years before.

We find in the census of 1901 that the population of Llanelli was 25,553, shared among three wards roughly corresponding to the old divisions of Town, Wern and Seaside (including the New Dock district). One of the features of the census, in spite of an increase in population of nearly 2,000 over the previous decade, was the number of unoccupied houses. This was due, in part, to the emigration of tinplate and steel workers to the USA. The American tinplate industry was now making rapid strides as a result of the McKinley tariff and,

Painting, by John Wynne Hopkins, of Stepney Street, about 1890.

with an increasing demand for steel, Llanelli workers emigrated in numbers to the USA with their families following them once they were settled.

The Llanelli Rugby Club continued to make great strides and, by 1902, 27 of its players had been capped for Wales,

Stepney Street, 1909. (Brian Cripps collection)

several on more than one occasion. There now arose a controversy as to the suitability of the game as far as Christians were concerned. No Nonconformist minister would be seen dead at a rugby match, let alone play in one. S.B. Williams, however, was a curate at St Paul's and was one of many Anglican priests to play for Llanelli. Among them, C.B. Nicholl and J. Strand Jones[3] had already played and they would be followed by many more, including W.T. Havard who, after a curacy in Llanelli, became Bishop of St Asaph and, later, Bishop of St David's. At a banquet held to celebrate a victory over Swansea, on 6 March 1902, S.B. Williams[4] rose to condemn the attitude of Christians who objected to the game of rugby. He said, somewhat mischievously, that there was less rowdyism among the 12,000 spectators at the Swansea game than one would find in a Gymanfa Ganu or Eisteddfod. A stinging reply came in the following week's *Mercury*: 'This is a fine specimen of a Christian, standing in a pulpit preaching Christ on a Sunday and the previous Saturday enticing hundreds of people to witness the smashing of noses, the breaking of ribs and collar-bones, swearing, cursing and gambling.' The controversy rumbled on and though chapel members watched and played for Llanelli, ministers were very rarely seen at Stradey until after World War Two, and I cannot trace anyone who actually participated apart from the Revd Elwyn Jenkins, Aberystwyth, who played for Swansea and Llanelli.

The hostility between church and chapel was manifested not only on the rugby field but also in the pages of history. 1 January 1902, saw the publication of *Old Llanelly* by John Innes. He was the son of R.V. Innes, Collector of Customs at the port of Llanelli, who also kept a school at the Thomas Arms and the Athenaeum. John Innes' son was James Dickson Innes, Llanelli's most famous artist and friend of Augustus John. He spent most of his life in London and travelled widely in Ireland, France, Spain and Morocco. He was very fond of the Arenig mountain near

Furnace Pond, 1900. (Willis Walker)

Bala and made several studies of it. He was a typical bohemian and spent a lot of time with the gypsies encamped near Furnace Pond when painting at the nearby quarry. He was a tall, gaunt young man with long hair and was invariably dressed in a long black coat and black hat. Harry Davies, the doyen of local news reporters, once interviewed Mrs Alice Ley who was in service with the family at their New Road home. She said: 'Dickie only came home once or twice a year and that was only to clean up.' He had two brothers, Frank and Jack, and his mother was French. Mrs Ley said that his mother's bedroom was filled with her son's pictures and that many were lost when the family moved to Tavistock. The artist lived a debauched life, had a severe alcohol problem and died, in 1914, at the age of 27. A colourful booklet was published by Llanelli Council on the centenary of his birth in 1987 which contains some of his best paintings, including those of local scenes.

Nonconformity was offended by *Old Llanelly* because John Innes had devoted insufficient space to the influence of the chapel in the town's history. Innes drew heavily on the histories of David Bowen and James Lane Bowen as well as on the manuscript work of Thomas Mainwaring. There were several contributions also from Arthur Mee,[5] the author of the History of the Parish Church. From the point of

Gypsies at Furnace, 1907. (Brian Cripps collection)

'Furnace Quarry' by J.D. Innes.

view of illustrations, for example, there is not a single one of a chapel or minister whereas there are seven illustrations to do with the church. To be fair, Innes never claimed to have produced a historical masterpiece. 'My attempt is necessarily fragmentary', he said. He had been persuaded to publish a popular lecture he had delivered on seven occasions since 1899 'intended as reminiscences, gossip and anecdote.' These features are, indeed, his strong point and are brought together in the tale of Wil Bach, the Shoemaker, the last man to be put in the stocks outside the parish church for insulting behaviour towards William Chambers. Wil was drunk when he cheekily approached the big man and tried to shake his hand saying (in Welsh): 'Wil you are, and Wil I am.' We find a letter, in the *Guardian* claiming, with fairness, that the book contained many errors: 'They are obvious, here and there, throughout the whole work.'[6] Innes, himself, showed little confidence in his own abilities in dedicating the book to his mother as: 'My first (and doubtless my last) literary attempt.' The *Guardian* letter quoted above goes on to complain about the price of the book (6s) as: 'Too much for working-class Welshmen to be able to afford and it would be good to have a cheaper edition. But, better still would be to have it in Welsh. Will that ever come to pass?' It did – nearly a hundred years later!

The National Eisteddfod held in Llanelli of 1903[7] was an outstanding success with one of the highlights being a presidential address given, in Welsh, by David Lloyd George. John Innes, a non-Welsh speaker among several others, was received into the Gorsedd of Bards under the clever name Ynyshir. Letters in the

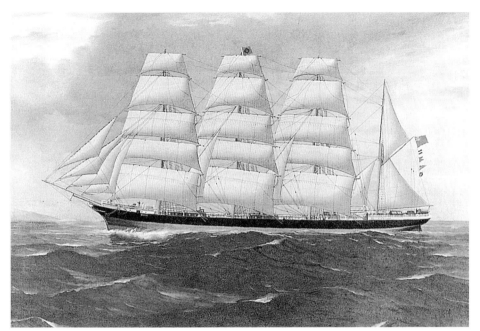

The 'Cissie' in 1903. Owned by William Bowen, junior, of Llanelli. Iron ship of 1,907 tons.
(Robin Craig collection)

local press were at the time of the Proclamation critical of 'honouring English-speaking Welshmen who had not bothered to learn our language.' In fact, about three-quarters of the proceedings were in English in spite of a plea that it was unfair and was intended only to obtain the support of a small minority of wealthy people.[8] W.H. Protheroe, secretary of the 1902 Eisteddfod Committee in Barmouth had stated that 'the Eisteddfod should be more Welsh in every way in order to nurture the language, raise the nation's standards and educate the people in its literature, music and every branch of the arts and sciences.'

It is appropriate, at this point, to pause and consider the state of the Welsh language at the turn of the century. The end of the 19th century saw a radical Liberal Home Rule policy for Wales and Ireland. Even the local MP, Sir John Jones Jenkins,[9] considered a Liberal in Llanelli and a Tory at Westminster, was involved in negotiations on Home Rule with Lloyd George and T.E. Ellis on the basis that matters affecting Wales should be left to the Welsh people. He claimed that a central body based in Wales would be much better able to assess local needs than officials sent from London. He proposed a National Council of 50 representatives elected by Welsh County Councils. It caused the *Llanelly Mercury* to declare, in a headline to an editorial, 'We are all Nationalists now.' Lloyd George and T.E. Ellis led a demand for the disestablishment of the Church in Wales. The Sunday Closing Act was passed under pressure from Nonconformists

Eisteddfod audience in the Market Pavilion, 1903. (Llanelli Library)

making Wales an exception from the rest of the United Kingdom. The Cymru Fydd (Future Wales) movement was active in pursuit of Welsh aims. The Welsh Intermediate Act was passed giving Wales its own powers over Secondary education, and Wales now had its own University with its constituent colleges of Aberystwyth, Bangor and Cardiff. It could be claimed that the condition of the country and its language had never been healthier. In fact, in 1891, when the census first asked questions about the language, it showed 87 percent of Llanelli's population speaking Welsh.[10]

All this seemed to indicate a sure foundation for the building of a truly Welsh social structure in Llanelli, but this was not to be. The question, therefore, is how did 13 percent of the population succeed in imposing its will on the majority? In spite of the fact that the workers succeeded in working in Welsh by adapting English technical terms, the owners and managers were either English or English-speaking Welshmen. Anyone who was keen on furthering his ambitions in industry was obliged to adopt an English persona. Evan Roberts, for example, was recommended for a managerial position by the Llanelly Railway and Dock Company but the recommendation was queried by its London office on the grounds that he was 'a Welshman and chattering'. This meant that he was likely to converse in Welsh with the workers which meant that the barrier erected

Stepney Street, about 1905. (Llanelli Library)

between management and labour risked being breached.[11] This kind of linguistic apartheid was apparent throughout industry and commerce. Elementary and secondary education was wholly English and, in this context, it is worth remembering that, in the early years, even Welsh was taught through the medium of English at Aberystwyth. No Welsh history was taught; history meant English history. Local papers were printed almost entirely in English with the exception of one or two columns in Welsh, usually exclusively religious or literary in character. The chapels were content with Welsh as the language of worship, feeding the masses on the Bible and denominational magazines. Welsh was the language of the chapel and home; it was English which drove the engine of real life. Entertainment, in theatres and cinemas, was available in English. English was the language of getting on in the world. English was the language of the ever-spreading British Empire; Welsh was the language of an insignificantly small country. It was clear to all that wealthy English-speaking people lived in grand houses on the fringes of town while Welsh-speaking workers lived in terraced houses near their places of employment.

English was the language of all the town's institutions – of the Council and all its works, the Chamber of Trade and the Magistrates' Court. Most of the magistrates, themselves, were English-speaking Anglicans or members of English chapels. The family of David Rees, Capel Als, who worshipped at Park Church, became totally English with his grand-children knowing next to nothing about the great man.[12] William Thomas, Cwmbach, and his family moved from Capel

Stepney Street, 1904. (Brian Cripps collection)

Seion to Greenfield English Baptist Church as did Thomas Jones JP, Brynmair, from Moriah.[13] Both were influential in the town. We have already seen that English-speakers were accepted into the Gorsedd of Bards, not because of their enthusiasm for the Eisteddfod but so that they could influence its activities. This attitude can be clearly seen in an extract from the *Mercury*: 'The Eisteddfod does not arrest the attention of many of the rich of our land but it is well adapted to be the annual festival of the sons of toil.'[14] And there we have it – the two classes, masters and servants and, as in the Imperial colonies, in spite of their small numbers in comparison with the natives, it was the power of the English masters and their language which triumphed. It was thus that the 'imperial tongue' held sway at Llanelli's National Eisteddfod in 1903 as it had in 1895.

In July 1903, the new upper Lliedi reservoir was opened. It had a capacity of 200 million gallons, cost £38,000 and was accompanied by the junketing which had become synonymous with the opening of reservoirs.[15] Even this, however, paled into insignificance compared with the daily menu provided for the men and horses of the 'Greatest Show on Earth' when Buffalo Bill took Llanelli by storm at Stradey Park in the same month.[16] The new North Dock was formally opened at the end of the year with the first

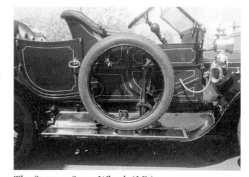

The Stepney Spare Wheel. (J.E.)

Railway disaster near Bynea, 1904. (Brian Cripps collection)

cargo arriving on Christmas morning.[17]

Numbers of cars were appearing on Llanelli's roads and punctured tyres were quite common on the roads. The Stepney Patent Spare Wheel Company[18] came up with an ingenious invention which was adopted worldwide. Instead of having to repair the puncture, the spare wheel could be fixed alongside the flat tyre simply by tightening two thumb-screws. The tyre was pumped hard and ready for use with the whole operation completed in minutes without the use of any tools. There was a reminder that railway travel was not without its dangers with the Bynea disaster of October 1904. The Milford express train had stopped at Llanelli and was passing Bynea when the 'banker' engine, at the front, was pushed off the rails by the heavier main engine. The main engine and some coaches also left the track. The banker engine was required to help pull the train up the Gowerton bank. Both driver and fireman, Llanelli men, were killed, three others died subsequently and about 20 were seriously injured. People waited anxiously for news at Llanelli station then made their way to the scene of the accident by walking along the track to assist in any way they could. The tragedy is often referred to as the Loughor Disaster. More of a blessing came from Loughor, in the same year, in the form of a religious revival led by Evan Roberts[19] whose evangelical fire swept through Llanelli and the rest of Wales in subsequent years. Many of Llanelli's chapels witnessed scenes of incredible religious fervour during this period.

Llanelli life moved along in a fairly leisurely way until the end of the decade. The last echo of the South African war was heard when Earl Roberts (former

Commander-in-Chief in South Africa) came to Llanelli in October 1905, to unveil a monument to local soldiers killed in the war. The war had come to an end in 1902 and the local papers urged people to contribute money for a memorial. In spite of pouring rain, thousands came to see the ceremony and the famous

Looking down towards Station Road. (Brian Cripps collection)

general. The monument still stands in the Town Hall grounds. A very different kind of monument was unveiled by William Abraham (Mabon) in January 1906, over the grave of Thomas Phillips at the Box Cemetery. Thomas Phillips had died in 1904. He was a tin-worker who became secretary of the national Tinplate Workers' Union.[20] In June 1906, the town was hit by a minor earthquake. Chimneys toppled in the Furnace area, New Dock was shaken, and the Town Hall clock-tower was seen to sway visibly. The tremors lasted several seconds but no one was hurt. Felinfoel Brewery was listed as a registered company in October 1906, competing with Buckley to slake Llanelli's enormous thirst. Buckley's beer was famous by this time, having won the Gold Medal at a Brewers' Exhibition in London, open to Britain and the Empire. Buckley's would also win the Grand Prix and Gold Medal at the Paris Exhibition in 1911.[21]

As if in response to the fervour of the Nonconformist religious revival, the Anglicans embarked upon the restoration of the Parish Church which had fallen into disrepair. The formal reopening of the old Church took place in January 1907, and the restoration was much admired by the crowded congregation. Services were conducted by the Bishop of St David's who paid tribute to the work of Arthur Mee in tracing the history of the building. A much-appreciated feature of the restoration was the building of a little turret where the late lamented second tower had stood. The Llanelli Choir covered itself with glory in November 1907, by giving a performance before the King and his cousin, the German Kaiser, at Windsor Castle. The choir was 230 strong and was conducted by John Thomas with his predecessor, R.C. Jenkins, sitting in the audience. It was the first occasion on which a mixed choir had been invited to Windsor and both King and Kaiser were delighted with the performance, according to newspaper reports. The choir was to gain further honours in the following year by winning the Chief Choral competition at the Llangollen National Eistcddfod.

Vaughan Street, 1910. (Llanelli Library)

Horse fair in Thomas Street, about 1911. (Brian Cripps collection)

News of the wanderings of Sir Arthur Cowell-Stepney reached Llanelli in 1908. He had been MP for Llanelli between 1876 and 1878 and was High Sheriff of Carmarthenshire in 1884 although he spent very little time in the area. He had married his wife Margaret, the daughter of Lord de Tabley, in London in 1875[22] and they had one daughter, Catherine Meriel. Their

Rees the Baker's cart, Station Road, 1906. (Brian Cripps collection)

home was at the Dell, Furnace, the old Raby residence. There were obviously strains in the marriage and Lady Margaret had petitioned for divorce in May 1903 because of desertion. He had also accused her, in writing, of bringing up Meriel, then aged 28, in an improper manner. Sir Arthur had written to Meriel, known as Alcie, urging her to join him in the USA where he now lived.[23] Lady Margaret wrote to him to try to persuade him to return home. In fact, she had been divorced by Sir Arthur in the US courts, in March, also for desertion, although there were doubts on the grounds of validity. He claimed to have invited his wife several times to join him in the USA but, in fact, he had no fixed domicile to offer her. A report from the *Los Angeles Examiner* in 1908 said that Sir Arthur was then living at the Hollenbeck Hotel, in that city. He had become a US citizen and was known as Mr Stepney. He was then 74 years old and was quoted as saying 'I prefer America. I am just plain A.C. Stepney, American

Market Street about 1900. (Llanelli Library)

Cowell Street, 1905. (Llanelli Library)

citizen, and I want the world, as well as myself, to forget that I was ever Sir Emile Arthur Cowell-Stepney. I could keep the title if I desired, but I don't want it.' It appears that he was, more or less, tramping across America and the poor man was found dead at Yuma railway station, Arizona, in July of the following year, having left Los Angeles six months previously.

'It was a great game and a great victory and Llanelly stands higher than ever on the pedestal of football fame.' It was thus that the *Guardian* recorded the victory of the Scarlets over the touring Wallabies from Australia at Stradey Park on 17 October 1908.

The score was 8-3 and the win also gave rise to the first additional English verse to Sospan Fach: 'Who beat the Wallabies?'

The year 1911 dawned brightly for Llanelli in a very real sense. On 1 January, the town was lit by electricity for the first time. A new electric tramway system was inaugurated by Alfred Holland who remarked: 'Every time I visit Llanelli, I am struck by some new mark of improvement. Llanelli is one of the most go-ahead and fastest rising towns in Wales, if not in the United Kingdom.' A fine new YMCA building was being raised in Stepney Street, costing £4,000, with a quarter of that sum coming from workers' collections. Vint's new Palace

On Llanelli beach, about 1900. (Llanelli Library)

Pier and Lighthouse, 1896. (Llanelli Library)

Cinema was being built in Market Street, there was a new Drill Hall in Murray Street, the Glenalla district was being developed and a fine new GPO building was taking shape at the top of John Street.

The summer had been the hottest in living memory with 100F being recorded at Greenwich. There had been much industrial unrest; the country had been torn by strikes during the past year and, on Thursday, 17 August, the railway unions called on all its members to come out on strike after negotiations with the railway companies in London had broken down. The call was answered to a man in Llanelli and although there were only 500 railwaymen employed in the area, crowds of between 1,500 and 5,000 were soon apparent at the station approaches. It was obvious that other Llanelli workers were showing complete support for the strike which was mainly called to demand pay increases.[24] Many of the lower-paid railway workers were earning less than £1 a week. On Thursday night there were only 18 policemen in town; the rest had been sent to Cardiff and Tonypandy where trouble had been anticipated. No one expected trouble at Llanelli. The police found a good-natured crowd and there was friendly banter between them and Superintendent Rogers and Sergeant Britten. Two trains

Crowd at the eastern crossing, 1911. (Llanelli Library)

were held up outside the eastern gates but the mail-train and a cattle-train were allowed to pass and proceed towards London.

At 5am in the morning, Thomas Jones (JP and GWR shareholder) arrived at the station. The suspicion is that he had requested troops to be sent to Llanelli and, at 7.45 on Friday morning, 127 soldiers of the North Lancashire Regiment arrived from Cardiff under Captain Burrows. There were some scuffles at the eastern level-crossing but the crowd held firm and kept the gates closed, although the two trains held up overnight were allowed to proceed. By the afternoon, the police were again at full strength but the strikers and supporters were still in control of the crossing. Thomas Jones and Frank Nevill, JP, sent a telegram to the Home Office asking for more soldiers and 250 men of the Devon Regiment and the Worcester Regiment arrived at 4.30 p.m. under the command of Major Brownlow Stuart. Frank Nevill then read the Riot Act and the troops reoccupied the crossing. From this moment, the strike turned ugly and passing trains were stoned.

On Saturday afternoon, a train had been standing for some time beside the down platform while the strikers were holding a meeting at Copperworks school,

Two trams at the bottom of Stepney Street, 1911. (Brian Cripps collection)

a mere 100 yards away. A large crowd had gathered on the western crossing. Suddenly, the train started out and was immediately pursued by the strikers and the crowd. It stopped about 600 yards down the line while the guard walked some 200 yards to the Old Castle crossing to open the gate. This gave the strikers time to reach the engine and the railwaymen's leader, John Bevan, in a symbolic gesture, lay his head on the track in front of the engine. The fire was effectively drawn from the engine by railway workers before Brownlow Stuart and 80 soldiers arrived on the scene. The crowd dispersed and climbed about 20ft up the embankments behind High Street and Bryn Road. Stones were thrown at the engine and Brownlow Stuart drew up his soldiers, ready to fire after he had tried to speak to some of the crowd on the High Street bank. A bugle was blown, Henry Wilkins, JP, read the Riot Act and the troops fired at a group of young men sitting on a low garden wall at No. 6. Two men were shot dead, one was wounded in the neck and another in the hand.[25] Brownlow Stuart marched his men back to the station at once.

After the news reached a public meeting in the town, a crowd marched down to the station where the soldiers and police were now hiding. They broke all the station windows and smashed the points on the up and down lines so that Llanelli was now effectively cut off. A train was stopped some distance away from the eastern crossing and was found to contain army uniforms and stores. The engine was quickly immobilised, windows were smashed and the contents of the train ransacked. This led to general looting in the sidings. Later, fires were started and night was turned to day while neither soldiers nor police intervened. There was looting in the town as well and a particular target was the wholesale grocery warehouse of Thomas Jones. Forty soldiers and 100 policemen, outside the police station in Market Street, looked on while Thomas Jones' stores were emptied, and the rest of the soldiers stayed inside the station while chaos reigned at the sidings. Fires were raging in the sidings when the Fire Brigade arrived at 10.45.[26] At 10.30, 350 men of the Sussex Regiment, on their way home from Ireland by train, got off at the Old Castle crossing and cleared the town streets. There was a tremendous explosion in one of the trucks at the siding and four people were

Cilymaenllwyd. Home of Sir Stafford and Lady Howard. (Llanelli Library)

killed before soldiers cleared the area.[27] The time was 11.15 and, a quarter of an hour earlier, the strike had been called off in London. It had been Llanelli's darkest day. A conspiracy of silence followed the events of that terrible Saturday and the story remained untold to future generations for 75 years.[28]

Autumn, 1911, saw Llanelli return to cooler weather and cooler tempers. Life in the town slowly returned to a measure of normality helped by the wedding of Catherine Meriel Stepney to Sir Stafford Howard on Thursday, 21 September.[29] Since the death of her father, Sir Arthur Stepney, in America, Meriel and her mother had returned to live at the Dell,[30] in Furnace, Meriel having succeeded to the Stepney estate. She became increasingly aware of her Welsh background and of her position in the life of the town. Although born in London and privately educated, she now spoke fluent Welsh thanks to the tuition of the Vicar of Llangennech, the Revd T. Geler Jones, and had been admitted to the Gorsedd of Bards under the name of Meriel Carnwallon. She had been very distressed at the death of the family chauffeur, Alfred Morris,[31] after the explosion at the railway sidings and took an active interest in the progress of other injured victims at the hospital. She was a person genuinely loved by the people of Llanelli and they were determined that nothing should spoil her wedding day. Meriel's bridegroom was Sir Edward Stafford Howard of Thornbury in Gloucestershire. He had been a Liberal MP and had held office in Liberal governments.[32] He was a 60-year-old widower when he married Meriel and the local press portrayed the occasion as a

Bryncaerau Mansion, Parc Howard. (Llanelli Library)

marriage of Autumn and Spring. The bride and her mother stayed at Llanelli House on the eve of the wedding which took place at the Parish Church just across the road around which large crowds had assembled. The service was conducted entirely in Welsh and there were two receptions, one for invited guests at Llanelli House and the other for 500 tenants of the estate at the Drill Hall.[33] The new Lady Howard addressed the tenants in Welsh and even Sir Stafford spoke enough of the language to express himself in Welsh saying: 'I am not a Welshman but my heart has been stolen completely by a beloved Welsh lady. Today, I dedicate myself to her and to her country.'[34]

The glittering reception at Llanelli House began and ended with the orchestra playing Hen Wlad Fy Nhadau and the three-tier wedding cake was decorated entirely with harps, leeks, daffodils and other Welsh symbols. Meriel was one of the few Stepneys who dedicated herself to the town and in her first engagement on her return from honeymoon, she said: 'I would never dream of living anywhere but in Llanelly.'[35] Sir Stafford and Lady Howard went to live at the newly-built Cilymaenllwyd[36] in Pwll and, at the end of the year, they bought Bryncaerau Mansion from the Buckley family and presented it, together with its spacious grounds, as a gift to the people of Llanelli on the occasion of their first wedding anniversary in 1912.[37] Known as Parc Howard, it continues to be greatly enjoyed and appreciated by the people of Llanelli to this day.

Notes to Chapter XII

1. Canrif hirfaith giliodd heibio
   I'r gorffenol du,
   Gweled gwawr un arall
   Wnaeth aneirif lu;
   Llawer calon, fu mewn pryder,
   Bellach lawenha,
   Am fod ffydd yn chwifio baner
   Canrif Newydd Dda.
   The words are by Blodeufryn of Mountain Ash and appeared, appropriately, in 1901.

2. Dr John Rhys Morgan, D.D., was succeeded by E.T. Jones until 1931 and then by J. Jubilee Young who was minister until 1957 thus providing a triumvirate of truly remarkable preachers over a period of more than a century. The same can be said of Capel Als with David Rees, Thomas Johns and D.J. Davies and of many other chapels in the town.

3. C.B. Nicholl was capped 15 times and J. Strand Jones five times, the first in 1902. W.T. Havard was Bishop of St Asaph from 1934 to 1950 and Bishop of St David's from 1950 to 1956, the year of his death. He married into the Holmes family of Penyfai, directors of the Llanelli Tinstamping Works.

4. Later Chancellor Williams, Rector of Laugharne.

5. His father, George Mee, was born in Aberdeen and had edited the *Bradford Observer* before coming to Llanelli as the editor and part-owner of the *South Wales Press*. It was here that Arthur learned his trade as a journalist. He left for Cardiff in 1892 and worked for the *Western*

Mail. His book *Llanelly Parish Church* was published in 1888 and his *Carmarthenshire Notes* (1889, 1890 and 1891) were published by Carmarthenshire County Council in 1997.

6   *Llanelly County Guardian*, 25 July 1907. A similar letter in the *Mercury* stated: 'It would be a shame if this book were passed down to the next generation as a history of Llanelly.' (Written in Welsh).

7   The Crown was won by the Revd J.E. Davies for a poem on 'Vicar Pritchard' and the Chair by the Revd J.T. Job for an ode on 'The Celt'. The Eisteddfod Choir, under the direction of John Thomas, gave a memorable performance of Handel's 'Israel in Egypt'.

8   William Evans quoted in *Llanelly Mercury,* 3 April 1902. W.H. Protheroe quoted in same paper 24 April 1902.

9   Later, Lord Glantawe. Worked in the tinplate works and later became a tinplate works owner. Related to my family on my father's side and worked alongside my great-grandfather in tinplate. His daughter married Lord Bledisloe, Governor General of Australia. New Zealand and Australia play rugby for the Bledisloe Cup.

10 Three questions were asked: Do you speak Welsh only? Do you speak English and Welsh? Do you speak English only?'

11 Correspondence books of Llanelly Railway and Dock Company in Llanelli Public Library. Written in exquisite copperplate. L.C. 1789.

12 Iorwerth Jones: *David Rees y Cynhyrfwr* (Swansea, 1971).

13 Thomas Jones became a crucial figure in the Railway Riots, 1911.

14 *Llanelly Mercury*, 10 July 1903.

15 'A large marquee was set aside for a luncheon sufficient for and abundantly to spare of everything for councillors and friends'. *Llanelly Guardian* 30 July 1903.

16 'Travelling with the show are a trained army of cooks and the meals are spread in a spacious dining tent where 500 can sit down at the same time. To provide food for 800 men, the daily requirements are 1,400lbs of meat, 7 cwts of potatoes, 450lbs of bread, and 500lbs of vegetables. The 500 horses required 7 tons of hay (with the same amount of straw) 6 cwts of bran and 3½ cwts of oats.' *Llanelly Guardian,* 16 July 1903.

17 The dock was 1,000ft. long and 400ft. across, with an entrance 53ft wide. The SS *Ravenscroft*, ironically, brought about 1,000 steel bars from Germany for the Richard Thomas Mills. These were produced for about £1 a ton less than local steel. The dock was sited at a very difficult location next to the Carmarthenshire Dock, yet, out of 11 million tons of exports from Llanelli between 1904 and 1947, 9 million tons were shipped from the North Dock. It closed in 1951 and was used, for some years, to berth a 'mothballed fleet' of Royal Naval vessels.

18 The spare-wheel was invented by T. Morris Davies, senior partner in the firm of Davies Bros., Stepney Works, Copperworks Road. It was so successful that works manufacturing the wheel were set up in other parts of Britain, France, Germany, Belgium, Austria, Italy, Canada and the USA. The company's proudest boast was: 'Nearly all the motor-cars of the world are fitted with Stepney Wheels.'

19 I heard many stories of the 1904 Revival from an aunt of mine, Mary Rees of Gorseinon, who was one of Evan Roberts' devoted female 'disciples'. She had a daughter, Tydfil, and three sons: Alwyn Rees of Aberystwyth; Brinley Rees of Bangor (both well-known in academic Welsh circles); and Myrddin Rees who was English master at Llanelli Grammar School.

20 Thomas Phillips was secretary of the Tin and Sheet Millmen's Association. He also devised a Ready Reckoner in 1889 to be used by millmen.

21 Beer has been brewed on the present brewery site at Felinfoel since 1878. The original owner was David John who also had interests in the tinplate industry.

22 In August 1875, at Holy Trinity Church, Brompton. W.E. Gladstone was a family friend.

23 He was naturalised American in 1906 and was an able man, being a Fellow of the Royal Geographical Society and a Doctor of Civil Law.

24 For a full account of the strike, read John Edwards, *Remembrance of a Riot*. (Llanelli Borough Council, 1988).

25 John John, aged 22 and Leonard Worsell, aged 20 were killed. John Francis, aged 24, was wounded in the throat and John Hanbury, aged 19, in the hand.

26 They were called out as early as 8.30 p.m. Police Supt. Rogers was in charge of a Brigade of 15 men.

27 Joseph Plant, aged 31, was killed when the truck exploded. William Harries, aged 48; Alfred Morris, aged 23 (Chauffeur to Lady Stepney); and Mrs A.M. Fisher, aged 30 and pregnant, all died in hospital the next day. 16 people were treated at the hospital for serious injuries received at the sidings or in the town.

28 This was largely because more emphasis was placed on the looting than on the shooting. Press reports and the pronouncements of religious and civic leaders dwelt on the shame brought on the town. The event was never mentioned by any of my family and a blanket silence covered the whole town.

29 It had a similar effect to that of royal and celebrity weddings, taking people's minds off difficult circumstances.

30 This was Alexander Raby's old residence known as Furnace House, now demolished for housing development.

31 He was to have driven the happy couple on their honeymoon. Like hundreds of others, he was simply a curious onlooker.

32 Entered Parliament in 1876 and was Commissioner of Her Majesty's Woods, Forests and Land Revenues. Honoured as CB in 1900 and KCB in 1909.

33 The land on which the Drill Hall was built had been given by Meriel Stepney among several other plots in the town.

34 'Nid wyf yn Gymro, ond arglwyddes Gymreig annwyl a ddygodd fy nghalon yn llwyr. Heddiw yr wyf yn cyflwyno fy hun iddi hi ac i'w gwlad.'

35 At St Joseph's Convent where she opened a bazaar.

36 Built by T.P. Jones at an estimated cost of £15,000.

37 The house and land was bought for £7,500.

Chapter XIII
From One War to Another

SIR Stafford Howard was elected the first Mayor of Llanelli[1] when it became a Borough in 1913 and Lady Howard presented the town and people with a new coat-of-arms, later given the motto 'Ymlaen Llanelli'.[2] When World War One broke out in August 1914, Llanelli men rallied to the cause and served on many fronts.[3] Italians in the town, mainly café proprietors, went home to enlist in the allied cause but German and Austrian workers at the Stamping Works were forced to leave their employment after a strike of employees.[4] Stebonheath School was converted into a military hospital and Parc Howard mansion became a home for Belgian refugees before being used as a Red Cross Hospital. A shell factory was set up at the Burry Extension Works in 1915, employing mainly women, making shells which were sent to the Royal Ordnance Factory at Pembrey.[5] Sadly, Sir Stafford Howard died in April 1916, and Lady Howard was asked to replace him as Mayor for the remainder of his term of office. A Llanelli man, Ivor Rees, gained the Victoria Cross in 1917[6] and many more were decorated for bravery. Throughout

Stepney Street, 1913. (Llanelli Library)

the war years the local papers carried photographs of servicemen killed in action. In September 1918, the Prime Minister, David Lloyd George, was proposed as the first Freeman of the Borough and, on 11 November, news of the armistice was joyously received by crowds in the streets with the ringing of church bells and the sounding of works' hooters. Llanelli's councillors were moved to start their proceedings that evening by singing 'God Save The King' led by Councillor T. Hay Samuel. 'The National Anthem was sung with great

War Memorial opposite Town Hall in 1968. (Llanelli Library)

patriotic fervour' according to both the *Mercury* and the *Guardian*. A telegram of congratulations was sent to Lloyd George, but there is no record of gratitude for the hundreds of Llanelli's sons who had given their lives in the war.

This was left to the churches and chapels while awaiting the setting-up of another war memorial. Amid all the jubilation, the *Mercury* struck a prescient note: 'We must not run away with the idea that, because the Germans have been crushed, they will never be able to raise their heads again.' It would take just over 20 years before another world war would break out after 'the war to end all wars.'

Another, more peaceable Army was making its presence felt in Llanelli at this time in the form of the Salvation Army. General Booth had visited the town in 1907 and a large crowd had gathered to see him pass in his famous white car in spite of heavy rain. There was some criticism of the Council for failing to accord him an official welcome – the only local authority not to do so. The Army had been operating in Llanelly since the end of the 19th century and hired Haggar's Theatre for Sunday meetings. It had occupied premises at Llanelli House before

moving into its newly-built Citadel in Swansea Road in 1915 with Sir Stafford Howard contributing £500 towards the cost. Its work involved open-air meetings with hymns accompanied by its popular brass band. Its officers, men and women, were a familiar sight in local public houses, especially on Saturday nights, cheerfully selling the 'War Cry' and the 'Young Soldier'. Its active work among the poor and needy made it a model of practical Christianity and members of the armed forces were very appreciative of its services during both World Wars.

Although the Parish Church had been a Catholic Church up until the Reformation, there was no further sign of Catholic

Memorial to 4th Welch Regiment in Parish Church graveyard. (J.E.)

Salvation Army band outside the Citadel in Swansea Road, 1937. (Llanelli Library)

activity in Llanelli for about 300 years. There is evidence that there were Irish people keeping Irish lodgers in Llanelli in the mid-19th century and that one of them, Peter O'Neill of Water Street, had a room fitted out as a chapel. Ann Griffin kept a school in Old Castle Road which probably taught children of the Catholic faith. Llanelli was, at the time, part of the Swansea Catholic parish and a priest was sent here once a month to celebrate mass, at Ann Griffin's house or at Peter O'Neill's. Eventually, Llanelli became a separate parish in 1862 with Fr. William Marshall as priest. A church was built in Lloyd Street in 1860 and an adjoining school in 1862. Fr. McLoughlin (1898-1912) proved to be a very popular priest as well as being an accomplished sportsman, becoming captain of the Ashburnham Golf Club, Pembrey. Fr. Carew was parish priest for almost a quarter of a century between 1912 and 1935 and was followed by Canon Moran, another long-serving priest who stood the parish in good stead.[8]

In 1909, the Jewish community in Llanelli opened their synagogue at the junction of Erw Road and Queen Victoria Road. Present at the ceremony was the Chief Rabbi, Dr Adler who said; 'The one potent factor that has preserved the nationality of the Welsh is their earnest desire to preserve their language' in comparing the Welsh and Hebrew languages. Jews

Bottom end of Stepney Street, 1925. Cars are now in evidence. (Brian Cripps collection)

Water Street, 1970. (Llanelli Library)

had been resident in Llanelli for about 100 years by this time but had been attached to the Swansea synagogue, built in 1859. As their numbers grew in Llanelli, they felt it right and proper that they should have their own place of worship. Before this they had met for services at the house of Mr Rubinstein in Murray Street and in a room in Castle Buildings. By 1916, they had acquired a burial site on the outskirts of Five Roads. The community was a thriving one, mainly concerned in trade of one kind or another. The contract for glass in the windows of the Town Hall was undertaken by Mr Benjamin in 1896. Like other immigrant populations from the continent of Europe, 'they caused little or no trouble by crime, drunkenness or any other misdemeanour' and many attained positions of authority in various fields.[9]

Soccer in Llanelli was given a boost in 1923 with the opening of Stebonheath Park. Llanelli AFC had experienced a chequered career since 1893 when a group of people came together at the Black Lion in Market Street consisting mainly of English immigrants into the town. They played friendly games, one in the Stradey area, but the club folded after a year or so. It was reformed in 1896 and played at Highfield, Tyisha. A full-time manager was appointed in 1904 and the team played in the Swansea and District League. They were referred to as the 'Tinplaters' in the press and played at a new venue behind Tunnel Road. W.J. Morris, from Llanidloes, came to town in 1910 and opened 'The Realm' in Stepney Street and soon became club chairman. He was largely instrumental in clearing the club's debts and brought in better-quality players. After playing at Cae Fflat, Llwynwhilwg, they moved to Halfway Park and, in 1914, reached the Final of

The Synagogue in Erw Road. (Llanelli Rural Council)

H.P. Wilkins (left) and Arthur Mee photographed in the mid-twenties by Owen Jones. Percy Wilkins was a famous astronomer who lived in James Street and Bradford Street. His special interest was the moon and his maps were used by NASA. He moved to Bexley Heath and died there in 1960, aged 64.

the Welsh Cup. After the war they played in the Welsh League and, from time to time, in the Southern League. They even reached the Third Round of the FA Cup in 1924 before being beaten 2-0 by Fulham at Craven Cottage. The move to Stebonheath with its natural bank and grandstand, however, did not draw the anticipated crowds and the club found itself, once again, in financial difficulties. It was destined forever, it seemed, to play second fiddle to rugby.[10]

The rugby club, on the other hand experienced something of a golden era in the early twenties in spite of losing very many talented players to the rugby league code in the North of England. The Scarlets probably fielded their best three-quarter line ever with Bryn Williams and Frank Evans on the wings and Albert Jenkins and Bryn Evans at centre. The most famous of all was the peerless Albert whose running, passing, tackling and kicking was the stuff of which legends were made. Crowds at Stradey could be halved when he was not playing. He was capped for Wales on 14 occasions, captained Llanelli for three seasons and played

for 13 years between 1919 and 1932. His exploits are still talked about and he was one of the greatest footballers ever to play for Llanelli. Albert Jenkins worked as a docker locally and, in his first season, was offered £500 to turn professional – a tremendous sum for a soldier newly returned from the war.[11] By this time, the rugby club was recognised as being among the best in Britain and, in 1924, they were beaten only by 8-3 by New Zealand just after Wales had been defeated by 19 points. The *Guardian* said it was 'one of the finest exhibitions of rugby ever played on the classic slope of Stradey'. In the 1925-26 season, Llanelli never lost a home game and in November 1926, they defeated a touring Maori side 3-0, the only

Dai Davies. The first Welshman to become a professional cricketer.

Welsh team to beat them.

Although rugby started as a gentleman's game it was not long before it became the workers' game too. Cricket proved to be more resistant in this respect but we see the doors of opportunity opening a little during the period following World War One. In the early twenties, Dai Davies was being described as 'the Albert Jenkins of cricket.'[12] He first played for Llanelli in 1919 and he joined

Llanelli rugby star, Albert Jenkins.

'Gipsy' Daniels. Llanelli's most famous boxer between the two World Wars. (Llanelli Library)

Glamorgan in 1923, two years after they had been accepted into the County Championship. He was the first Welshman ever to become a professional cricketer, after having been unexpectedly called on one Saturday morning after three hours' sleep following a double-shift of 16 hours at Llanelli Steelworks. He played for Glamorgan until the outbreak of World War Two in 1939. Dai was soon joined in the Glamorgan ranks by Emrys Davies who had played for the Llanelli Steel XI and the two proved to be the backbone of the side for many years. Both came from the Sandy area, a remarkable breeding-ground of cricketers, near to Stradey; both became Test cricket umpires when they had finished playing; and both were living within 300 yards of each other in their latter years. The Stradey ground, incidentally, also had a share in aviation history.

In the middle of a match between Llanelli and Briton Ferry Steel, an aeroplane was sighted coming in to land on the cricket pitch. The pilot was a Frenchman named M. Salmet and his Blériot plane was the first to land in the town. People were amazed to learn that he had made the trip from Swansea in 10 minutes.

Llanelli's most famous light industry came to an end in 1923 with the closure of the Pottery. Although principally produced for domestic use, porcelain of the highest quality was made there and exported to Australia, USA, France, Spain, Portugal and

Llanelli pottery on an old Welsh dresser. (Carmarthen Museum)

Exchange Buildings, about 1925. (Llanelli Library)

West Africa. After William Chambers left the town in 1855, the Pottery was run by Charles William Coombs and William Thomas Holland. Coombs, whose son William became an important Llanelli shipowner, soon left the partnership and Holland carried on alone until 1875. The Pottery was then closed for two years and reopened in 1877 under David Guest and Richard Dewsberry. Several families came to Llanelli from the area around Stoke-on-Trent and their descendants are still here.[13] Most were of the Nonconformist persuasion, many attending the English Congregational Park Church and others Hall Street English Wesleyan Methodist Church. Sarah Jane Roberts[14] was the renowned painter of 'cockerel plates' while the most famous painter of all was Samuel Walter Shufflebotham[15] who worked at the Pottery between 1908 and 1915. In 1927, Lady Howard Stepney intervened to rescue some of the potters' tools and other items just before the Pottery buildings were demolished.[16] She housed them in one of the rooms of Llanelli House 'until such time as the town would take an interest in them.' This action led to offers of Llanelli pottery to Lady Howard Stepney who was attempting to build up a collection on behalf of the town. These items were the beginnings of the magnificent collection now housed at the Parc Howard Museum.[17]

By the time that the Freedom of the Borough was conferred on Lloyd George, he was no longer Prime Minister. It took five years before the ceremony took place on 10 September 1923. It proved to be a fine day, as opposed to other damper occasions, and a large crowd turned out to cheer their hero. The Market Hall was packed to overflowing. In spite of the jubilation, Llanelli was

Hippodrome staff and performers. Haggar's Theatre.
(Brian Cripps collection)

undergoing a severe industrial slump at this stage which caused great hardship. Workers organised six-hour shifts instead of the normal eight hours so that the little work available could be shared more widely. There were thousands on the dole by 1925 and, in April 1926, the Richard Thomas Steelworks (previously Morewoods) closed four furnaces to throw another 500 out of work at a stroke.[18]

The General Strike came into operation at midnight on Monday, 3 May 1926, in support of locked-out miners. The town was at a standstill on the following day with the local *South Wales Press* observing that 'people walked about the streets in aimless fashion.' Bus services came to a halt and no trams were running.[19] Both Felinfoel and Buckley's breweries continued to deliver supplies 'with the consent of the TUC' and this caused an uproar when buses were not permitted to carry students from outlying areas to the Intermediate School. This caused the TUC to call a halt to brewery deliveries by the end of the week. People volunteered to drive lorries for essential services with 400 being recruited within a week. There were meetings at Town Hall Square where the Red Flag was sung with gusto and Arthur Horner of the South Wales Miners' Federation addressed a Communist Party gathering at the Town Hall. Nevertheless the strike had little impact on the town itself. Local papers reported brisk trade in shops selling wallpaper and paint suggesting that strikers were taking the opportunity of decorating their homes. Others made the most of leisure activities with great demand being made on the bowling greens and tennis courts of Parc Howard.

Borough Council Steam Waggon, 1926.
(Brian Cripps collection)

The strike collapsed on Wednesday, 12 May, with the miners once more standing alone.

An historic moment in the history of aviation happened in the area in June 1928. In the words of the local *Guardian*: 'The name of Llanelly was flashed all over the world on Monday morning (18th) when news got abroad that the American seaplane 'Friendship' had effected a safe landing near Pwll.' It was a momentous occasion as the co-pilot was Amelia Earhart who thus became the first woman to fly the Atlantic. With her was the pilot, Commander Stultz, and the engineer, Lou Gordon. Since the tide was far out at the time, it was

Demolition of Spring Gardens, 1929. (Llanelli Library)

easy for a boat to row out to the seaplane and bring the crew back to Burry Port, even though they believed they had landed in Ireland. Reports were carried to the General Post Office in Llanelli and relayed from there to America. Photographs and a summary of the story can be seen in the 'Friendship Bar' of the George Hotel in Burry Port which attracts a great number of visitors, especially from America.

Unemployment had reached such a pitch by the end of the Twenties that Llanelli was officially designated as a 'Distressed Area' in February 1929. Government money was released for public works and, in the town, this was channelled into the task of culverting the Lliedi river from Vaughan Street to Town Hall Square. The slums of Spring Gardens and King's Square were demolished and this made room for the new 'Broadway' in Frederick Street leading to the 'Bullring' (with room for parking 50 cars) and the laying out of the Town Hall Square gardens. The old Raby houses in Caerelms and Forge Row were knocked down as was Custom House Bank in the Seaside. New council housing was started in the Morfa, Llanerch, Capel and Penyfan areas and was further extended to Felinfoel by 1939.

The National Eisteddfod again visited Llanelli in 1930 when Gwilym Myrddin, an Ammanford miner won the Crown and Dewi Emrys the Chair. The Eisteddfod choir, under the baton of Edgar Thomas, gave a magnificent performance of Handel's 'Solomon' while Capel Als won first prize in the competition for orchestral playing. The Australian Cricket XI, who were playing Glamorgan at Swansea,

Footbridge across the Lliedi near the Arcade, 1930. (Llanelli Library)

Capel Als Choir trip, 1930s. (Brian Cripps collection)

visited the Eisteddfod thanks to the prompting of Dai and Emrys Davies and the highlight of the week was, once again, the appearance of David Lloyd George. The following year saw the passing of C.W. Mansel Lewis of Stradey. He held the remarkable record of having been chairman of the Arts and Crafts Committee three times on the Eisteddfod's successive visits to Llanelli.[20] More eisteddfodic honours came to the town when the Revd D. J. Davies, Capel Als, won the Chair at Aberavon in 1932 and in 1937 when Llanelli won the Chief Choral competition at Machynlleth.

The unemployment situation worsened in Llanelli at the beginning of the 1930s with 7,000 out of work in 1931. In December of that year, a Mayor's Fund was set up to provide boots and clothing for needy children. There was real poverty in the town and many workers joined up with groups from other towns in South Wales to organise hunger marches to London. Illness was, obviously, more prevalent at this time and a Workers' Medical Committee was set up in 1934 with a surgery opened in Station Road. For 18 months there was conflict between the 'new doctors' and the 'old doctors' but this was settled in 1935 and the Public Medical Service was set up.[21] The workers' scheme proved to be one of the best in the country and was used, along with other Medical Schemes, as a pattern for a later National Health Service.

An interesting development took place towards the end of 1935 when both local breweries considered putting beer into cans. In October, the possibility was discussed by Buckleys, and T.R. Mills, the managing director went on record as saying: 'It would be a wonderful thing for the future of the Welsh tinplate industry.' The industry's great weakness was that, in the main, the finished product was sent away to be processed. The only exceptions were the Tinstamping Works[22] which made kitchen utensils including the famous

Houses on the Wern, Ann Street, 1956. (Llanelli Library)

Stradey Castle. (Llanelli Rural Council).

saucepans, and the small Richmond and Greenfield Works on the Wern which turned out wheelbarrows and shovels.[23] The Buckley family had shares in the Old Castle Tinplate Works and using its product to make beer-cans would have given the works a great boost.[24] In the event, Buckleys did not pursue the idea. On the other hand, Felinfoel Brewery went ahead and successfully canned beer for the first time in December 1935. The John family, which owned the brewery, had interests in both the Dafen and Bynea works. Felinfoel can proudly lay claim to be the oldest existing brewery in the world to put beer into cans.[25] The general public was slow to take to canned beer and it was only when war came, and the product was despatched to servicemen all over the world, that the idea took off.[26] Industry, in fact, began to recover in 1936 but this was due, not to the canning of beer, but to preparations for World War Two which seemed to be inevitable from this time onward.[27] The Spanish Civil War was seen as a training ground for German and Italian forces as they helped Franco to overturn the legitimate government of Spain. There was great support for the Republican side in Wales and hundreds of men, including many from the Llanelli area volunteered to fight against Fascism. Most were members of the Communist Party which was a rising force at the time and was represented by three members on Llanelli Borough Council. In 1936, James Griffiths, of Ammanford was elected Labour Member of Parliament on the death of J. H. Williams. In his early career Jim Griffiths had spoken on Communist platforms. There was, in fact, little to choose between the Communist and Labour parties during this period of depression.

All was not gloom, however, and, as a boy growing up in the 1930s, life was

Eisteddfod Choir at Steboneath Park, 1930. The conductor, Edgar Thomas is seated (right).
(Brian Cripps collection)

quite pleasant. The old market was a magical place with its variety of stalls. There were beautiful shops which sold everything that any heart could desire. Fish-and-chip shops provided wholesome fare and Italian cafés served ice cream and coffee among other delights.[28] Sartori's in Park Street was a favourite meeting place on Sunday nights after a stroll on Monkey's Parade. The YMCA proved a haven of rest and relaxation with a beautifully furnished lounge and snooker room.[29] Concerts were held regularly, mainly in chapels, and we were given the opportunity of seeing and hearing world-famous singers performing solo roles in oratorios. Most of us

Row of houses opposite South Star Inn, 1938.
(Llanelli Library)

Gorsedd stones at Parc Howard overlooking Pentrepoeth, 1930. (Brian Cripps collection)

were poor but we did not realise it because everyone else we knew was in the same boat. Christmas was always made special by hanging paper chains on the walls and there were usually a few trinkets in our stocking and a fabulous turkey dinner. Sixpence a week deposited in the Sunday School bank would yield an

Custom House Bank, Seaside. (Llanelli Library)

amazing 25s in time for Christmas and New Year's morning would see us out singing for a 'calennig' which would add, at least, another 5s. The magnificent Odeon cinema opened in 1938, the last word in luxury, making a total of five cinemas in which people could indulge in their favourite entertainment, and escape from the troubles of everyday life.[30]

By July 1939, gas-masks had arrived in Llanelli and were stored at Prospect Place School, Dafen School and Parc Howard Mansion, ready for distribution. In January, the Llanelli Sheetworks had been given an order for 120,000 tons of

Heolfawr, a row of houses behind Copperworks School. The trolleybus is passing trucks on the railway lines.

Mill Lane in the 1930s. (Llanelli Library)

galvanised steel sheets for the making of Anderson shelters to be put up in house gardens.[31] In March, the Council received a letter from the Minister of Health telling them to draw up detailed plans for the reception of 3,000 evacuees from English cities. By now, it was clear that war was inevitable.

The 'Bullring' and Rose Garden in 1932. (Llanelli Library)

Notes to Chapter XIII

1 Charter of Incorporation, 23 August 1913. Alderman D.J. Davies became Deputy Mayor.

2 The coat of arms contains a female figure to represent Saint Elli.

3 Over 4,000 men enlisted. One batch of 150 men enlisted together from the Burry Tinplate Works.

4 One German worker, Paul Meyer, had worked there for 14 years.

5 My mother-in-law, Mary Elizabeth Davies worked there. She remembered being told by the foreman to be extremely careful in her work because a mistake could result in the shell 'blowing up in our boys' faces'.

6 A native of Pwll. I remember him living in Limekiln Row, New Dock.

7 I am grateful to a group of senior Salvationists whom I met at their Citadel for information and a welcome cup of tea. Since 1986 they have occupied their new Citadel in Bryntirion Terrace.

Clifford Evans, Llanelli's best known actor greets T.V. Shaw, headmaster of the Intermediate School, about 1939. (Llanelli Library)

8 I would like to thank Andrew Parkinson of Lliedi Crescent for valuable information on the Catholic church in Llanelli. Our Lady of Peace was built on the Waunlanyrafon site in 1938.

9 Michael Howard, MP, became Home Secretary; Isaac Cohen was Chief Rabbi of Ireland; Wilfred Miron was a Director of the National Coal Board; Ronnie Cass is still well-known as a composer. Other prominent Jewish families included Solomon, Benjamin, Palto and Landy. See article by Sidney Wilson in the *Llanelli Star,* 16 October 1965.

10 I am grateful to Graham Williams, Alban Road, for information on the history of soccer in Llanelli.

11 Albert Jenkins, is probably the all-time star of Llanelli rugby. Bryn Evans was awarded the MC in World War One and was my first headmaster at Stradey School. Bryn Williams was a tin-worker whose mother, known to all as 'Mrs Williams, Long Row', was a wonderful herbal healer. Bryn joined Batley Rugby League Club and was known, thereafter, as Bryn Batley. Frank Evans signed for Swinton RLFC, was also a tin-worker, known throughout his life as Frankie Dafen.

12 See *Dai Davies: Not out… 78* by John Edwards, (Dyfed Publications, 1975). Dai was my father-in-law. Llanelli players who followed Dai and Emrys into County Cricket in the 1930s were Trevor Every and Haydn Davies (Glamorgan) and Cliff Owen (Surrey).

13 Some of the familiar names are Henshall, Auckland, Marsh, Tunstall, Toft, Ellerton, Bryant, Newark (owned a china shop in Market Street) and Boulton (Jonathan Boulton was the town's first Librarian). There were many china shops in town, the best known were Williams and Edwards, trading in the market.

14 The Roberts family also came from the Midlands.

15 He worked apart from other painters and was obviously of superior talent. He joined the Army in 1915 and never returned to Llanelli. His work is marked 'S.W.S.' Other marks on Llanelli pottery are 'William Chambers'; 'South Wales Pottery' or 'S.W.P.'; 'C and H' (Coombs and Holland); 'W.T.H.' (W.T. Holland) and G and D (Guest and Dewsberry). Most of the 20th century production is unmarked.

16 Lady Howard now went by the name of Lady Howard Stepney. Her mother, Lady Stepney, died in 1921. There is no trace of this original collection.

17 Mr Robert Pugh has done much to foster interest in Llanelli Pottery and, in his capacity as an antique-dealer, has kept a sharp look-out for items far and wide. From an old Llanelli family, he is co-author with the late Gareth Hughes of *Llanelly Pottery* (Llanelli, 1990) the authoritative work on the subject.

18 There were 10 furnaces in all but only 6 were in operation at this time. Closing another 4 meant that 2 furnaces only were now working. The Richard Thomas and Baldwin group were in the process of buying up a great number of steelworks and tinplate works in the area. For a remarkable portrayal of the poverty of this period, read Tabitha John, *Tabitha* (Gwerin, Llanelli, 1979).

19 Electric trams had been introduced in 1911. Buses had been evident since 1914 when S.W. Thomas started a service to Swansea. James Hughes, Carway, and Samuel Eynon, Trimsaran, among others, ran services to outlying areas while Sage (yellow buses) and Gimblett (red buses) ran an efficient town service.

20 His body was one of the first from Llanelli to be cremated at Pontypridd. C.W. Mansel Lewis had studied art in London under Herkomer, among others. He was a talented artist.

21 See article by Roy Davies in *Tinopolis*, op. cit.

22 See article by John Simon in *Tinopolis*.

23 Producing shovels for various purposes including collieries. Also made the famous 'lazy back' shovel with long handle ideal for opening rows in gardening. Ladles were also made for precious metal companies like Rothschild. See article by Harry Davies in *Tinopolis*.

24 The Old Castle (1866) was the first works in Llanelli to be built by local capital. Its shareholders included industrialists, merchants and professional people including Dr Morgan (Lleurwg) the minister of Zion Baptist Chapel.

25 The very first in the field was an American company in January 1935. This company is no longer in existence. See article by Peter Donaldson in *Tinopolis*.

26 Cardboard boxes containing a dozen cans could be sent post-free to members of the armed forces during World War Two. While I was in the Royal Navy, a box was sent to me at Singapore for Christmas 1945. I had sailed by that time and the consignment caught up with me on St David's Day in Samarang, Indonesia. The beer was in perfect condition.

27 In 1936, the four furnaces closed at the Richard Thomas Works were reopened. In the same year, the Morfa Works was bought by Richard Thomas. By 1939, almost all the remaining tinworks joined together to form the Llanelli Associated Tinplate Co. The only remaining independent works by then were the Old Lodge and the Pemberton. The Pemberton produced plates for the Stamping Works. Dorothy Squires, the popular singer, worked there – so did my father and my grandfather.

28 The Italian cafés were more like clubs with their regular customers. One of the first was Rabaiotti who was a friend of my grandfather's. My father was friendly with the Perego family as I was with the Sartoris. Among others were Allegri, Orsi, Cavalli, Strinati and, of course, Bracchi.

29 Snooker was a very popular game at this time. The largest snooker-halls were the Lucania, Hatcher's and the Welcome while tables were to be found in clubs of every kind. Boxing was also popular with 'Gipsy' Daniels a local hero.

30 The Regal was also a luxurious cinema where people could drink tea in a Palm-Court lounge. It was built, in 1929, at a cost of £50,000, the same as the Odeon cost in 1938. Other cinemas were the Hippodrome (Haggar's), the Palace (Vint's), the Llanelly Cinema and the Astoria (Dock).

31 This order was to provide 400,000 shelters. There were, therefore, three tons of steel in every shelter. The shelters were named after the Home Secretary, Sir John Anderson.

Chapter XIV
The End of Heavy Industry 1939-70

WAR was declared on 3 September 1939, and 5,000 gas-masks were distributed on the same day. As distribution was completed, it became a common sight to see everyone carrying their masks in a cardboard box with the cord slung over their shoulders. On 4 September, 1,115 Liverpool children arrived in Llanelli.[1] They came in three trains, and fleets of buses and cars awaited them outside the railway station. They were taken to dispersal centres and given refreshments before being sent out to their billets. Two of the three trains arrived during hours of darkness but, in spite of the difficulties caused by enforced black-out, the Welsh Board of Health Inspector declared 'the arrangements had worked perfectly.' Most of these children had returned to their homes by Christmas because there was so little enemy activity during this period known as 'the phoney war'.

Life in Llanelli was affected by the war on several levels. Unlike World War One, which was fought, almost exclusively in far-away places, this war was literally brought home to us and involved civilian populations as never before. Identity cards were issued which everyone had to carry, and ration books ensured a fair distribution of food.[2] Air-raid shelters were built in the town centre[3] and a severe black-out imposed after dark. Wardens patrolled the streets to ensure that not a single chink of light showed which could be to the advantage of enemy bombers.[4] Heavy black-out curtains were used in the home and shutters put up on shop windows. Cars, buses and lorries travelled at

'Caeffair' (Fair Field), Felinfoel Road. (J.E.)

night with masked headlights while blinds were pulled down on trains. Windows were criss-crossed with sticky tape to prevent shattering in explosions and large buildings, like the Town Hall and Parc Howard Mansion, were heavily sand-bagged. Children were dispersed from school during air-raids and were allocated to nearby homes in which to shelter, and school canteens were set up for the first time.

Units of the Air Training Corps and Army Cadet Corps were organised in the town and a civilian militia, the Home Guard, was trained to repel invasion.[5] A National Fire Service was organised and fire-watching squads guarded unoccupied buildings at night with pumps and sand-buckets at the ready to deal with incendiary bombs.[6] When serious German bombing started in June 1940 1,200 London evacuees came to Llanelli[7] and the town saw an influx of airmen from RAF Pembrey as well as soldiers from all over the world. Huge collections were made during the war with £5,000 being raised for a Spitfire Fund in 1940, £300,000 during Warship Week in 1941 and, in the same year, £746,000 for War Weapons Week. This was in addition to pots and pans collected for aluminium to make aeroplanes and iron railings torn down for scrap to make steel. Lawns were dug up and every available piece of ground was used to grow vegetables. Pigs and chickens were, once more, seen in back gardens in the town and weird and wonderful concoctions made from strange ingredients like powdered milk and powdered egg. Women knitted woollen garments for troops[8] and, because of clothing rations, recycled their own clothes in most ingenious ways. On a more sombre note, Henry Thomas, the Builders, were producing 40 plain wooden coffins a day for military and civilian burials.[9] Swansea suffered a heavy three-night blitz in February 1941, with the reddened sky clearly visible from Llanelli. Our town itself, apart from a stray bomb or two, escaped unscathed.[10]

Llanelli men served in all branches of the services and were represented on all war-fronts. Many were never to return, others were wounded, some suffered great hardship as prisoners of war. It was reckoned that 70 percent of all men in Britain born between 1915 and 1927 served in the war and that figure probably held true for Llanelli. In all, 357,000[11] were killed and, although the figure is appalling, three times as many were killed in World War One. Women also served in the Forces, joined the Land Army to work on farms or replaced men in various occupations.

Some men continued to work in reserved occupations and others were sent to work in the mines.[12] One must not forget the Conscientious Objectors who had to appear before Tribunals and were sent to non-combatant units of the services or to work on the land. They often faced hostility and derision and they, too, displayed a certain kind of bravery. It was also sad to see many of our Italian and

The Elwyn Jones family home, 142, Old Castle Road.
(Llanelli Rural Council)

German friends interned as 'enemy aliens.'[13]

When the war in Europe came to an end on Tuesday, 8 May, joy was unbounded. The news came at three o'clock in the afternoon and almost everyone left work for the day. There were thanksgiving services in some churches and chapels and the Parish Church was floodlit. Thousands thronged Town Hall Square and the Bullring car park was put to good use as a dance-floor where dancing went on into the early hours of the morning. The celebrations went on throughout Wednesday and it was Thursday before most people returned to work. It was not until 14 August that the war ended against Japan but the rain interfered with the celebrations on this occasion and people remembered the numbers of Llanelli's sons who would never return home.[14] Llanelli, like most other towns, did not erect a new war memorial but simply added a tribute to the fallen on the 1914-18 memorial which, at this time, stood opposite the Town Hall.

The Labour party won a sweeping victory in the 1945 Election and James Griffiths was returned as MP for Llanelli with a massive majority of 34,117. He was appointed Minister of National Insurance and subsequently held the post of Commonwealth Secretary before becoming the first Secretary of State for Wales. Elected for English constituencies were three other Llanelli men including Elwyn Jones, Labour MP for Plaistow.[15] Elwyn was the son of Fred and Elizabeth Jones of Old Castle Road, both of whom had worked in the Old Castle tinworks.[16] Elwyn Jones was born in 1909, the youngest of a family of four; the others were Winifred, Idris and Gwyn.[17] It was a remarkable family with its roots firmly planted in Tabernacle chapel.

Winifred went to the Intermediate School and University College, Aberystwyth, where she graduated before becoming a teacher. How many girls from a working-class background received a college education at the beginning of the century? Idris followed her to study chemistry before winning a Cambridge Scholarship and gaining a Ph.D. While at Cambridge, he won three rugby 'blues' in successive years. He was a hooker, despite being over 6ft tall, and played for Llanelli, London Welsh and Wales.[18] At the peak of his career, he was appointed Director of Research at the National Coal Board in 1946. Gwyn followed along the same tracks before becoming head of Unilever in Brazil. Unfortunately, he was killed in a car crash in Milan in 1952 when he was only 48 years old. Like his sister and brothers, Elwyn went to the Intermediate School, Aberystwyth and Cambridge. He chose a career in Law and became prominent as a prosecutor at the Nuremberg Trials which followed World War Two. He became Attorney General in a Labour government, and ended his career in the House of

Zion Vestry. First home of Dewi Sant School. (Llanelli Library)

Lords as Lord Chancellor.[19] He was a product of a remarkable family which is probably the finest example of the effort and sacrifice made by many other ordinary families to educate and inspire their children to reach their potential.

When the Butler Education Act (1944) came into operation, there were two Grammar schools in Llanelli, one for boys and one for girls. Entry to these schools was by examination at the age of 11. At the same age, the rest of Llanelli's children went to three Secondary Modern Schools, Coleshill, Stebonheath and Lakefield. Coleshill and Stebonheath had separate departments for boys and girls but Lakefield was co-educational as was Stradey, on the edge of town, whose catchment area was the surrounding villages. This was the school where one found a distinctly Welsh atmosphere in a town in which education, both primary and secondary, had become almost wholly English.

Grain Ships at the North Dock, 1972. (Llanelli Library)

Although Llanelli's Welsh-speaking population still numbered over 60 percent, there was almost complete acceptance of the situation. Then, suddenly, came an awakening when a local HMI, Dr Matthew Williams, noticed that there was a clause in the Butler Act which said that parents should have a voice in their children's education. He

Horse-trough, West End, 1956. (Llanelli Library)

realised, at once, that this clause was of significance to Welsh-speakers. In the course of a chance meeting on one of Carmarthen's streets, he mentioned this fact to Olwen Williams, a teacher in Market Street School who was also active with the Urdd Aelwyd in Goring Road. Olwen Williams immediately saw to the formation of a parents' Committee with Loti Hopkin as Chairman and Aneurin Williams as Secretary.[20] A petition was prepared and signed by over 200 parents. It was sent to the Ministry of Education in London and the Director of Education in Carmarthen. Parts of the petition, in Aneurin Williams' handwriting, are worth translating; 'We request an education for our children in their mother-tongue… in accordance with the spirit of the Butler Education Act … Welsh is the language of our homes and it is appropriate that our children be given the opportunity to attend a school where Welsh is the first language… We feel certain that it is worthwhile setting up a Welsh School in the town of Llanelli and we are ready to risk the welfare and future of our children for its sake.' The

petition was despatched in October 1945, but it was not until St David's Day, 1947, that Zion chapel's vestry opened its doors to 34 children between the ages of three and eight. The inspirational Olwen Williams was appointed headteacher with Rachel Ann Evans as teacher. When Miss Evans failed to gain release from a teaching post

The Thomas Arms and Georgian houses in Goring Road. (Llanelli Library)

in England, Inez Thomas, on the staff at Felinfoel, was appointed temporarily. Fortunately, Miss Thomas' appointment was made permanent and she went on to inspire generations of children.

Although Lluest School, in Aberystwyth, had been established as a Welsh School during the war-years, it was a

South Wales Transport bus in Stepney Street in the 1960s. (Llanelli Library)

private school. Dewi Sant – or 'Olwen's School' as it was known – was the first Welsh School to be set up by a local authority and blazed a trail which others soon followed. It was ironic that the school should have opened exactly 100 years after the low-point of the *Treachery of the Blue Books*, but it was the beginning of a revolution in our country's education which led to subsequent developments in Welsh secondary schools and Welsh courses in higher education. It also tended to temper the hostility of opposition groups by its teachers' dedication and pupils' subsequent successes by helping to foster a more sympathetic attitude towards the language on the part of English-speaking Welsh people.[21]

Following World War Two, there were hopes that Llanelli's industrial future could be bright. The Nuffield Works came to Felinfoel and 1,000 workers were employed there by 1946.[22] In 1947, the decision was made to build a modern tinplate plant at Trostre to replace the old mills which were coming to the end of their usefulness.[23] There were plans to build an electricity power-station at Burry Port and to sink a new coal-mine in Cynheidre, both offering jobs to local people.[24] Down at the harbour, it was a different story and, in 1951, the North Dock closed following massive financial difficulties following a prolonged slump in trade.[25] For a town which had seen ships come and go for centuries, and which had built ships of all types, it was sad to see that the only successful maritime activity now was a ship-breakers' yard.[26]

1952 proved to be quite a significant year in Llanelli's history. The rugby club finally purchased its Stradey ground from David Mansel Lewis, the owner of the Stradey estate. A development appeal committee was set up 'to ensure that Stradey should be the home of the Scarlets for all time.' This somewhat brightened the gloom cast over Stradey by the departure of Lewis Jones for Leeds, in November, to play Rugby League. Lewis Jones had become the idol of Llanelli supporters during past seasons and his drawing power was second only to Albert Jenkins. It awaited only the arrival of Phil Bennett to complete a triumvirate of Scarlet immortals.

In May, a scheme was inaugurated to extract water from the River Tywi from a pumping-station at Nantgaredig.[27] Officials,

Old Lodge flats on the site of the old works. (Llanelli Library)

councillors and others were carried to Nantgaredig in a fleet of cars and were lavishly entertained by the Mayor at the Ritz Ballroom on their return. Thus continued the tradition of celebrating the inauguration of water-works with anything but water in the history of our town.

In June, Llanelli mourned the death of Meriel, Lady Howard-Stepney. She was one of Llanelli's greatest benefactors and was held in the highest regard. She died quietly in her sleep at her home in Cilymaenllwyd secure in the rites of the Roman Catholic Church, her mother's faith, to which she had returned. Meriel had taken an active part in the civic life of the town and was the first lady member to sit on Carmarthenshire County Council. She was made a Freeman of the Borough in 1934 and had donated to the Borough Council a magnificent coat of arms, a silver mace, chains of office and mayoral and aldermanic robes. She also gave her wonderful collection of Wesley relics to Hall Street Methodist Church which are now housed in the museum at Parc Howard. She was survived by a daughter, popularly known as Marged Fach,[28] who lived in London for most of her short life, and a son named Stafford. Her death effectively severed Llanelli's long connection with the Stepney family.

Llanelli's famous trolleybuses had taken over from electric trams in 1932. Their routes ran from the railway station to Loughor, Felinfoel and Pwll.[29] In 1934, there was even talk of an extension to Pembrey, but it never materialised. These beautiful buses glided along our roads, humming on their overhead wires. This state of transport bliss came to an end in July 1952, when the Llanelly and District Transport Undertaking sold out to South Wales Transport in a change to noisy,

'The Doubler'. Sculpture by Adriano Candelori.

Railway Place, 1962. (Llanelli Library)

smelly buses and a huge rise in fares. In 1952 began the task of clearing-up derelict tinworks, a task which involved the Council's legal department in complicated dealings with various owners. A start was made in Station Road, the first sight of the town for many visitors. The Old Lodge Works and Nevill's Foundry were the first to go and a housing estate and old people's complex were built on the site.[30] The nearby Marshfield was next to make way for the Maesgors housing development. These were the first of many industrial clearances which were soon to change the face of Llanelli. In October, the Trostre Works was opened and was heralded as 'one of the world's finest.'

1953 was the year of the coronation and the occasion of the Queen's visit, the first royal visit since that of the Prince of Wales, later Edward VIII, in 1936.[31] The coronation was also the occasion for an upsurge in the buying and renting of television sets which had a definite effect on the social life of Llanelli as it did everywhere else. From now on, people would not be so keen on leaving their homes, especially on dark winter nights. There was a marked drop in cinema attendances and, one by one, nearly all Llanelli's cinemas were forced to close. One saw a lack of support for grand concerts held in chapels with well-known soloists singing with local choirs. Even politics now depended more on television image than on the cut and thrust of open-air speakers and hecklers on Town Hall Square at weekends. Television was, indeed, an historic turning point, in mid-century, for good as well as for bad.

By 1955 the town became ashamed of its industrial relics and was determined to change an image which was now a deterrent to the hopes of attracting new light industries. Harold Prescott, the Llanelli Borough librarian was only just in time when he decided to film the St David's steelworks and tinworks at Bynea towards the end of 1957.[32] There were now only three tinplate works left out of 18 which had once produced tinplate in the area between Kidwelly and Hendy. The situation was so hopeless that workers were recruited from Italy[33] during the demise of the old hand-mills. When the Old Castle

Eisteddfod Pavilion at Penygaer, 1962. (Brian Cripps collection)

Works closed in 1957,[34] there were 50 Italians working there. New industrial estates were set up near the North Dock and, on the outskirts of town in Dafen and Felinfoel. Even the rugby club was conscious of its image and opened a new grandstand at Stradey Park at a cost of £15,000, to be followed by a new clubhouse in 1958, with the money coming from its own supporters. The club also widened its horizons in 1957 when a team went to play in Moscow with Carwyn James as the most important member of the squad, not because he was a genius at playing or coaching, but because he could speak Russian, which he had learnt during his period of National Service in the Royal Navy. As the works closed, one by one, the numbers of unemployed steadily mounted and, in January 1958, more than 15,000 marched in protest through the streets of the town under the lead of James Griffiths, MP. Neither the Trostre Works nor the new light industries were capable of quenching the town's hunger for work. In 1959, the Dafen tinworks, the first in the area, ground to a halt after 113 years.

In 1962, the Eisteddfod came to Llanelli once again. As it happened, it was a week of unrelenting rain which turned the Penygaer site into a morass of squelching mud. In spite of the rain beating a constant drumbeat on the pavilion roof, there were keenly-contested competitions throughout the week with the rain ensuring packed audiences

Crowning ceremony, National Eisteddfod, 1962. The Archdruid, Trefin, and the crowned bard, Revd D. Emlyn Lewis. (Brian Cripps collection)

every single day. The crown was won by the Revd Emlyn Lewis, Vicar of Llanddarog on the appropriate subject of 'The Cloud', and the chair went to Caradog Pritchard for 'Crying in the Wilderness'.[35] Caradog Pritchard chose the nom-de-plume 'Idris' in honour of Dr Idris Jones who had donated the chair in memory of his parents, Fred and Elizabeth Jones. One of the great nightly attractions was the community singing in Town Hall Square with about 3,000 people coming together after the evening concert, drama or Noson Lawen at about 10.30 p.m. to sing non-stop until about two in the morning. The well-known actor, Clifford Evans, spoke on his life-long ambition to see a National Theatre for Wales and paid eloquent tribute to two of his teachers at Llanelli Grammar School, J. Afan Jones and Morgan Rees, for giving him the confidence necessary to pursue an acting career. The large gathering of Welsh exiles were led by Tom Jeffreys of Baltimore, a man who had worked at the Old Castle tinworks before emigrating to North America 40 years before.[36] It really was an outstanding Eisteddfod in spite of the weather and I quote T. Llew Jones in a rough translation:[37]

> 'I say to you quite honestly
> "This was the best one yet";
> I leave Llanelli's Festival
> But its joy I'll not forget.'

Once again, Llanelli had exceeded all expectations in spite of the fact that the town presented a sorry sight. Sir Ben Bowen Thomas said: 'Open your eyes. If you're satisfied with the state of the town, you should be ashamed of yourselves!' The Eisteddfod did no good to one disgruntled local contributor quoting Matthew Arnold in the *Llanelli Star*: 'The sooner the Welsh language disappears from the political and social life of Wales, the better... The language of a Welshman is, and must be, English.' Bydded i'r hen iaith barhau!

Llanelli celebrated its Jubilee Year in 1963 – 50 years since its designation as a chartered borough. Llanelli had long discussed the possibility of a swimming-pool and this came to fruition in April 1963, with the opening of the Jubilee Pool on the Waunlanyrafon site. In August, a huge Jubilee Exhibition was held

at nearby People's Park with 60 stands inside what was described as the biggest marquee in Europe. The hugely successful exhibition went on for 10 days and

Jubilee Swimming Pool, 1963.
(Llanelli Library)

attracted 70,000 visitors. 1965 saw the historic purchase, by the Borough Council, of the Stepney Estate. It was an immensely complicated transaction involving land, houses, shops, chapels, businesses, offices, public houses and a bank. It was the largest acquisition of land by the town since the Enclosures of 1810. The preparation of the conveyance was done by the Town Clerk, Selwyn

Ceremony granting Elwyn Jones the Freedom of the Borough. (Llanelli Library)

Samuel, and his Deputy, Hugh Williams, at the head of the Council's legal department. On 29 September 1965, Mark Stepney Murray Threipland,[38] the grandson of Sir Stafford and Lady Howard, came down from Scotland and signed away the Stepney Estate's rights for the very reasonable sum of £350,000. In 1966, the Council decided that the spelling of the town's name should be Llanelli, in its Welsh form. Plans were also under way for the new Gelli Onn roadway linking West End and Thomas Street which also meant the demolition of the Old Town Hall[39] as well as Jerusalem Welsh Wesleyan Chapel. Some of Llanelli's oldest streets similarly fell prey to the bulldozers; Wind Street, Edgar Street (previously Oxen Street), Union Square and Cilheol. Whatever the pros and cons of the scheme, it was pleasant to approach the town from the west and get a clear view of the Parish Church, with its magnificent tower. In the mid-1960s, unemployment in Llanelli reached almost 20 percent and crime seemed to be on the increase. One sad aspect was the fact that churches and chapels had to lock their doors when no services were being held. Many people, including visitors complained about the practice but times had changed and there would be no going back.

Churches and chapels themselves were experiencing a drastic drop in numbers by this time. In a *Guardian* survey conducted on a November Sunday in 1881, it was estimated that over 50 percent of the population attended Sunday services. By 1970, this figure was down to 20 percent and the slide continued.[40] There were expensive repairs to be undertaken as well as bills for heating and lighting and members were having a difficult time trying to make ends meet. Realistically, no denomination had need of more than one chapel. The first Nonconformist chapel to fall was Siloh, still some years short of a century of existence in spite of the fact that, like most other chapels, it had the appearance of being capable of lasting for ever. Its small congregation bowed to the inevitable and Siloh was closed as a place of worship. It was taken over by the

Trostre works from the air, 1962. (Llanelli Library)

Council and converted for use as a Community Centre for the Lakefield area. The Anglican Church were not immune either and St Paul's was later closed and demolished. Siloh and St Paul's were the first; others would follow. It seemed that all the old certainties were being shaken at this time. The grand old Market Pavilion, Llanelli's Crystal Palace, was pulled down in 1968 and a new market replaced it by 1970, topped by a monstrous concrete car park.[41] Old family shops were disappearing in 1967 and being replaced by multiple stores.[42] Individuality gave way to conformity and Llanelli became a look-alike for any other town. Even our dream-factories, the cinemas, were either demolished, closed or they scraped along as bingo-halls. In fact, the Regal Cinema, once the height of luxury and the fourth largest in Wales, died of shame as a bingo hall in Llanelli's biggest blaze of the 1960s just before Christmas, 1969. One certainty, however, remained and, although James Griffiths had resigned as our Member of Parliament, Denzil Davies, a young barrister from Cynwyl Elfed retained the seat in the 1970 General Election. He polled 31,000 votes with his nearest rival, Carwyn James, polling 8,000 for Plaid Cymru. Three other contestants, Conservative, Liberal and Communists, all lost their deposits. Politically, nothing had changed in Llanelli since 1922.

Notes to Chapter XIV

1   Many were Catholic schoolchildren from La Sagesse Girls' Secondary School and St Edmund's College for Boys. There were also young children accompanied by their mothers. For a full account, read the *Llanelly Guardian*, 7 September 1939.

2 Food rationing began in January 1940. Coupons entitled each individual, per week, to meat amounting to 1s 10d (9p) though offal was exempt, 6oz of sugar, 4oz of butter, 2oz of bacon, 2oz of tea, 2 eggs and 1oz of cheese were allowed. Statistics showed that Welsh children were healthier after 1939 than they had been before.

3 Nine shelters were built to provide for 450 persons. Anderson shelters usually housed about 12 persons but were few and far between in Llanelli. They were 7ft below ground-level and had 4ft of earth on top.

The old Fire Station in Hall Street, 1968. (Llanelli Library)

4 Llanelli's Air Raid Precaution plans dated from 1938. Air-Raid Wardens wore steel-helmets bearing the letters ARP. They were well-known for their stentorian cry: 'Put that light out!'

5 The Home Guard were first known as Local Defence Volunteers. Firearms were slow in arriving and they drilled with broomsticks and pikes.

Inside the Arcade. (Llanelli Library)

6 As a County School sixth-former and a member of the School Squadron (556) of the ATC, I did fire-watching duty at Market Street School.

7 One London Girls' School, Mary Datchelor, shared the County School facilities until the end of the war. See article in *Llanelli Miscellany*. No 11.

8 Wool was provided for this purpose and women knitted gloves, scarves and balaclava helmets.

9 The firm was known locally as Harry Bach and was situated in Pottery Street.

10 One or two fell in the Docks area and I remember going to see a bomb crater on the fields of Soho Farm. These were stray bombs jettisoned by bombers after raiding Swansea. An intentional attack was made on the ROF Factory at Pembrey where there were casualties.

11 White Paper CMD 6832. Ten percent of women in the same age-group served in the Forces.

12 These were called 'Bevin Boys' after the Minister for Labour, Ernest Bevin. Local Bevin Boys were sent to train at Oakdale Colliery, Rhondda.

13 This was under Regulation 18B. They were interned in camps for the duration of the war.

14 There are no official figures for Llanelli but 357,000 was the United Kingdom total of those killed in the war. This represents one-third of World War One fatalities. White Paper CMD 6832.

15 Of the other two, one was Edward Evans, Labour MP for Lowestoft. He was educated at Park Street school and the Higher Grade School before becoming a teacher. The other was Tom O'Brien (later Sir Tom) who was educated at St Mary's Catholic School. He became General Secretary of NATKE. (National Association of Theatrical and Kine Employees).

16 Elizabeth was employed at 'sorting' plates. She started at the age of 13 and worked for 10 years before marriage. Fred went through every department of the hot-mill before becoming a rollerman.

17 Winifred was born in 1896, Idris in 1890 and Gwyn in 1904. Three other children died at under a year old. Elizabeth maintained that these three were brighter than the ones who survived!

18 He was captain of Wales against Ireland in 1925. See article on Idris Jones by John Edwards in *Llanelli Miscellany*, No. 9.

19 Read his autobiography *In My Time* (Weidenfeld and Nicolson, 1983).

20 Loti Hopkin was a local councillor and the mother of Dr Deian Hopkin who was one of the first intake into the school. Welsh-readers should consult *Ysgol Gymraeg Dewi Sant, Llanelli, 1947-1987*. Ed. Deian Hopkin, 1987. Also *Fel y Cadwer I'r Oesoedd a Ddêl* by Elenid Jones. Llanelli 1997. Elenid was another pioneer pupil and was the daughter of Dr Matthew Williams. Aneurin Williams lived in Tyisha Road.

21 As numbers grew, the school moved to Old Road and then to Copperworks schools before having a new school of its own at Penygaer in 1976. John Morris Williams became head teacher when Olwen Williams retired in 1973. He was head teacher until his premature death in 1985 when Meirion Davies, took over. The school numbered 440 in 1999, the largest primary school in Carmarthenshire.

22 Producing car radiators for Morris Motors at Cowley, Oxford.

23 Opened in 1952 under Steel Company of Wales, then under British Steel and now under CORUS, a firm with Dutch connections.

24 Carmarthen Bay Power Station started in 1959 (closed 1983) and Cynheidre Colliery in 1954 (closed 1989).

25 21 tank-landing craft of the Royal Navy were mothballed in the North Dock between 1953 and 1956. It was used briefly in 1970 to unload grain for chicken factories in the Pembrey area.

26 Edgar Rees' yard. This, too, finished in 1962.

27 Water is no longer drawn from this source but is held in reserve. Trostre gets its water from the Upper Cwmlliedi Reservoir.

28 Margaret lived in Cheyne Walk, London. There was also a son, Stafford, who lived at Greystoke Castle, Cumbria.

29 No. 1 went to Loughor, 2 to Bynea, 3 to Pemberton, 4 to the Depot, 5 to Felinfoel and 6 to Pwll. See Geoff Griffiths: *Llanelli Trolley Buses* (Trolleybooks, 1992) and article by Stuart Cole in *Llanelli Miscellany* No. 6.

30 Old Lodge Estate and Hafan Complex.

31 It was the first-ever visit by a reigning monarch.

32 We are indebted to Harold Prescott for his foresight in filming the town's changing character during this period.

33 Many Italians settled here. Among them was the sculptor Adriano Candelori.

34 One of Llanelli's largest tinworks, it once employed 550, was now down to 440 of whom 70 were women.

35 He used Jubilee Young, the minister of Zion, to illustrate a section of his poems. He was probably the greatest preacher of his day.

36 One of the Canadian exiles was my sister Nansi who emigrated in 1956. She was accompanied by her husband and baby daughter just over 18 months old.

37 'Yn ddidwyll mi ddywedaf
    "R'orau rioed a gofiaf;"
    O dre'r Wŷl adref af
    A'i hafiaith nid anghofiaf.'

38 Margaret Stepney had been married twice. This was the son from her first husband.

39 The Old Town Hall had ben used by the Health Department for some years. It was here that children came to see the School Dentist.

40 Survey made by local journalist, Harry Davies, who worked for the *Swansea Evening Post*. See Harry Davies; *Looking Around Llanelli*. Ed. Gareth Hughes. 1985.

41 Letter in the *Llanelli Star*, 15 May 1989, from Dudley Gershon returning after an absence of 21 years: 'Then (in 1968) shops were kept in good repair, were presentable and had individuality… Stepney Street is now in a state of dilapidation… The multi-storey car park is hideous…the town lacks character. What had happened to make people lose pride in appearance?' It was one of many.

42 Morris the Realm disappeared in 1967 although it had been taken over by Macowards of Swansea since 1956. The Realm was the largest store in Stepney Street and some of the others were Lewis the York, James Ready-Made and David Evans, Bradford House.

Chapter XV
Change of Direction: New Horizons

THE 1970s witnessed a drastic change in Llanelli's town centre. In 1970, the first stage of the new market was opened and, in the following year, Stepney Street was closed to traffic and pedestrianised. By this time, the Public Library had become far too small and an extension was added to it in 1972 which enabled it to continue its second-to-none service to the community. In October 1972, came the unforgettable day when the Scarlets beat the All Blacks, 9-3. J.B.G. Thomas, writing in the *Western Mail*, said: 'Llanelli achieved their finest hour and most historical win in the cauldron of Stradey Park. No praise can be too great for the 15 scarlet-jerseyed heroes who played magnificently from first to last.' The town celebrated, as never before, until the early hours of the morning and the pubs ran dry.[1] The 1970s proved to be a golden age for the Scarlets who played in five Welsh Cup Finals from the inception of the competition in 1972 and won it four

The 'Tanner Bank' at Stradey. (Llanelli Library)

seasons in succession.[2] This was the era of Carwyn James as coach and Phil Bennett as captain. The man who captained Llanelli to victory against the All Blacks was the gentle giant, Delme Thomas.

Unfortunately, no such striking successes came to way of the soccer club. Its players were paid but it was not a professional club in the true sense. The Reds found themselves in constant financial difficulties. From time to time, Llanelli played in the Southern League and in the Welsh League and they were Welsh League Champions in 1930 and in 1933. They also won the Welsh League Challenge Cup two years in succession in 1930 and 1932. The Reds' best home-grown player was Billy Hughes of Andrew Street who played for Swansea, Birmingham City and Wales and was considered the finest back of his day.[3] Probably, the club's most glamorous era was in the 1950s when a number of Scottish players were recruited including Doug Wallace and Jock Stein who later became manager of the Celtic and the Scottish international teams. By 1957, however, financial troubles and a poor playing record saw them ejected from both Southern and Welsh Leagues. The team never returned to the Southern League but they gained readmission to the Welsh League to win the championship three times again and lift the League Challenge Cup in 1975.

In 1974, Llanelli Cricket Club celebrated 100 years of cricket at Stradey Park. The club had played in the South Wales Association since its inception in 1926 and had won the championship for the first time in 1928. Peter Jenkins captained the side for a remarkable period of 16 years in the 1960s and 1970s but the team's performances were

Traffic jam in Stepney Street, 1962. (Llanelli Library)

generally inconsistent. Too often, they would end up on the bottom of Division One and would be relegated to Division Two only to be promoted again the following season. Apart from Dai and Emrys Davies, several local players have served Glamorgan well throughout the years, among them being Trevor Every, Haydn Davies, Hugh Davies of Pembrey and Euros Lewis and Jeff Jones of Dafen. Most glory must go to Jeff Jones, a fast bowler who played in 15 Test matches for England between 1964 and 1969 before an elbow injury brought his career to a premature end. During the winter men's and

Multi-storey car park above the Market. (Llanelli Library)

women's hockey was played on the cricket field by Llanelli teams and one of our ablest players was Lynne Thomas who played hockey for Wales and women's cricket for England. The Welsh women's hockey team played international matches at Stradey and claimed that it was the finest pitch in Wales. The wonderful Stradey playing fields were also shared by the Llanelli Tennis Club, formed in 1880, where national competitions and international matches were held. The club later added a squash court which became a popular venue with Adrian Davies becoming a world-class player.

The redevelopment of Llanelli's town centre took place at the same time as plans were put forward for a massive reorganisation of local government. The town had been part of Carmarthenshire since 1535 but now, in 1974, it found itself in a new administrative unit called Dyfed which comprised the counties of Pembrokeshire and Cardiganshire in addition to Carmarthenshire. Llanelli became one of six District Councils within the county of Dyfed and, although the first meeting of the reorganised Borough Council was held in April 1974, the new authority did not officially become a borough until the following November when a new charter was handed over to the Mayor, Councillor Edgar J. Thomas. The new council ruled over a much-enlarged Llanelli which had swallowed up the Llanelli Rural Council and, much to their chagrin, the Burry Port and Kidwelly Councils. Alun Bowen Thomas took up the post of Chief Executive of the Council, replacing Selwyn Samuel who had served as Town Clerk to the previous administration. Mr Samuel had resigned in March 1974, a few days after having been elected a Freeman of the Borough, the only officer of the Council ever to receive the honour.[4]

In February 1975, Llanelli was given complete control over the running of its Public Library in spite of opposition from Dyfed County Council. A temporary order had been granted to this purpose in 1974 but now the order was made permanent to the delight of the townspeople who had treasured their Library and truly valued its services over a very long period of time. One of the Library's prize collections was the gift of the author Theodore Nicholl who died in 1973.[5] The donation of 220 volumes included signed editions of works by Walter de la Mare, T.S. Eliot, Aldous Huxley, John Masefield, Siegfried Sassoon, Stephen Spender and Rhys Davies, many of whom were friends. Theodore Nicholl was a distinguished novelist, poet, playwright, critic and journalist and was a grandson of Jeremiah Williams, agent to the Stepney estate. After the death of his parents, he lived with his grandmother in Greenfield Villas and attended the local Intermediate School. Another Llanelli author, from a quite different background, was making his living by writing in London at this time. He was a man who had profited greatly from using Llanelli's Public Library and his name was William Glynne Jones.[6] He lived in Andrew Street and worked as a moulder at Glanmor Foundry for almost 20 years until 1942. He drew deeply on his foundry experience, especially in his book 'Farewell Innocence', and also on his childhood in Llanelli in 'The Childhood Land' which, in the opinion of the eminent critic, L.A.G. Strong, was: 'Surely one of the great books of childhood.' W. Glynne Jones died in 1977.

During 1975, members of the Round Table came together to prepare for a winter Carnival to start the Christmas celebrations in the town. Together with the switching-on of the lights in the town centre, it proved to be a real antidote for the winter blues brought on by the long dark nights. Thousands of people turned up in spite of unfavourable weather, had an enjoyable time and gave generously to local charities. The Carnival has grown tremendously since then and is now a date to be noted in the town's social calendar. A great upheaval was caused in the town's centre at this time when Tesco built a supermarket where the Tinopolis Studios are today. Unfortunately, the lower end of Market Street was lost as well as shops in Park Street but the greatest advantage to shoppers was the provision of a car park on top of the building. Even though negotiations began in 1976, it was 1979 before the supermarket opened its doors.

In 1976, a new Comprehensive system of education was introduced which meant the demise of the Grammar and Secondary Modern schools and an end to the examination at 11 years of age on which a child's educational future depended. This resulted in the creation of a new Welsh-language Comprehensive School at Stradey and four English-medium schools, Graig, Coedcae, Bryngwyn and St John Lloyd Roman Catholic School in Havard Road. It was the end of the Boys' Grammar School and Girls' Grammar School and of Secondary Modern Schools such as Coleshill, Stebonheath and Stradey.[7] The change was made as a result of government policy and was not universally accepted at the beginning. The Grammar schools claimed they were not trained to teach less-gifted children, and much was made of the strain imposed on children by the 11+ examination. Failure at this juncture, however, was not always crucial as there was a 13+ examination to allow pupils a second chance at gaining Grammar

School entrance. By this time, some Secondary Modern Schools were preparing pupils for GCE 'O' Level examinations and gaining very good results. An interesting sidelight to this educational change was seen in its effect on the production of future rugby stars. Up to now, all the schools played against each other on a regular basis and a very strong Llanelli Schoolboys team was among the best in Wales, while the Grammar School proved supreme at seven-a-side rugby. Rugby was predominantly the winter game and Physical Education lessons, outside the gymnasium, meant organised inter-form rugby matches.[8] Introducing other sports such as soccer and cross-country running might be seen as broadening sporting horizons but it was disaster as far as rugby was concerned and its effects soon became evident throughout Wales with Comprehensive Schools being blamed for the decline of Welsh rugby at senior level. Still, change was inevitable and the Comprehensive Schools have excelled themselves on both academic and sporting fronts as well as being instrumental in teaching social skills. No one, today, would seriously consider reverting to a system based on selection.

One of the reasons for the delay in opening the Tesco supermarket was the opposition of the Argos bingo-ball on the corner of Market Street and Water Street. The Argos had seen better days as the famous Royalty Theatre, built by a Llanelli impresario J.B. Noakes in 1892. Many famous artists trod its boards including Charlie Chaplin (who lodged in Andrew Street)[9] Henry Irving, Charles Coburn and Marie Lloyd. It later came into the possession of the pioneer film-maker, William Haggar and, very early in the 1900s, short films were shown interspersed with plays (including Shakespeare), operas, musical comedies and music-hall variety bills. The nearby Angel Hotel in Water Street served as a theatre bar and a bell rang there at the end of intervals. When films became the predominant entertainment, the place changed its name to the Hippodrome but it was as Haggar's that the cinema was known to generations of Llanelli people.

There had, for many years, been plans afoot to provide Llanelli with a civic theatre but nothing came of them until 1976 when the Borough Council bought the Classic Cinema, previously the Odeon, in Station Road. The price paid was £65,000 and £50,000 of this came from the Civic Theatre Appeal Trust which had been assiduously collecting money since 1972. The first live shows were seen at the new venue in 1978 and it has been a stage for many local theatre groups, including successful youth companies and school groups, ever since. Concerts of all kinds have taken place there including appearances by Llanelli's two best-known choirs, Côr Meibion and the Hywel Girls Choir who have both been marvellous ambassadors for Llanelli on their various European and overseas tours.

It was a proud moment for Llanelli Borough Council when Pembrey Country Park was opened in July 1980. The Mayor, Councillor Harry Richards, said; 'This is the single most important environmental and ideological decision.' It had been a long struggle, going back for more than a decade to the threatened removal of a Ministry of Defence gunnery range from Shoeburyness to Pembrey. Grass-roots opinion was galvanised into action by voluntary groups. Anti-Gunnery Range Committees bearing the motto 'SOS' (Save our Sands) were formed to protest against the plans. Public inquiries were held over a period of eight weeks in 1970 under the chairmanship of Sir Alun Talfan Davies and the move was rejected by the Welsh Office.[10] From 1975, onwards, there was a threat of development by private enterprise of the old Royal Ordnance Factory site but this was thwarted by Llanelli Borough Council which bought the site outright, in two stages, by 1978 together with areas of forest and foreshore. This was in spite of the fact that the development of the proposed Country Park was not supported by Dyfed County Council. The Country Park was soon one of the major tourist attractions in Wales and still remains so with activities to suit all tastes and vast parking areas fronted by the seven-mile-long Cefn Sidan Beach and magnificent views of Gower.

In 1979, Llanelli industry suffered yet another blow with the closure of the Glanmorfa Foundry which had been in existence for 130 years.[11] In 1980, Duport Steelworks laid off 575 workers and, in 1981, closed altogether with the loss of 1,100 workers. These closures were all opposed by unions, support groups, the Borough Council and the MP, Denzil Davies, but the fight was in vain. There was even a call for God's help when 400 people turned up for divine service near the Sunken Gardens in the hope of reversing the Duport decision. Works closures meant not only the loss of jobs and the abandonment of skills honed in almost 200 years of making iron and steel in the town, but they also had an impact on ancillary services like haulage and affected trade right down to the smallest corner shop. The worst effect was on the morale of the workers themselves and, indirectly, on their families. The situation was made even more hopeless by an almost complete lack of alternative employment even for those prepared to leave the town. At this stage, the Council's unemployment figure stood at 19.3 percent. It is no coincidence that this is the period when hard drugs first made their appearance in Llanelli, a problem which, once established, would spread rapidly.

By the 1980s it was obvious that the Town Hall had become too small to accommodate all the Council's departments and several of them found themselves housed in different buildings all over town. It was, therefore, decided to erect a new administrative building to bring all departments together under the same roof. The site chosen was that of the old Regal cinema which had burnt

Ty Elwyn. (Llanelli Library)

to the ground in 1969, a site which was also convenient because it stood adjacent to the Town Hall. Work on the project was started in 1980 and the building was opened exactly two years later.[12] The name chosen for it was Tŷ Elwyn in honour of Frederick Elwyn Jones, one of the town's most distinguished sons and it was Elwyn Jones himself who came to perform the opening ceremony. He had become Sir Elwyn Jones in 1964 and entered the House of Lords in 1974, taking the title of Lord Elwyn Jones of Llanelli and Newnham, his former London constituency. In his speech he said that this occasion was one of the two greatest honours ever conferred on him; the second was that he was a Llanelli man and that Llanelli people had been generous enough to make him a Freeman in 1967.

In 1984, work was started on the Wildfowl and Wetlands site at Penclacwydd near Bynea and, when the last Llanelli foundry at Machynys was closed in 1985, the vision slowly came into view of developing the coastal area between Bynea and Kidwelly as a resort facility. As far back as May 1982, the retiring Mayor, Councillor Vincent Lewis, had predicted that Llanelli would be changing into a seaside town between then and the end of the century saying: 'It is extremely important that we constantly remind ourselves that, while Llanelli has always been a town by the sea, it has never been a seaside town.' By 1986, the whole of the old Duport Steelworks site had been purchased by the Borough Council. Demolition was swiftly carried out and the area was landscaped in 1987. It was a rare pleasure to drive over Sandy Bridge and see the sea again but, alas, the view was obscured once more when the soil excavated to make a lake where the steelworks had stood was used to make a

Sandy Water Park on the old Steelworks site. (Llanelli Library)

landscape of rolling hillocks between the lake and the sea. Soon afterwards, a new housing development arose on the lake's shore together with a modern restaurant complex called the Sandpiper a feature of whose interior are walls of unadorned old 'Klondike' bricks.

It was not only old industrial buildings which were being demolished at this time. Coleshill School, which looked as if it had been built to last for centuries, was demolished on the orders of Dyfed County Council in 1984 after the remaining school population had moved on to Coedcae Comprehensive. It was a sound, substantial building made of local stone which could surely have been used for some good purpose and had recently been renovated and painted. In spite of protests from the Borough Council, however, it was unceremoniously torn down. The same happened to fine Victorian buildings, including the York Hotel at the lower end of Stepney Street. These were removed to make way for the dubious Sunken Gardens while, having demolished perfectly good genuine Victorian buildings, it was later decided to adorn the main streets, ironically, with mock Victorian lamp-posts and litter-bins. It was for a better reason that Our Lady of Peace, the Roman Catholic Church at Waunlanyrafon, was

York Hotel, Stepney Street. (Brian Cripps collection)

171

The Sunken Gardens, 1980. (Llanelli Library)

demolished in 1985 because the building had been structurally unsound almost from the beginning in 1937. A new church on the same site, was dedicated in 1995. St Paul's Church, Tyisha, another fine Victorian edifice, was demolished in 1987, the church having been closed since 1980.

During the 1980s, with unemployment running at around 20 percent, Llanelli was hit by two industrial closures which were different from those experienced in the past. They were outside the town area but within the jurisdiction of Llanelli Borough Council and gave employment to numbers of Llanelli workers. They were new and expensive projects and much was expected of them. The £12 million Carmarthen Bay Electricity Generating Station at Pembrey started producing electricity in 1950. The site had been cleared in 1947 and the magnificent structure with its massive chimneys was visible all around the Burry estuary. It closed in 1983. Specialist German technicians were brought over in 1954 to sink deep shafts for mining anthracite coal at the new Cynheidre Colliery between Five Roads and Pontyates. The total cost of this enterprise was estimated at £18 million. It closed in 1989. When Carmarthen Bay Power Station was demolished in 1991 and the tall towers of Cynheidre toppled a year later, we saw industrial buildings come and go within a single generation. Most of the old heavy industries had been here for over a century and we had grown up with them. This was an altogether different experience.

Within the scope of this work, it is quite impossible to catalogue all the sporting activities in the town but it should by no means be assumed that they were confined to rugby, soccer and cricket. Bowls had become a favourite summer game since the beginning of the 20th century and it is probable that more people actively took part in bowls than in any other single game.

Carmarthen Bay Power Station. (Llanelli Library)

The Llanelli Bowling Club had been formed in 1906 and played on the tennis-courts of the Thomas Arms Hotel before its own green was laid in 1911. When Parc Howard was presented to the town in 1912 a green was laid there which was open to the public and another added later. These were followed by greens at People's Park and Havelock Park, New Dock, within the town boundaries. There were also greens in surrounding villages as well as works greens such as RTB at Tyisha, BSC at Trostre and Morris Motors in Felinfoel. Leagues were formed and the game was played to a very high standard and Llanelli provided internationals too numerous to mention. It was therefore fitting that the British Isles Internationals were held at Park Howard in 1987 and pronounced a great success.[13]

1986 had seen a further development on the bowling scene when Llanelli Town Council built the first indoor arena on the edge of People's Park. International matches and competitions with worldwide appeal are regularly televised from the Selwyn Samuel Centre. The centre can be transformed into a concert venue and exhibition hall during the summer months and a banqueting suite has recently been added. This, in addition to a revamped Leisure Centre, built around the nearby Jubilee Swimming Pool, has added much to the enjoyment of Llanelli people as well as visitors to the town. The game of snooker has also been very popular, taking over from billiards in the 1920s. The present centre is the Matchroom at Waunlanyrafon run by our own Terry Griffiths who won the World Snooker Championship at his first attempt in 1979. There is a thriving Snooker League and many clubs dotted around the town in clubs and institutes but one still nostalgically looks back at the long-gone snooker halls of the Lucania in Stepney Street, the Welcome in Murray Street and Hatcher's on the river bank behind Vaughan Street.

The Borough Council put forward their plan for South Llanelli in 1988 to develop the old industrial area between the rivers Loughor and Gwendraeth. £10 million of EEC money had been used to clear most of the industrial sites between 1985 and 1987 and now a further £3 million was immediately made available by the Welsh Office. Tourism was now the main aim and after clearing away the old Eastwood Poultry Factory at Pembrey, the Welsh Motor Sports Council set up a race-track there. The same year saw the opening of the Industrial Museum at Kidwelly[14] in 1988. In 1991, the Wildfowl and Wetland Centre was opened at Penclacwydd, Bynea. All have since proved to be popular tourist attractions.

A new hospital at Bryngwynmawr was ready by 1990 and caused great anger by being named Prince Philip Hospital after the person who declared it officially open in June of that year.[15] The name of the old Hospital had been Llanelli General Hospital and the original building had been largely paid for by the townspeople and workers. A whole hospital wing had been added from the J.C. Williams Trust Fund and, If the new hospital were to be named after any single person, then he should be the one. There was a tremendous amount of correspondence on the subject in the *Llanelli Star* with one letter only defending the choice of name imposed on the town by the local Health Authority. They were all in vain as was the protest against the lack of maternity provision at the hospital organised by MUMS. (Mothers Unite for Maternity Services). There was also a demand for a Hospice alongside the hospital and money for Tŷ Bryngwyn was painstakingly raised over a number of years.

J.C. Williams, local benefactor. Portrait at Llanelli Public Library.

There cannot be many towns anywhere in the world which could boast two breweries both started and still largely controlled by local families. Felinfoel and Buckley Breweries had maintained proud traditions in Llanelli over countless generations but the beginning of the end for Buckley's came in 1989 when they were taken over by Crown Brewery of Pontyclun under the name of Crown Buckley. It was seen as a means of expansion at the time but beer ceased to be brewed in Llanelli and the new concern was itself taken over by Brains of Cardiff within 10 years and the brewery building at present lies empty and forlorn as the Lliedi passes quietly by. This was the age of take-overs and, also in 1989, Calsonic, a Japanese firm, took over the Llanelli Radiator Factory in Felinfoel. This was, in fact, the first of the modern light industries to come to Llanelli as the Nuffield Factory[16] in 1942 when it was erected on a green-field site in Felinfoel and made parts for the aircraft industry. When the war ended in 1945, it switched to making radiators for Morris cars assembled at Oxford and was considerably enlarged in 1965. The original hope was for car-production at Llanelli but that never came to reality. Morris became amalgamated with Austin cars who, in turn combined with Rover and closure of the factory was threatened in 1986. This was averted by a remarkable buy-out of the factory spearheaded by the manager Mike Reilly with the support of the workers. Three years later, Llanelli Radiators was taken over by Calsonic with Mike Reilly later becoming the only non-Japanese to sit on the Board as Head of Calsonic (Europe). He saved the factory and made sure it expanded under new control and he deserves to be remembered as one of the best among modern managers who have lived and worked at Llanelli in the latter part of the 20th century.[17]

Another large factory at Felinfoel is that of Thyssen Krupp Camford. It was built in 1962 and was then known as Fisher and Ludlow, a Birmingham firm which was part of the British Motor Corporation – a combine of Austin Morris and Rover. Over the years it had several changes of name, among them Pressed Steel Fisher. The firm produced car doors and other pressings for British cars but it now supplies car manufacturers all over the world. The 1990s saw the expansion of Industrial Parks in the area with the largest at Cross Hands, then under the control of Llanelli Borough Council. Nearer home, Industrial Parks were established at Trostre, North Dock, Dafen, and Bynea housing important industries such as I.N.A. Needle Bearings, Hunstman's Chemicals, F.C. Taylor (Aerospace) and Avon Inflatables among others. Most firms came in from outside but some were locally owned, notably Dyfed Steel and Daniel Fans and three sizeable haulage firms, Owens, North, and John Evans. Scores of smaller home-grown firms are also established on these parks. Heavy industry is still represented by the Trostre works, now owned by Corus. A Dutch firm, Draka, has taken over from Delta Crompton at the Copper Works which, remarkably, is producing copper wire in a works where copper has been produced for nearly 200 years with some of the work still being carried on in the original buildings.

After barely 10 years, the Tesco supermarket left the town centre for its new site in the new Trostre Retail Park in 1989, leaving behind it a contract which, unbelievably, prohibited the premises from being sold to anyone selling food in competition with Tesco for 99 years. The building was more or less abandoned except for very casual occupancy by the cheaper end of the clothing market. It left the town without a single large grocery store and even though Tesco provided free transport to Trostre, it made things very difficult for people who did not have cars. Even so, for those with cars, it proved an ideal location with plenty of room for parking. The Trostre Retail Park, in fact, became a magnet for shoppers when firms such as Halford, Great Mills, MFI and the inevitable McDonalds also made their presence felt. During the 1980s, Trostre had become the hub of two new roads, one linking with the M4 motorway at Hendy and the other, a direct road to Swansea, linking with the M4 at Penllergaer. The old Tesco building in the town became an eyesore until it was rescued by Agenda TV and tastefully renovated to house television studios in 1998.

Plans were unveiled in 1992 for yet another reorganisation in local government which was to become effective in 1995. It appeared that David Hunt, the Welsh Secretary had 22 unitary authorities in mind, including Llanelli.[18] As time went on, however, it looked increasingly likely that Llanelli was to be included in a resurrected Carmarthenshire and that Wales would be served by 21 unitary authorities. An organisation named SOL. (Save Our Llanelli) was formed with support from all political parties, the Chamber of Trade and NALGO (The National Association of Local Government Officers). The *Llanelli Star* vigorously backed the campaign and weekly reports of activities appeared in its pages. John Redwood had replaced David Hunt by July 1993, when a Llanelli Borough Council deputation arranged to meet him to plead its case. In the event, Redwood did not even turn up, and the deputation was met by a Junior Minister, Gwilym Jones.

The local MP was not part of the deputation and his support was luke-warm to say the least.[19] The SOL movement, however, found support in the House of Lords where Lord Howe and Lord Hooson spoke in favour and Lord Chalfont[20] stated: 'I believe Llanelli, in every way, is sufficiently large and important to create a viable unitary authority of its own.' The crucial weakness in the Llanelli case was that it was, at the time, an extended borough which included nine Community Councils, only four of which supported SOL. There was an attempt to forge an alternative unitary authority by joining Llanelli with Ammanford and Lliw Valley but nothing came of this proposal. Thus the Local Government (Wales) Act was passed on 7 July 1994, and the new Carmarthenshire came into being on 1 April 1995. Strangely enough, Llanelli's campaign led to a revival of the case for devolution which had been so crushingly rejected in 1979. Marc Phillips, Plaid Cymru's candidate for Llanelli, put the matter succinctly in 1993: 'Even if all 38 Welsh MP's voted against, it could be imposed by the strength of the Conservative Party in England. Has there ever been a clearer example of Welsh impotence? The need for a Welsh Parliament grows more urgent by the day!' As it proved, Llanelli's loss was Wales' gain.

Probably the most exciting project of the 1990s was that of the Millennium Park started in 1995 by Llanelli Borough Council assisted by the Welsh Development Agency and Welsh Water. The scheme attracted £13.75 million of Lottery funding matched by an equal amount of money by the public and private sector. Thus a £27.5 million project was in place to regenerate and beautify 22 kilometres of coastline comprising 2,000 acres of land along the coastal plain including 200 acres of lakes and 200 acres of forest. Four hundred new homes have already been built in the area and the £1 million Sandpiper restaurant complex stands on the Sandy Water Park lakeside. A Jack Nicklaus golf course is scheduled for Machynys, the North Dock has been emptied and will be filled to a depth of 1½ metres to provide for watersports and sail training. There will also be a major visitor centre in the North Dock area as well as a covered leisure facility. Improvements will be made at Burry Port harbour and all these facilities will be joined by the Sustrans[21] Celtic Trail for pedestrians and cycles which will run from Newport in the east to Fishguard in the west.

Further changes in the education system occurred when it was decided in 1989, to take away the sixth forms of Llanelli's comprehensive schools and transfer them to a Tertiary College at the CCTA Campus in Pwll. The only exception was Ysgol y Strade which retained its sixth form since its medium of instruction was Welsh. The Carmarthenshire College of Technology and Art had been set up in 1985 by amalgamating the Technical Colleges of Llanelli, Ammanford, Pibwrlwyd, Gelli Aur and Dyfed College of Art, Carmarthen, into which the Llanelli College of Art had been absorbed. The Llanelli College of Art had occupied premises in the old Prospect Place School and in Coleshill Terrace (next to Tabernacle) before moving to the building which now houses Pentip Primary School. Llanelli's first Technical College, however, was built in Stebonheath Terrace in 1936 before extending into the old Grammar School buildings in Marble Hall Road when the school moved to Pwll in stages during the 1970s.[22] The college teaches a range of courses to 'A' Level, Diploma and Honours Levels and offers numerous adult courses which afford great opportunities to local people.

A revolution overtook the game of rugby in 1995 when it turned professional almost overnight and huge sums of money were paid for the services of quite ordinary players. Llanelli Rugby Club soon found itself in financial straits by spending money it did not possess. There were many twists and turns while millionaire sponsors proved elusive during which time the club almost sold its car park as a supermarket site. In the end, the unthinkable happened when the ground itself had to be sold to the Welsh Rugby Union in exchange for an annual rent.

Ieuan Evans was a popular captain and was chosen as captain of Wales in the 1991 World Cup. Llanelli beat Australia in 1992 and, this season (1999–2000), the Club is doing well in the Welsh Cup, the Scottish-Welsh League and in the European Cup. We have men from all over the world playing for Llanelli today but, among our few local players, Scott Quinnell keeps the flag flying as did his father Derek before him. The Stradey ground is now considered one of the finest in Wales. The soccer ground at Stebonheath has improved considerably since being taken over by Llanelli Town Council and Llanelli AFC are near the top of the Welsh National League. The club suffered a great loss when their player-manager, Robbie James, died while playing against Porthcawl in February 1998. The cricket ground also saw an improvement when a new pavilion was built in 1981, though no great improvement in playing standards followed. The players and spectators, however, continue to enjoy the game and

the club is a warm and welcoming place in winter as well as in summer. Llanelli continues to produce players for Glamorgan and Darren Thomas has played for the England 'A' team while Wayne Law is beginning his county career under the watchful eye of Hugh Davies who is currently chairman of Glamorgan Cricket Club. The most successful of all local players is Robert Croft of Hendy who has played for England while Simon Jones of Dafen, son of Jeff Jones, is beginning to make his mark for Glamorgan as a fast bowler like his father.[23] Unfortunately, Glamorgan have not played a match at Stradey since 1993.

Llanelli, therefore, found itself back in Carmarthenshire's bosom even though it had never lain comfortably there. With the extinction of the Borough Council, authority moved out of the Town Hall and Tŷ Elwyn with the town finding itself confined within smaller boundaries at Sandy Bridge, Furnace, Trostre, Panteg and Halfway. The Llanelli Town Community Council came into being in 1974 with its responsibilities for such matters as Community Halls and footpaths. This Council took the opportunity of twinning Llanelli with Agen in south-west France in 1989, it built the Selwyn Samuel Centre and took over Stebonheath Park. It has recently purchased Llanelli House in the hope of restoring it gradually and making it into a civic centre. The Council has good relations with the Llanelli Rural community Council and both share responsibility for the Public Cemetery (no longer the Box Cemetery) and for the Senior Citizens'

St Elli Shopping Centre, 1999.

Centre at the YMCA in Stepney Street. Llanelli's population at the present time is 41,600, according to the County Council, with 20 councillors representing five wards, Bigyn, Elli, Glanymor, Lliedi and Tyisha. J.C. Williams was the Council's hard-working Clerk until his retirement a year ago and he has been

Vaughan Street today. (Carms County Council)

replaced by Lynn Davies who promises to be just as conscientious. Llanelli Rural Community Council is responsible for 20,000 people living outside the town's boundaries, represented by 20 councillors representing the wards of Bynea, Dafen, Felinfoel, Glyn, Hengoed, Pembrey, Pwll and Swiss Valley. Note that the divisions of Glyn and Hengoed go back to the early Middle Ages. The council's headquarters are in the town of Llanelli and the office is efficiently run by the Clerk, Richard Thomas.[24]

The new St Elli shopping centre was opened in 1999 with the Asda Supermarket as its centrepiece. Improvements have been made in Stepney Street and Vaughan Street by attractive paving and the provision of seats, useful for resting in fine weather and canopies placed over the shops to protect people in wet weather. A rather ornate market entrance was created in Stepney Street at the cost of £300,000 but the general tone of a once-grand shopping street has been diminished by closures or by relocation in the St Elli Shopping Centre and to Trostre Retail Park. The main difference between now and 50 years ago is the disappearance of local family firms and their replacement by chain stores.[25]

Even so, it is still a pleasure to shop in Llanelli and talk to old friends and it is often still possible to do so entirely in Welsh. Between town centre attractions and the beauty of the outlying areas, Llanelli and its surroundings are well worth visiting with all our local authorities placing a very high priority on tourism. Visitors can travel quickly along a new network of roads linking up with the M4 motorway or they can let the train take the strain as we are on the main line between London and Fishguard as well as on the Central Wales line which runs between Swansea and Shrewsbury. It is now also possible to fly in and out of Pembrey airport and there are hopes for further expansion at Pembrey.[26] Cardiff International Airport is only an hour away and, with the Amsterdam Link, visitors will be able to arrive from all parts of the globe. Who knows but that, with continuing global warming, people will be flocking here from the Mediterranean countries and reversing present trends. Let's be ready to receive them!

Looking forward to the year 2000, there are great expectations for the coming of the Eisteddfod. A beautiful site has been chosen in the middle of the Millennium Park and the Gorsedd stones lie between the sea and the lake at

Shopping in the Market. (Carms County Council)

Sandy. It is bound to be a successful Eisteddfod because all the others held in Llanelli have been great successes. Also, the preparations have been very thorough, stretching back over a number of years. It was towards the end of 1992 when Heward Rees, of Felinfoel, came to lecture to the local branch of the WEA[27] at the Thomas Arms. His subject was 'Music in Wales' and he was, at the time, Director of the Welsh Music Information Centre at Cardiff. The Eisteddfod had been on his mind for some time and, out of the blue, towards the end of his talk, he suggested that it might be a good idea to invite the Eisteddfod to Llanelli and district in the year 2000. He had not planned to say anything on the subject but when he saw a strong representation from various local authorities sitting in the front rows, he suddenly realised he would never have a better opportunity.

After the meeting, the Llanelli Rural Community Council had arranged refreshments for the speaker and officials of the WEA and the Council Clerk, Richard Thomas got into conversation with Heward Rees. Richard Thomas said that he thought his Council would be interested in initiating a campaign to invite the Eisteddfod to Llanelli. Also present was Brenda Lewis, a member of both the Gorsedd and the WEA. The Rural Council then called a meeting in February 1993, but there was a disappointing turn-out of 19 people. A second meeting was called in June and this time the response was more heartening. The *Llanelli Star* then got involved and when a third meeting took place in July, it proved possible to elect a steering committee at which the Rural Council promised £1,000 as a first contribution to the Eisteddfod Fund. It was this early start and subsequent preparation which led to Llanelli beating Cardiff and St David's to the prize of Eisteddfod 2000. The Proclamation Ceremony was held at the recently-laid Gorsedd Stones in June 1999, led by the Archdruid, Meirion Evans, minister of Jerusalem, Burry Port. In spite of lowering clouds and a bitterly cold breeze, a

Gorsedd Stones, Sandy Water Park. (Carms County Council)

good crowd came together to watch the colourful proceedings. The rain stayed away during both the Procession from town and the Proclamation Ceremony and one hopes it does the same in August, 2000. In 1962, the Eisteddfod experienced a week of unremitting rain. We hope for sunshine this time.

How, therefore, does one sum up the general situation in Llanelli at the end of 1999? First of all, there was the political earthquake when Plaid Cymru's Helen Mary Jones was elected as Member for the new Welsh Assembly in 1998 when Llanelli had been a Labour stronghold since 1922. It is not a matter of party politics, however, when we sense a growing perception of Welshness which has

Proclaiming Eisteddfod 2000. The Archdruid, the Revd Meirion Evans with Swordbearer, Ray Gravell.

Aerial view of St Elli Shopping Centre.

brought us a long way since the 1950s when Trefor and Eileen Beasley of Llangennech battled for the right to receive rate-demands in Welsh from the old Llanelli Rural Council. It was a long, lonely struggle which continued into the 1960s and was generally received with scorn and contempt. Today, we find much more sympathy from non-Welsh speakers as well as a clearer perception of nationality. There is no doubt that Welsh-medium schools such as Dewi Sant and Brynsierfel have played their part as has the outstanding success of Ysgol y Strade. But it is not purely a matter of language either; there is a marked contrast between now and the beginning of the century when people felt far more British than Welsh. Since the end of World War Two, our Red Dragons have out-numbered the Union Jacks and the Assembly, though barely a year old, is helping to restore our national self-respect and making us more self-confident.

Organised religion is in decline with most of our churches and chapels sparsely attended. Lloyd Street was the latest chapel to be torn down although a new Catholic church has been built in Waunlanyrafon and an Evangelical congregation occupies the abandoned Jewish synagogue in Erw Road. It is easy to connect the decline in religious observance with rising crime especially when so many people today are ignorant of the old values of Christian teaching. But the history of our town, like every other, has been riddled with crime over the centuries, with violence and robbery being constantly evident and drunkenness a contributing factor, as it still is today. What is different now is the effect of drugs and the money needed to feed the habit. Dr Cledwyn Thomas, acting as a police doctor as far back as 1993, stated that 40 percent of all crime in Llanelli was drug-related. What is also different is the scale of violence inflicted on the old, the infirm and the disabled and even on doctors and nurses in hospitals. We see theft from churches and chapels as well as from homes and some of our streets have become no-go areas at night. Mindless vandalism is still an ongoing curse. Sometimes, it seems as if civilisation itself is in danger and that the Barbarians are at the gates. But this is the traditional verdict of every generation on that which follows.

The old works, which created our industrial town, have all been swept away. De-industrialisation is a strange experience but, in historical terms, it is of little significance. The first works were planted here on green fields 200 years ago and many more were added in the following 100 years. Now, they have all disappeared and we are back to green fields again. This time, however, we are more in tune with the environment and are conscious of the fact that the balance of nature is a very precarious one and that we must be very careful of it. Our surroundings, today, have been made more beautiful and our responsibility is to stand guard over them. Let us therefore remember our motto 'Ymlaen Llanelli' and go forward with every faith in our future.[28]

Notes to Chapter XV

1   The match is immortalised in Max Boyce's song '*9-3*'. Scorers for Llanelli were Roy Bergiers, try, converted by Phil Bennett, and a penalty-goal by Andy Hill. New Zealand scored a penalty by Joe Karam, their full-back.

2   Full reports of all these matches will be found in *One Hundred Years of Scarlet*, compiled by Gareth Hughes (Llanelli RFC, 1983).

3   'The best back in the three countries'. This was the unanimous opinion of the secretaries of the Welsh FA, English FA, and Scottish FA (Ted Robbins, Stanley Rous and George Graham). Reported in *Coventry Evening Telegraph*, May 1946.

4   Mainly for his work in seeking to attract new industries to Llanelli. He had been Town Clerk since 1952, following D.J. Phillips in the post.

5   He was a prolific writer and his work includes *Sung Before the Bridal*, Lane, 1930; *Wild Swans*, Duckworth, 1939; and *Immortal Ease*, Hutchinson, 1947. He was a regular contributor to periodicals such as *Adelphi* and *Argosy* and to newspapers including the *Observer* and *London Evening News*. He was 71 when he died. His father was an ex-Scarlet, D.W. Nicholl, who was capped against Ireland in 1894.

6   He was born in 1907 in Llewellyn Street. He left Llanelli in 1943 and lived in Hornsey, London, from 1948 onwards. *Farewell Innocence* was published by Werner Laurie in 1950 and reprinted by Pan Books in 1973. *The Childhood Land* was published by Batsford in 1960. His other novels were *Ride the White Stallion*, Werner Laurie, 1951; and *Summer Long Ago*, Peter Neville, 1954. He wrote a dozen children's books in addition to school readers and contributed to 50 magazines worldwide. For further information, read *William Glynne Jones* by E.D. Jones and L.D. Jones, a booklet published by Llanelli Borough Council in 1995.

7   Burry Port Secondary Modern School became Glanymor Comprehensive. A Roman Catholic Secondary School was built in Havard Road in 1963. It was named Blessed John Lloyd and was changed to St John Lloyd in 1970, consequent upon canonisation. St Michael's, Bryn, was a private secondary school. Lakefield had become a primary school.

8 Llanelli Secondary schools had produced international players at Senior level. The most striking example was that of Phil Bennett and Derek Quinnell playing in the same side at Coleshill and going on to play in the same British Lions team.

9 Harry Davies interviewed a member of the orchestra who said he took him to No. 8. See *Looking Around Llanelli,* op. cit.

10 The full story of this heroic stand can be read in J.R. Ladd, *S.O.S.* (Llanelli Borough Council, 1992.)

11 For a history, read *The Glanmorfa Foundry and Engineering Co. Ltd.* by Byron Davies, (Carmarthenshire County Council, 1999.)

12 Work was started in March 1980. The building cost £2,000,000.

Welcome to Llanelli sign on Sandy Bridge. (Carms. County Council)

13 Probably the most famous of all Llanelli bowlers was A.J. Stacey who was at his peak in the 1930s.

14 The museum was the brainchild of W.H. Morris of Kidwelly. It is open to the public from March to September. It is on the site of the old Kidwelly Tinworks.

15 The opening was boycotted by many invited guests including the local MP, Denzil Davies.

16 After William Richard Morris, later Lord Nuffield, who owned Morris Motors at Cowley, Oxford.

17 Mike Reilly died on Christmas Day, 1999, after falling on ice while walking his dog near his home at Five Roads.

18 It was listed as a Unitary Authority in the Government's Green Paper.

19 His support became stronger towards the end of the campaign and he moved an amendment to the Local Government (Wales) Bill in April 1994, which was defeated by only one vote (13-12) at the Committee stage.

20 Geoffrey Howe came from Aberavon, Emlyn Hooson had been MP for Montgomery while Alun Glynne Jones (a former Minister of Defence) was a patron of Llanelli RFC.

21 Sustrans means Sustainable Transport. A branch route is scheduled to run along the old Mynydd Mawr railway line from Sandy eventually reaching the National Botanical Garden of Wales at Middleton Hall.

22 Llanelli Grammar School became Graig Comprehensive in 1977 and Graig was phased out in 1997 when the entire campus was taken over by CCTA.

23 Robert Croft attended St John Lloyd School, Llanelli while Simon Jones was a pupil at Coedcae Comprehensive. Both came through the Llanelli and Dyfed school system.

24 The Rural offices are in Vauxhall and the Town's at the Old Vicarage, near the Public Library.

25 In 1914, there were 46 locally owned shops in Stepney Street. Now, there are fewer than half a dozen.

26 The airport was being developed by Winston Thomas of Five Roads who made his fortune in the field of engineering in Dallas, Texas, US. Progress had since been stalled.

27 The branch has held a series of public lectures since its inception in 1913. Its history is outlined in various volumes of its magazine, *Llanelli Miscellany.*

28 We can expect to live longer to enjoy our improved environment. In 1901, life expectancy was 45 years for men and 49 for women. In 2001, it is likely to be 74 for men and 79 for women. *Britain 2000; Official Yearbook of the UK* (Office of National Statistics, 1999).

Chapter XVI
Into the third Millennium

At last, the year 2000 was upon us, the year in which the National Eisteddfod was to return to Llanelli. Preparations were afoot to prepare the site which was magnificently situated alongside Sandy Water Park. Fundraising had proceeded apace and, by June, the target of £250,000 had been reached. Now, all that was needed was fine weather and, when August came, we were truly blessed. The Maes was well set out and was a most congenial meeting-place, and from the wonderful performance of Joseff by Ysgol y Strade on the opening Friday evening to the rousing closing Gymanfa Ganu on the Sunday of the following week, we would glory in the finest of daytime competitions and evening concerts. Never to be forgotten also was the tribute paid to Gwynfor Evans, patriot and former President of Plaid Cymru in a ceremony which transpired to be his last public appearance. In the two main literary events, the Chair was won by Llion Jones of Bangor and the Crown by Dylan Iorwerth of Lampeter. It was truly a wonderful Eisteddfod – one which will set the standard for a long time to come.

The same year, however, also brought its disappointment. There had been high hopes of a fully operational airport at Pembrey but the project was finally abandoned in 2000. There had also been plans to develop a racecourse near the airport which had been approved by the British Horse-Racing Board, but this also came to nothing. A second plan to resite the racetrack in Trimsaran was put forward in 2002 but the planning application is still gathering dust on the shelves of County Hall.

Llanelli was still continuing to make history in rugby terms, and, in 2001, the Scarlets became the first Welsh club to win on French soil in the Heineken Cup when they beat Bourgoin 36–30. They went on to the semi-finals only to be beaten by Northampton at Reading by a last-minute penalty, 31–28. Lady Luck again deserted them at Nottingham against Leicester when a penalty was given against them in the dying minutes to send Llanelli to defeat by 13–12. The Scarlets are on target again in 2006 under new coach, Phil Davies and captain Simon Easterby, having won all their pool matches so far and are looking forward to a home tie in the quarter-finals.

The Welsh Rugby Union undertook a restructuring exercise in 2002 when regional rugby was introduced. Five regional clubs were formed, since reduced to four, and the new Llanelli Scarlets were launched in July 2003. As much attention has been focussed off the field as on it since the Scarlets, in partnership with Carmarthenshire County Council, proposed the move to a new ground at Pemberton in 2004. The club was in debt to the tune of £8 million and the intention was to build 450 houses on the Stradey site to offset the debt. Strong arguments were put forward by those in favour as well as by objectors and before Carmarthenshire County Council could consider planning consent, the application was called in by the Welsh Assembly. A public inquiry is due to be held in January 2007 and the result announced in May.

Dwayne Peel, Stephen Jones and Simon Easterby toured with the British Lions in New Zealand in 2005 and, by 2006, Scarlets' coaches Gareth Jenkins, Nigel Davies and Robin McBryde had left Llanelli to work with the Welsh International XV. It is also pleasing to note that Llanelli legend Phil Bennet was admitted to Rugby's Hall of Fame in 2006, which lists just 30 players worldwide.

It must be remembered, however, that rugby is not the only winter game. Robert Jones[1] of Swansea had taken charge of Llanelli's soccer club in 1996 with the intention of making it one of the leading clubs in the League of Wales but his ambition had not been realised. Much improvement had been made to the clubhouse and to the ground, which was owned by Llanelli Town Council, but performance on the pitch fell short of the facilities until 2005 when the Jesco group acquired the majority shareholding under the club's new chairman, Nitin Parekh. The group made a spectacular coup by signing Luca Cazoria as Director of Football in June 2005, in preparation for the coming season. Cazoria had played for Atletico Madrid and soon set about signing players from the lower Spanish leagues. Soon, the Reds' team sheet contained names like Torres, Fernandez, Mingorance and Nofuentes, the first four Spaniards to join. The squad was boosted to 17 with 10 professional players. Peter Nicholas was appointed as coach; he had been manager in 2001-2 and was now signed on a full-time basis. Nicholas took over from Cazoria in February 2006, and took the club to second position in the Premier Welsh League. He was now looking forward to taking the club into UEFA Cup football for the first time in its history.

The club's first European foray was to Sweden in July 2006 where they played Gefle in Stockholm and won 2–1. The return game was played at Stradey Park because Stebonheath did not come up to UEFA standards. Here they drew 0–0 and so went forward to the second round. This time, their opponents were the considerably stronger Odense from Denmark, but the Reds performed creditably against the Danes and lost by only 1–0. The return match was played at the Liberty Stadium in Swansea where Llanelli were trounced 5–0. We hope for better luck next season.

Cricket and bowls continue to be Llanelli's favourite summer games, with the Cricket Club being the oldest sporting club in town. Tennis and bowls continue to be well supported – the Llanelli Bowls Club celebrated its centenary in 2006. Fishing enjoys a good following on the Cwmlliedi reservoirs, while the Ramblers are increasingly popular, attracting people from far and wide. Simon Jones of Dafen was one of the heroes of England's cricket team that won the Ashes in 2005 and his absence through injury played a big part in the team's humiliating whitewash in Australia in 2006.

In January 2001 Llanelli welcomed a new vicar to succeed Chancellor Anthony Williams, who had retired. The new man was Revd Ian Thomas who had served for 20 years as a chaplain in the RAF. He threw himself into his work with tremendous enthusiasm, seeing to the restoration of the church organ and the Parish Hall, both of which were showing signs of age. In March 2005 he set up an appeal to restore the Parish Church itself to coincide with the centenary of the 1906 restoration. During this time, the parish had been extended and now comprised St Elli, All Saints, St Alban's, St Peter's, Christ Church and the Furnace Mission. Revd Ian Thomas now found himself Rector of the new Benefice supervising a team of clergy, but in March 2006 he left for Eccleston in Cheshire and was succeeded by Revd Siân Jones, the first woman to serve in Llanelli. The new Rector had previously been Vicar of Llansteffan and had been among the first women ever to be ordained in the Church in Wales.

The decline of Nonconformity continues with Park Church[2] being sold for development as a retail outlet. It is the latest in a long line of chapel closures. Hall Street Methodist Church, on the other hand, celebrated its 150th anniversary in 2006 with renovations aided by a grant from the Heritage Lottery Fund.

Llanelli is a seriously musical town claiming choirs of many descriptions. The two best-known choirs are the male-voice Cor Meibion conducted by Eifion Thomas and the Hywel Girls' Choir and Boy Singers conducted by John Hywel Williams. Both groups are seasoned worldwide travellers. In October 2000 the Hywel Girls' Choir went on a tour of Italy, visiting Venice, Florence and Rome where they were invited to sing before Pope John II at the Vatican. In September 2001 Cor Meibion undertook a tour of the US. The tour started in San Jose where Eifion Thomas also conducted the 70th Welsh Cymanfa Ganu of North America. They then gave concerts in Salt Lake City, Denver and Kansas City. They were breakfasting in Kansas City when they saw highjacked planes crashing into New York's Twin Towers on TV.

In 2002 a new orchestra was formed called the Llanelli Symphony Orchestra, conducted by Rhodri Evans, which has given regular performances since that time. As recently as 2006, we have seen a new mixed choir called Baroc under the baton of Eifion Thomas, giving its first concert at All Saints Church. Numerous smaller choirs are also to be found in the nearby villages putting on concerts of high quality and singing regularly to support charitable causes.

A surge of regeneration was initiated in 2001 when it was disclosed that the Buckleys' Brewery site was to be demolished and that Aldi was to build a supermarket with the Gwalia Housing

Section of Buckleys' Brewery building, scheduled for development. (J.E.)

Association building new homes. Llanelli's largest tinworks of the old hand-mill era, the Old Castle, still remained a ruinous eyesore. It had lain derelict for many years and there was renewed talk of demolition in 2000 before the National Eisteddfod came to town and again in 2002 before the Queen's visit. Nothing was done, however, until 2005 when the County Council purchased the site.[3] Plans were unveiled for the future of the eight-acre site which showed what was described as a projected cultural village giving access to several areas of creativity. We await developments.[4]

The top end of Stepney Street leading on to Upper Park Street has long been a sadly neglected part of town from the time when Tesco decamped to Trostre. Thankfully, the Tesco building was taken over by Agenda TV, which has since changed its name to Tinopolis and become a very big player in the media business. Now, the imposing but shabby Exchange Buildings opposite the studios has been renovated and some units have already been occupied. The very worst eyesore of Upper Park Street has been demolished to make way for what promises to be a very attractive area to comprise three anchor stores and 20 smaller shops. A new bus station will also be built as well as a car park, and covered ways will lead to St Elli Shopping Centre.[5]

Pugh Brothers' furniture store finally closed its doors at the end of

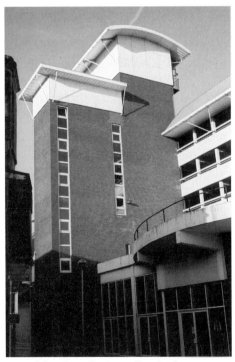

Part of the Tinopolis TV studios. (J.E.)

The imposing upper floors of Exchange Buildings. (J.E.)

The Bidding bar and restaurant, Cowell Street. The Pugh sign stands defiant. (J.E.)

January 2005. It was the last large family concern to succumb to the onslaught of the multinational colossus. The shop, extended over the years, had stood proudly in Cowell Street for over a hundred years, having started trading in Station Road in 1893. Developers moved in and opened an attractive bar and restaurant called The Bidding on the ground floor, leaving space for 26 apartments on the upper floors.

Several societies with interests in our history and heritage are in existence. The oldest is the Llanelli Civic Society which keeps a watching brief on new development and does its best to preserve what it thinks is important. It has also added to our historical archive by undertaking the reprinting of 'Old Llanelly' by John Innes, first published in 1902. The Friends of Llanelli Museum are active in the collection of local artefacts, among other activities, and are responsible for a section of the museum dedicated to Lord Elwyn Jones. The Llanelli Historical Society was formed in 2000 after Caroline De Abreu had brought together a group of historians and enthusiasts. By 2006 the Society numbers well over 100. An Open Day is held each year in order to display the ongoing work of various interest groups. The Society has recently been entrusted with part of Robin Craig's vast maritime collection and this is at present being catalogued. The Llanelli Community Heritage was formed on 1 March 2004. Since its inception, it has put up interpretive panels in Furnace, Felinfoel and in the Old Castle area. Almost 30 blue plaques have been set up to commemorate events, buildings, industrial sites and famous celebrities who have lived in the town. Material is also produced for use in schools. There

Shopping Centre, Llanelli Carmarthenshire County Council)

is also much activity in specific areas of the town as well, as we see in south Llanelli. In 2004 the Glanymor and Tyisha History Group was set up which has produced a magazine each year since mainly describing the lives of ordinary people in times gone by.

Llanelli House – Y Tŷ Mawr – came in for considerable attention in the year 2000. At last, it was realised that we had a priceless possession in

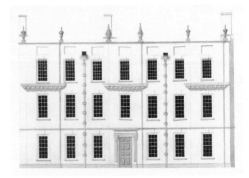

A sketch of the front of Llanelli House as it will appear after renovation. (Llanelli Town Council)

our midst even though the building had been neglected and misused for the greater part of its life. Ambitious plans for its future were put forward by its new owners, Llanelli Town Council, to be spearheaded by William Wilkins, late of the National Botanical Gardens and Aberglasney. In 2003 the house was entered into a BBC series called *Restoration* and was chosen as the winner of the Wales final. It came a creditable fourth in the UK final. The prize of £3 million, however, went to the Victoria Baths in Manchester. Some restoration work has been done with limited funds on the interior of the building, but much remains to be done on what is, without doubt, the finest 18th century town house in Wales. A large cash injection is needed and we can only hope that this will come about in the not too distant future.

In 2003 it was announced that a popular Indian restaurant named 'The Verandah' was to move from Market Street to the old Mansel Hotel. The owners said that they were looking for larger premises and were taking over the Mansel because 'We wanted to do something for the town because its people have been very good to us.' The old inn would certainly have been derelict in a year or so and its refurbishment is a credit to our friends from Bangladesh who have saved a valuable piece of our heritage. 'The Verandah', of course, is one of many Indian restaurants in the town. There are also Thai and Italian restaurants with pizza parlours and takeaways of all descriptions. Our hotels provide good food and other venues range from fine dining to tasty fish and chips. Most public houses also serve

'The Verandah' Indian Restaurant, formerly the Mansel Hotel. (J.E.)

very good food and there is a multiplicity of cafes and snack bars. No one need die of hunger in Llanelli. And talking of dying, we had our own crematorium at last, in 2003, built at a cost of £1.5 million.

After Tom Lewis had visited a friend in a Swansea hospice, he decided that Llanelli should have one. A committee was set up in 1986 which set to fundraising with tremendous enthusiasm under the chairmanship of Dr Mary Llewellyn Morgan. In just over 10 years, £1,100,000 had been raised through the generosity of the people of Llanelli. By 1999 more money had been raised to enable a residential wing to be built but, due to delays in the granting of resource funding from the National Assembly, the facility could only be opened for day-patients for three days a week. Michael Gimblett, secretary to the Hospice trustees, expressed everyone's anger and frustration when he declared 'The trustees were assured, before a brick was laid, that funding would be available on completion. The present situation is inexcusable, immoral and totally unfair to the people of Llanelli.' It was not until 2003 that the Hospice was officially opened as Tŷ Bryngwyn.

Llanelli's hospital (Prince Philip) has suffered from gradual downgrading with some specialist facilities available only in Swansea and Carmarthen. The Accident and Emergency Department was actually closed from 8pm to 8am in September, 2003. There was a huge protest campaign but it took a whole year before the unit was restored[6].

Among the many societies in the town, the Art Society is one of the oldest, having been formed in 1927 with a membership, at present, of 150. The society holds a Summer and Winter exhibition every year and also joins with Ammanford and Carmarthen Art Societies to hold an annual Three Towns Exhibition. Sadly, three leading Llanelli artists have died in recent years: Tony Evans, best known for his portrayals of industrial workers, died in 2002 and the same year saw the death of Vernon Hurford,[7] whose black and white drawings of local scenes are displayed in many homes, while John Bowen, the doyen of the Art Society and former Art master at Llanelli Grammar School, died in 2006. Llanelli has, in fact, a tremendous number of societies, far too many to catalogue here, which cater for all kinds of interests and hobbies.

The town is also well blessed with theatre groups. The two established ones are the Phoenix and Little Theatre groups, while among the others are the Academy Theatre, Llanelli Musical Players, Llanelli Youth Theatre and Curtain Up. These groups attract actors of all ages who stage productions to suit all tastes. On the cultural side, the Workers' Educational Association, which celebrated its 90th birthday in 2004, holds weekly classes and monthly public lectures which attract a good following. The Music and Drama Society is also a successful group which

Cyclists on Millennium Coastal Path. (Carmarthenshire County Council)

concentrates mainly on music and organises concerts locally and visits to concert venues further afield. The Llanelli Writers' Circle holds monthly meetings at which writers discuss their work and organises seminars addressed by established authors and poets during the year.[8]

The Millennium Park has proved to be a continuing attraction with its accompanying cycle path and glorious views across the estuary. A new Discovery Centre was built in 2004 on Llanelli's foreshore which houses tourist information, an exhibition centre and a restaurant. A housing development also provided 258 houses between the North Dock and the shore in blocks four and five-storeys high. Although providing wonderful accommodation, the development has not met with universal approval on architectural grounds.

The old industrial area of Machynys has been re-populated by expensive housing at Bwlchygwynt, now called Pentre Nicklaus after the nearby golf course designed by the famous American golfer. The course was built in 2003 and settled so quickly that it was chosen for the European Ladies' Golf Championship in 2005.[9] A lady named Edna Whitten, who has since died, was a native of the area and had a lengthy correspondence with various local authorities attempting

The restaurant area at Machynys Peninsula Golf Club. (J.E.)

to ensure that the name of Bwlchygwynt was not forgotten. Her dream was realised when a plaque was unveiled at the Golf Club recalling the old community which had once lived there. The last hole is called, appropriately, Bwlchygwynt.

The Public Library is one of Llanelli's treasured possessions. It has always been among the best in Wales and is moving ahead to cater for modern needs. It is no longer just a repository of books, maps and manuscripts, but has a new information technology unit housing 20 computers which are free of charge to all as well as a video conferencing room. The Library also has 10 village branches and a touring mobile van. It caters for hospitals and residential homes and even for housebound customers providing reading books, talking books and CDs, including music, free of charge. It even opens on Sundays to provide language lessons for Llanelli's growing Polish community.

Llanelli briefly found itself in the UK spotlight in 2003 when local boy Michael Howard was made leader of the Conservative Party. He chose his home town to kick-start his whistle-stop tour of the constituencies. He enjoyed his visit to Colêg Sir Gar on the site where he had attended the Grammar School and visited the premises in Cowell Street where his mother once had a fashion shop.[10] The National Assembly elections of 2003 proved to be a close-run affair, with Catherine Thomas, Labour, scraping in by 21 votes over Helen Mary Jones, Plaid Cymru. Denzil Davies, the sitting Labour Member of Parliament, announced that he was standing down at the next General Election and Nia Griffiths was

The Public Library, Llanelli. (J.E.)

A photograph of the Discovery Centre taken by night. (Derek Newton-Goverd)

selected to stand in his place. The new candidate was Head of Modern Languages at Morriston Comprehensive School and was bilingual as well as being fluent in French, Italian and Spanish. In the General Election of May 2005 she became Llanelli's MP by a majority of 7,200 votes.

This chapter has been a snapshot of Llanelli life at the beginning of the 21st century. It would be intriguing to read what a future historian might have to say in a hundred years' time.

Notes to Chapter XVI

1 An interesting fact concerning Robert Jones is that he is an uncle to the actress Catherine Zeta Jones, being her father's brother.
2 The closure affected several voluntary groups which occupied a section of the church called the Octagon. These had to find new homes.
3 Much of the delay was due to problems of ownership of the site.
4 Plans include three theatres of varying capacity as well as studios, workshops and rehearsal rooms.
5 Work is scheduled to start in 2007 with a projected opening in 2009.
6 According to the health authorities, closure was due to the difficulty in recruiting middle-grade doctors.
7 A book of Vernon Hurford's drawings called *Memories* was published by Llanelli Town Council in 2006.
8 Several members of Llanelli Writers' Circle contribute to a wide variety of magazines.
9 Competitors from 28 countries took part. The winner was Kirsty Taylor of England.
10 The shop is now occupied by A.J.'s restaurant.

(Among books written on the history of Llanelli in the past few years, the most important is *The Industrial and Maritime History of Llanelli and Burry Port, 1750 to 2000* by R.S Craig, R. Protheroe Jones and M.V. Symons, published by Carmarthenshire County Council in 2002. For other publications, consult Llanelli Public Library.)

Appendices

Appendix I

A list of contents of Llanelli House was made in 1776 in anticipation of a lease or sale.

Second Floor Guest Rooms

Wrought Room – One bedstead with wrought furniture

Plaid Room – One bedstead with plaid curtains

The following rooms were either on the first floor or second floors:

Red Room	*Red Cotton Room*
Blue Room	*Yellow Silk Room*
Papered Room	*Drawing Room*
Tapestry Room	*Study*

There was also a *Long Gallery* and on its walls hung 22 family portraits. Most of the following rooms would have been on the ground floor:

Breakfast Parlour	*Common Hall*
Beer Room	*Old Nursery*
Ante-Chamber	*Butler's Room*

The following were likely to be found in the outbuildings:

Steward's Hall	*Dairy*
Servants' Hall	*Larder/Pantry*
Kitchen	*Wash-house*
Brewing Kitchen	*Cold Bath Room*

A manuscript (S.L. 2131, dated 1764) in Llanelli Public Library also lists china, furniture, bed linen, wines and spirits among other items.

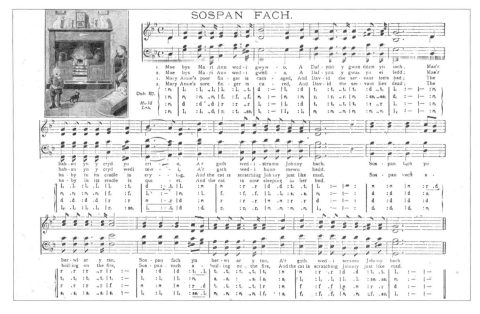

Appendix II

Sospan Fach (The Little Saucepan)

The origin of this song lies in the work of Mynyddog, a bard whose real name was Richard Davies of Llanbrynmair. These lines of his from Rheolau'r Aelwyd (Rules of the Hearth) were written in 1873:

Pan fo Catherine Ann wedi brifo	*When Catherine Ann is hurting*
A Dafydd a gwas ddim yn iach	*And John the servant isn't well*
A'r babi yn nadu a chrio	*And the baby is howling and crying*
A'r gath wedi crafu John bach.	*And the cat has scratched little John.*

In 1895, Talog Williams, a Dowlais accountant, wrote four comic verses at Llanwrtyd. Five or six verses are seen in some collections but apparently only four were written at that time. He may have collaborated with the Revd D.M. Davies as both claimed the work as their own. There is also a possibility that D.M. Davies wrote the music. He was a student at Bangor at the time. Incidentally, both later were ashamed of their association with the song and, having become pillars of society, put it down to the wildness of youth. The first verse is more or less a copy of Mynyddog:

Mae bys Mary Ann wedi brifo	*Mary Ann's finger is hurting*
A Dafydd y gwas ddim yn iach	*And Dafydd the servant isn't well*
Mae'r baban yn y crud yn crio	*The baby in the cradle is crying*
A'r gath wedi scrabin Joni bach.	*And the cat has scratched little John*

Only one of the other three verses is now heard:

Mae bys Mary Ann wedi gwella	*Mary Ann's finger is better*
A Dafydd y gwas yn ei fedd	*And Dafydd the servant's in his grave*
Mae'r baban yn y crud wedi tyfu	*The baby in the cradle has grown up*
A'r gath wedi huno mewn hedd.	*And the cat is resting in peace.*

What was important, however, was that a chorus was added:

Sospan Fach yn berwi ar y tân (2)	*Little saucepan boiling on the fire (2)*
A'r gath wedi huno.	*And the cat is dead.*

Notice that *scrabin* has now become *scrapio*. In Llanelli we say *scramo*, and similarly *gwywo* instead of *brifo* to describe Mary Ann's finger – withered rather than hurting.

The chorus as we now know it is:

Sospan fach yn berwi ar y tân	*Little Saucepan boiling on the fire*
Sospan fawr yn berwi ar y llawr	*Big saucepan boiling on the floor*
A'r gath wedi scramo Joni bach	*And the cat has scratched little Johnny.*

I remember reading in one of the local papers (but failed to record the reference) that the second line used to be:

Yn llawn sgadan ffres a rheiny ddim yn lân   *Full of fresh herring and those not clean.*

This makes more sense as far as rhyming is concerned although the current line has a nice internal rhyme. But whoever saw a saucepan boiling on the floor? Herrings were regularly sold on Llanelli's streets at this time to cries of 'Sgadan Aberporth' – 'Aberporth Herrings' In any case, the song is called the *Little Saucepan* so why should the big one have got into the act?

Be that as it may, Llanwrtyd was a magnet for Llanelli workers at holiday time and they loved to come together and sing. They took to the *Little Saucepan* probably because the Stamping Works had been established in Llanelli since 1892 and was famous for producing saucepans along with other kitchen utensils. They took the song back to Llanelli and it thus became the town's unofficial anthem. There is some opposition to the song's Llanwrtyd origins from Llanelli itself. A letter to the *Llanelly and County Guardian*, 24 December 1934, claimed that the song was composed in Llanelli in 1889 by Owen Rees of Lakefield Road. An eyewitness said that it was written in the York Hotel in response to a request from Johnny Noakes for a topical song for a Christmas pantomime to be staged at his wooden theatre at Waunlanyrafon. Maybe Johnny Noakes was little Johnny after all and, stranger still, the pantomime was Dick Whittington and his cat! The case is rather spoilt by the fact that the writer says the other three verses were written by a clergyman. This would point to the Rev D.M. Davies and we know that the first verse came from Mynyddog by way of Talog Williams.

If the origin of the words seem rather complicated, the source of the tune is even more so. The published version by Gwynn and Company of Llangollen gives it as 'an old Welsh air'. A note goes on to explain: 'This song in its present form is said to date from around 1890 and to have been popularized by Llanelli visitors to Llanwrtyd Wells.' The Rev H. Elvet Lewis (Elfed), who ministered at Park Church, gave a lecture to the Llanelli Cymmrodorion in October 1942. He said that Dr Alfred Daniell had told him that the tune appeared in the Myvyrian Archaeology and was over 500 years old. In a letter to the *Western Mail* in April 1947, Glyn Charles, the well-known chemist of New Dock Road, claimed that William Evans of Caroline Street was the composer. William Evans was organist and choirmaster of St John's church, Seaside. He said that he got the information from William Evan's daughter who also told him that a postcard, containing Welsh and English words and set out in Old Notation and Sol-fa, was published in 1906. Imagine my surprise when the very card turned up in Brian Cripps' vast collection. The card is reproduced at the beginning of this appendix.

During the Boer War at the turn of the century, an additional chorus was added:

Dai bach y sowldiwr (3)	*Dai Bach the soldier (3)*
A'i gwt i grys e mas.	*With his shirt tail hanging out.*

This was followed by the question:

Sut grys oedd ganddo?   *What kind of shirt did he have?*

To which came the answer:

Crys bach gwyn a streipen las.   *A little white shirt with a blue stripe.*

This describes the traditional flannel shirt of the period. There is a suggestion that the original might refer to Dai bach y soldrwr – the solderer, whose work was to solder handles on to the saucepans at the Stamping Works.

This was followed by the request:

    O, hwp e miwn te   *O, tuck it in then.*

And was answered by:

    Ond well 'da fi gal e mas   *But I'd rather leave it out*

And so the little nonsense song ended triumphantly more or less like a hymn-tune.

The song was soon adopted by Llanelli rugby supporters and, as early as February 1896, the *Cambrian Leader*, reporting on a game between Swansea and Llanelli said: '*Sospan Fach* does seem to have an extraordinary effect upon the Scarlets. The crowd began to sing the ballad of the *Little Saucepan*… and instantly the old spirit of the Scarlets began to reassert itself and before the strains had melted away, they were over with what had seemed an impossible try. It was another testimony to the efficacy of the epic of the withered finger and Llanelly's splendid pluck.'

With the victory over the Wallabies at Stradey in 1908, came the first English addition to the song: *Who beat the Wallabies but good old Sospan Fach*, and with the famous 9-3 win over the All Blacks in 1972, came *Who beat the All Blacks*.

Saucepans now stand proudly over the goal posts at Stradey and long may we continue to hear the stirring strains of *Sospan Fach* accompanying the Scarlets wherever they play.

Stop Press. Two publications regarding *Sospan Fach* were published during Eisteddfod 2000. One was an attractive bi-lingual booklet – *Sosban Fach* (Gomer Press) by Aeres Twigg and the other a printed version of a scintillating lecture by Professor Sioned Davies in Welsh, entitled *O'r Pair I'r Sosban* (Eisteddfod Court) (From the Cauldron to the Saucepan). Our little song is now obviously worthy of serious academic research.

Appendix III

Mayors of the Borough of Llanelli

1913-14	Sir Stafford Howard	1955-56	W.J. Davies
1914-15	Sir Stafford Howard	1956-57	Frederick Howells
1915-16	Sir Stafford Howard	1957-58	G.W. Every
1916 (May-November)	Lady Howard	1958-59	T.Glanville Williams
1916-17	D. James Davies	1959-60	Frank Griffiths
1917-18	D. James Davies	1960-61	A.J. Evans
1918-19	Daniel Williams	1961-62	W.A. Nurse
1919-20	Daniel Williams	1962-63	William Davies
1920-21	Joseph Roberts	1963-64	Robert E. Bonnell
1921-22	Joseph Roberts	1964-65	D.D. Williams
1922-23	Joseph Roberts	1965-66	J.H. Williams
1923-24	D.R. Jones	1966-67	Harry Morris
1924-25	Roland P. Jones	1967-68	D. Rees Williams
1925-26	John L. Jones	1968-69	Harold J. Thomas
1926-27	Frank J. Rees	1969 (May-July)	W.J. Thomas
1927-28	David Jennings	1969-70 (July-May)	W.C.U. Griffiths
1928-29	E. Willis Jones	1970-71	A. Mathonwy Jones
1929-30	Morgan Morgan	1971-72	C.R. Edwards
1930-31	T. Hay Samuel	1972-73	Gwilym Gibby
1931-32	W. Powell Rees	1973-74	Dewi H.R. Jones
1932-33	William Davies	1974-75	Edgar J. Thomas
1933-34	Martin R. Richards	1975-76	C. McLoughlin
1934-35	John Hughes	1976-77	A. Bowen
1935-36	Tom Charles	1977-78	G. Thomas
1936-37	J.H. Williams	1978-79	L.A. Davies
1937-38	Elias Davies	1979-80	T. George Thomas
1938-39	Daniel Roberts	1980-81	Harry J. Richards
1939-40	Theophilus Jenkins	1981-82	R.H.V. Lewis
1940-41	W.E. Davies	1982-83	Terry G. Evans
1941-42	H.W. Bowen	1983-84	Richard T. Peregrine
1942-43	W.H. Charles	1984-85	Frederick Owens
1943-44	A.H. Olive	1985-86	Griffith J. Jones
1944-45	W. Douglas Hughes	1986 (May-October)	R.J. James
1945-46	Daniel Rees	1986-87 (Nov.-May)	W.R. Thomas
1946-47	John Griffiths	1987-88	G.G. Jones
1947-48	David J. Joseph	1988-89	W. Mathonwy Jones
1948-49	David J. Joseph	1989-90	Dewi H.R. Jones
1949-50	Dr. H.D. Llewellyn	1990-91	Leonard R. McDonagh
1950-51	D.L. Richards	1991-92	H. John Evans
1951-52	Gwilym Thomas	1992-93	Mrs Elinor G. Lloyd
1952-53	W.E. Payne	1993-94	H. Wynn Jenkins
1953-54	D.J. Davies	1994-95	S.R. Coslett
1954-55	J. Zammitt	1995-96	D.T. James

Appendix IV

Freemen of the Borough of Llanelli

	Date of Proposal
David Lloyd George	2 September 1918
Richard Austin Nevill	3 September 1923
Alfred Daniell	1 May 1925
Francis John Rees	4 December 1934
Lady Catherine Meriel Howard Stepney	4 June 1939
David Jennings	19 June 1939
Martin Rees Richards	8 October 1945
James Griffiths	8 October 1945
William Douglas Hughes	22 December 1949
4th Batt. Welsh Regiment	4 February 1950
Mrs Anna D. Williams (USA)	8 June 1959
Lord Elwyn Jones	11 May 1966
Glyn Williams Every	5 May 1971
David Dan Williams	16 April 1973
Selwyn Samuel	29 March 1974
Royal Regiment of Wales	23 June 1975
Edgar James Thomas	19 July 1976
Thomas George Thomas	29 April 1987

Index

Index